D1048050

LULA
OF BRAZIL

LULA

OF BRAZIL

THE STORY SO FAR

RICHARD BOURNE

UNIVERSITY OF CALIFORNIA PRESS

BERKELEY   LOS ANGELES

University of California Press, one of the most distinguished university presses in the United States, enriches lives around the world by advancing scholarship in the humanities, social sciences, and natural sciences. Its activities are supported by the UC Press Foundation and by philanthropic contributions from individuals and institutions. For more information, visit www.ucpress.edu.

University of California Press
Berkeley and Los Angeles, California

© 2008 by The Regents of the University of California

Library of Congress Cataloging-in-Publication Data

Bourne, Richard.
    Lula of Brazil : the story so far / Richard Bourne.
        p.   cm.
    Includes bibliographical references and index.
    ISBN: 978-0-520-26155-6 (pbk. : alk. paper)
        1. Lula, 1945–   2. Brazil—Politics and government—2003–
3. Brazil—Politics and government—19852002   4. Presidents—
Brazil—Biography.   I. Title.

F2538.5.L5B68   2007
981.06092—dc22
[B]   2007024079

Manufactured in the United States of America

17 16 15 14 13 12 11
10 9 8 7 6 5 4 3 2

This book is printed on Natures Book, which contains 50% post-consumer waste and meets the minimum requirements of ANSI/NISO z39.48-1992 (R 1997) (Permanence of Paper). ⊖

For Emily, Daniel, Max, James, and Isabel, my
grandchildren, who will know another Brazil

CONTENTS

ILLUSTRATIONS

(following page 162)

PREFACE AND
ACKNOWLEDGMENTS

I have to start with a confession: I lost my heart to Brazil at the age of nearly twenty-five, in 1965, when I was lucky enough to win a scholarship to spend six months in Brazil, theoretically linked to the Catholic University in Rio de Janeiro but in reality free to work as an independent journalist. The scholarship was awarded by the Brazilian Foreign Ministry, the Itamaraty, and was handled on behalf of the Brazilian Embassy in London by the British Council. At the time, I was a staff reporter for *The Guardian*, which generously gave me a leave of absence.

The period was exciting for a young journalist interested in politics. The military government that had overthrown President Goulart had not quite congealed into the brutal regime it became later, and there was still active civilian opposition and a relatively free press. Over the following decade I made further visits, collecting material for three books. Then, in the early 1980s, my own career took a different turn. I left journalism and immersed myself in the affairs of the Commonwealth of Nations, undertaking a series of different activities.

It was only in 2005, when I was due to retire from the last of these, the Commonwealth Policy Studies Unit at London University, that I was free to return to a Brazilian topic. The extraordinary and controversial life of Lula, the president of Brazil since the beginning of 2003, beckoned as a subject for a life-and-times biography.

What follows, therefore, is an attempt to provide a readable account of the current Brazilian president, set against the recent history of his country. The questions asked here relate not only to the unprecedented arrival in the presidency of an industrial worker who grew up poor, with many disadvantages, but also to the democratization of Brazil after the military was forced out; a new kind of leftist party built on a renewed union movement; the difficulties of progressive politics in an era of globalization and the free movement of capital; corrupt aspects of the Brazilian political system; and the ambition of Lula and many others that Brazil should become a major world power in the twenty-first century.

This aims to be an accessible political biography, eschewing psychological profiling or minutiae about what the president likes for breakfast. It assumes that many English-speaking readers will start with only a vague knowledge of modern Brazil or its politics. Translations from Portuguese are mine. I have depended heavily on books, articles, and those I have interviewed, particularly for the period in which my own knowledge of Brazil was secondhand and remote. Mistakes are all my own.

Nonetheless, in seeking to provide a balanced view of the Lula presidency up to the point of his reelection in October 2006, I hope that his own vital personality shines through, as well as my own affection and concern for his country.

I owe many people my thanks for their help, starting with my wife, Juliet, who has been enormously patient as I have researched this book, and Naomi Schneider, my editor at the University of California Press. The Leverhulme Trust generously funded my research in Brazil, under its scheme for Emeritus Fellows. I would also like to thank Dr. Sue Cunningham, who kindly read a draft, and was one of those who encouraged me to persevere when I was having difficulty in persuading publishers.

I would also like to remember with affection those who helped me in Brazil when I first arrived in 1965, most of whom are no longer with us: Jane Braga, who was with Reuters; Henry Hogg, who was a local correspondent for the *Daily Express* (and recorded the view then of the Duke of Edinburgh that "the *Express* is a bloody awful newspaper");

Michael Field of the *Daily Telegraph;* Roman Skowronski, son of the Polish Ambassador to Brazil in 1939; Dora Basilio, artist; and Carlos Widmann, then with *Suddeutsche Zeitung.*

Others I should like to thank by name include:

In northeast Brazil: Edson Barreto, who drove me around and helped with interviews; Eraldo Ferreira, secretary-general of the Garanhuns executive of the PT; Gilberto Ferreira in Caetés; Beti of Radio Sete Colinas, Garanhuns, and Aldo of Radio Marana, Garanhuns; Luciano Godoy and Vali Vicente, guides to the site of Lula's birthplace; Alamir Cardoso, president of the Partido Comunista do Brasil, Pernambuco; and Moacir Paulino Silveira, José Inácio Barbosa, and Augusto dos Santos Semente, all members of the Pernambuco state committee of the PCdoB.

In São Paulo: Maria Laura Canineu, invaluable research assistant; Denise Paraná, author of the comprehensive biography *Lula, o filho do Brasil;* "Gijo"—Juno Rodrigues Silva, São Bernardo restaurateur and former union activist; Denise Brito, journalist, invaluable for picture research; Epaminondas Neto Filho, journalist; Marco Moretto, director for Paranapiacaba in Santo André; André Skowronski; Flamarion Maues, editorial coordinator, Editora Fundação Perseu Abramo; Ana Stuart, coordinator for international relations, PT; Ana Luiza Leão, advocate; Heather Sutton, Sou de Paz; and Expedito Soares Batista of the Sindicato dos Metalurgicos, ABCD.

In Brasília: Renato Janine Ribeiro, CAPES; Marco Aurélio de Garcia, special adviser on external affairs to the presidency, and subsequently president, PT; Senator Aloizio Mercadante; Senator Marco Maciel, former vice president; José Graziano da Silva; Oswaldo Bargas; Deputy Vicentinho (Vicente Paulo da Silva); Celsius Lodder; Denise Neddermayor; Hamilton Pereira, president, Fundação Perseu Abramo; Dr. Peter Collecott; United Kingdom ambassador; Winston Moore, ambassador of Trinidad and Tobago; Professor João Paulo Peixoto; David Cordingley, Brazil director, British Council; Minister Paulo Roberto de Almeida, Nucleo de Assuntos Estrategicos; Bernardo Kucinski, journalist; Kennedy Alencar, journalist; and Vicente y Plã Trevas, deputy minister of federative affairs.

In Rio de Janeiro: Nelson Franco Jobim, journalist; Carlos Magno, journalist; Minister Gilberto Gil, minister of culture; João Moreira Salles, filmmaker; Silvia Skowronski; and Tom Phillips, journalist.

In the United Kingdom: Sue Branford, journalist; Sue Cunningham, economic commentator on Brazil; Fernando de Mello Barreto, then Brazilian consul-general, now ambassador to Australia; Graça Fish; Edna Crepaldi, chief executive of Brazilian Contemporary Arts; Carlos Feres, who assisted me in researching foreign policy; Jan Rocha; Fiona Macauley; Professor Leslie Bethell, director, Oxford Centre for Brazilian Studies; Professor Andrew Williams, St. Andrews University; and Ian Cooke.

I   A TOUGH START IN LIFE

Lula was born on 27 October 1945 in the neighborhood of Garanhuns, a small town about 150 miles inland from Recife, the state capital of Pernambuco.[1] It was a Saturday. His father had left a month before to find work in São Paulo, and his mother, Dona Lindu, was already bringing up six children. Lula, Luiz Inácio da Silva, was the seventh.[2] They were living in a small house, and she was scraping together a living by growing maize and manioc, potatoes, beans, and fruit.

The house where Lula was born no longer exists. But its site, up a dirt track some way off the main road from Garanhuns to Caetés, was pointed out to me in September 2005 by two boys on motorcycles, one a distant cousin of Lula's. Technically, the land is semiarid, but there are pools of water nearby and the soil is fertile.

A few of the farmhouses now have satellite TV dishes. But there is still much unemployment, and there are armed holdups on some of the rural roads at night. Garanhuns, "the city of flowers," was founded in 1879; its railway station, long closed, has become a cultural center. It is a region of *minifundios* (smallholdings), not natural territory for the Partido dos Trabalhadores (the PT, the Workers' Party), and it was not until twenty-five years after the party's foundation that it managed to elect its first town councilor (*vereador*).[3]

It is an area that has seen a steady flow of out-migration for more than a half century. In 2005, as president, Lula opened a law school at the state university of Pernambuco in the town, in part a contribution to keeping young people in the area. At the dedication there was a crowd of ten thousand, and fifty of his relations were photographed alongside him.

If Garanhuns today looks tidy, with some new buildings, the smaller town of Caetés is closer to the history of forgotten places in Brazil's impoverished northeast.[4] There are still donkey carts to be seen, and the occasional *pau-de-arara* (literally, "parrot's perch"), which is a truck converted to a people-transport with hard wooden benches.[5] It is hard to know what anyone does for a living in Caetés, aside from subsistence agriculture. But the da Silva family of the president is acknowledged. Opposite the home of Lula's cousin Gilberto Ferreira is a new public health clinic named for Dona Lindu.

It does not take a lot of imagination to realize that when Lula was born this was a harsh region. There was no electricity in the countryside. People heated their homes and cooked with charcoal and firewood. They got water from wells and washed their clothes in streams. Whole families squeezed into self-built two-room houses. Lula's had been built by his father and uncle, with a wooden roof, a cement floor under the main room, and beaten earth elsewhere. Cobras would sit on the roof. There was no radio.

Surplus produce barely stretched to buy essentials, such as clothing or salt, and game was hunted to add to the diet. Brazil may have been among the victors in World War II, its expeditionary force coming home from Italy to a country that was sick of its semifascist Estado Novo regime, but in the northeast, regularly stricken by droughts, there was often hunger.

When she felt her labor pains beginning, Lula's mother, Euridíce Ferreira de Melo, asked her brother-in-law José to fetch a midwife from Caetés. He was thin, she was large, and they fell off the horse more than once on the way back; by the time they arrived, Lula was in the process of being born. His mother was thirty. Her eldest son, José Inácio, known as Zé Cuia, was nine; Jaime was eight; Marinete was seven; Genival, known as Vavá, was six; another José—later known as Frei Chico because his baldness made him look like a monk—was three; and Maria was two. Two other babies had died before Lula's birth; Lindu also lost twins later, after Lula's birth. Large families and child mortality were sadly common in an era prior to birth control and in a region lacking health services.

What Dona Lindu did not know, when she cried as she waved her dry-eyed husband, Aristides Inácio da Silva, off on foot to pick up a *pau-de-arara* in Garanhuns to find his fortune in the southeast—he had sold two horses to raise the fare—was that he was not leaving alone. He was traveling with a young female cousin of Lindu's, Mocinha,[6] already pregnant, with whom he would raise a second family. Nordestino migrants to the richer central south often started second families. In the case of the da Silvas, this led to trouble.

Although Aristides sent money back for Lindu, which was crucial for two years when her smallholding was wracked by drought, he did not return to the northeast even to visit until 1949. He had won funds for a trip from *jogo de bicho,* the illegal but popular gambling game, and he brought his second wife and their two sons back to Pernambuco to see their homeland. Although he kept Mocinha apart from Lindu, Lindu felt humiliated, and Vavá made a point of throwing his well-dressed half-brothers into the nettles. They did not come again.

Nonetheless, Lindu accepted Aristides. He made her pregnant once more, with Sebastiana, or Tiana, who was baptized as Ruth. Lula therefore met his father for the first time when he was four. He was not to get to know him until he was seven, and he was only to live with him for three rather unhappy years altogether.

A certain amount is known of Lula's antecedents. His paternal grandfather had land in Pernambuco and, according to Lula himself, was very mean and died poor. His was a common Portuguese surname. On his mother's side, Lula had a grandmother who was a dressmaker of Italian origin, who drank too much. It is generally supposed that, as with other northeastern families, there had been intermarriage with the local natives (usually called Indians) in the past. Aristides looked like a *caboclo,* a rural man descended from a mixture of Indians and Portuguese. Lula's parents were poor and illiterate, and, though his father had some admiration for Getúlio Vargas (the former dictator who came back to be elected as president in 1950), they showed little interest in politics.

During his formative early years, Lula was brought up by his mother, brothers, and sisters, particularly his older sister Marinete. He adored his hardworking mother, a woman who never had enemies and who was loving without being demonstrative with her children. She was blue-eyed and physically strong, but a tough life and modest diet prematurely aged her.

It may not be right to describe Lula as her favorite child, though he may have had some advantages as her youngest son. But she seems to have spotted something about him—a kind of energy, if not exactly a gift for leadership—quite early on, and she strongly encouraged his education when she could. The family was poor, surrounded by other poor families, and therefore not always aware of its poverty. Lula does not remember having had much fun in his early childhood.

His life changed when he was seven. In 1952, his mother brought the whole family down to Santos, where his father was working at the port as a longshoreman. He was loading sacks of coffee (then and for much longer Brazil's principal export) onto the ships. This was hard manual labor. Aristides became too fond of alcohol and tried to conceal his illiteracy by buying newspapers, which he sometimes pretended to read while holding them upside down.

Aristides probably never wanted his first family to come south, and implied that the only member he would have liked to see was a favorite dog, who had had to be left behind. On a second visit to the northeast he collected his son Jaime, who then wrote to Lindu without his father's knowledge to say that Aristides wanted them all to join him. Lindu, telling the children that it would be better to die of hunger in São Paulo than in the northeast, sold everything and bought a ride on a *pau-de-arara*. Vavá, hiding in a tree, did not want to leave home.

The journey south was a classic migrant story of the era, lasting thirteen days and nights from 10 to 23 December 1952. Altogether eleven members of the family were on a crowded truck covered by a canvas top—Lindu and seven children, plus an uncle, his wife, and their son. Lula wore the same shirt throughout the trip.

This was Lula's first expedition away from home, and on it he caught his first sight of a bicycle, a car, and a truck. They started from Tonzinho's, a bar and corner shop, where they had to stay overnight because the *pau-de-arara* was behind schedule. On the journey they slept in the truck, in the open, or at gas stations; Lindu had packed chicken and biscuits, and they also lived off farinha (manioc flour), bananas, and jerked meat; they were chased by cattle; Lula and Frei Chico were nearly left behind when they stopped to relieve themselves, and had to run behind the truck at night for a half mile before they were spotted; they washed every three or four days. It was a huge adventure: sixty people packed together in two levels on an uncomfortable truck, driving on dirt roads, looking forward to a new life.

When the da Silvas reached their destination, the Brás bus station in São Paulo, all eleven of them piled into a new Chevrolet taxi and drove down to the Santos docks in search of Aristides. He was not particularly pleased to see them—he was living with Mocinha and their children—but rented a place for them to stay. This opened a new chapter in the life of the dysfunctional family. It offered the prospect of greater freedom for Lula, and this was the point at which he ceased to be a rather ignorant country child and began to grow up as a streetwise kid, close to Brazil's industrial heartland.

Lula never liked his father. He saw him as tyrannical, stupid, alcoholic, and favoring his second family over his first. When drunk—and he was overly fond of cachaça, a type of rough sugarcane liquor—he would beat his family, though his second wife and their son Rubens suffered more than Lindu's children. The only good things Lula had to say about Aristides were that he was a hard worker, that he tried to support both families, and that in certain ways he recognized the primacy of the first. Lula's other siblings were frightened of their father, but Frei Chico, who went hunting with him on the weekend, had a rather better opinion.

Lula's memories of his father in Santos, recounted to his biographer, Denise Paraná,[7] were largely negative. He gave two illustrations. One was when Aristides had asked Frei Chico and Lula to check on a small boat he had on the River Caraú, the far side of a Brazilian air force base from where they lived. It began to rain heavily when they were going there, they were afraid, and they turned back without seeing the boat. When Aristides came home, Lindu told him that the boat was safe.

The next day, however, a fellow worker told Aristides that he had seen someone rowing off in the boat—that it had been stolen. Aristides was furious. When he got home, he beat Frei Chico so hard with a hosepipe that he urinated in his school trousers, and he would have beaten Lula also had Lindu not stood between them. He struck Lindu instead; Lula thought this was the start of her determination to separate from him.

The other example was Aristides' meanness about food. Food was always in short supply, but in 1952, when Tiana was only three, he gave pieces of bread to his dogs even though she was begging for some. Lula also did not forgive Aristides for giving ice cream once to his two sons by Mocinha, but not to Lula, saying that he would not know how to lick it! Their father did not let them have much fun, would not let the older boys smoke, and was suspicious of education.

How did Aristides manage to keep the two households going? He alternated between them, spending two nights here and two there. But in fact he was a privileged worker, earning relatively good money as a stevedore. It was physically demanding to carry three sacks of coffee beans at a time. But longshoremen who loaded coffee beans onto the ships were able to dress well and were treated as aristocrats of labor.

Furthermore, every member of the family, except the youngest, had to work and bring in money. Vavá sold water from a barrel and worked in a bar, Jaime helped construct fishing boats in a shipyard, Zé Cuia worked in a coal yard, and Marinete and Maria both worked as domestics. When Lula was seven or eight, he started selling peanuts in the port with Frei Chico. They also sold oranges and Lindu's homemade tapioca. Lula was not very good at this to begin with; Frei Chico later recalled that he was too shy to shout his wares.

Child labor and children selling on the street were common then and are not unknown in Brazil now. An excellent film by Nelson Pereira dos Santos, *Rio, 40 Graus*, follows the fortunes of a group of child peanut sellers in Rio de Janeiro at about the time Lula and Frei Chico were selling peanuts in Santos. It depicts the intimidation of young street sellers by older boys and the police in a risky and potentially violent environment. Lula was not an orphan and had a large family and loving mother behind him, but his experiences on the quays of Santos only strengthened his knowledge of human nature, his street smarts, and his will to survive.

Lula and his siblings worked by day and studied by night. He and three others went to the same school, the Grupo Escolar Marcílio Dias. He remembers a teacher, Dona Terezinha, who was fond of him, and he recalls that Frei Chico won a translation of *Gulliver's Travels* as a prize.

But life in Santos, with a sometimes drunk father and a mother who was far from happy that she was sharing her husband with another, was no idyll. It involved much drudgery, which included hauling water and firewood. Within three years Lindu had had enough and decided to break away from Aristides. Although he tried to win her back with feasts and relatives' attempts at persuasion, and by hanging around her new home at night, she was finished with him. One day she and her family left the joint home early, leaving behind only a daughter to hand him the keys.

Lindu never married again, though she had an offer, and she bore Aristides little ill will after the separation, even bringing up one of his other children. For Lula and her other children, however, this separation was like a cry of liberty. They could begin to live a normal childhood and adolescence, go to the movies, play soccer, and have boyfriends and girlfriends.

But they were still toiling hard, and Lindu was sorting coffee beans and then washing clothes to make money. She got behind with her rent. Her fortunes changed in 1955, however, when Vavá found a package wrapped up in a newspaper on the ground at the market where he was working. It contained 5,855 cruzeiros—more than thirty-four times the legal minimum monthly salary.

After waiting a week to see whether anyone would claim the money and giving 500 cruzeiros to the man he had asked for advice, Vavá handed over the money to his mother. She promptly paid off the rent she owed and moved with four of her children to Vila Carioca, an industrial suburb of the city of São Paulo. Two of her daughters, working as domestics, stayed behind in Santos; Frei Chico and Lula lived with Aristides and Mocinha for an uncomfortable year—during which Aristides was stabbed in a drunken brawl and lost a kidney—before rejoining their mother in 1956.

What sort of a Brazil was it that Lula was growing up in, as he arrived in Brazil's industrial capital? It was an exciting time. In 1955, Juscelino Kubitschek had been elected president, backed by two parties, the Partido Social Democrático and the Partido Trabalhista Brasileira, both of which traced their origins to Getúlio Vargas. He promised fifty years of progress in five, a program of thirty *metas* (goals), rapid industrialization based on import substitution, and a deepening of Brazil's rather fragile democracy. This was a democracy that was only a decade old, where an elected president had committed suicide in 1954, blaming malign pressures, where illiterates such as Aristides could not vote, where there had been constant rumors of military intervention, and where Kubitschek could be elected with only 35.63 percent of the vote.

Historically, Brazil had been an exception in Latin America. It was Portuguese-speaking, largely surrounded by Spanish-speaking countries. It had been created by the diplomacy of Portugal and the ruthless westward advance of mixed-race *bandeirantes*, of Portuguese and American Indian heritage, in the era of Portuguese discovery and the following century. Two years after Columbus "discovered" the New World, Portugal persuaded the pope to arbitrate between the two Catholic powers, Spain and Portugal, in the Treaty of Tordesillas in 1494. Under the terms of the treaty, Portugal would get land 370 leagues west of the Cape Verde islands. Six years later, Pedro Cabral "discovered" Brazil, and a rather lackluster mother country oversaw a steadily expanding occupation by her more energetic offspring.

In the succeeding four centuries there was a gradual colonization of the vast space of modern Brazil. Rivals such as the Dutch, who briefly occupied the northeast in the seventeenth century, were defeated. Negro slaves were brought from Africa, after the local Indians proved resistant to coercion and manual labor. There were periodic booms in sugar, gold, and cotton, but Portugal, initially more interested in a route to India and the spice trade, took a while to find much economic advantage in its South American possession.

While the coastal strip saw a semifeudal world consolidate, with plantation houses and slavery, a more dynamic and lawless society was growing up in São Paulo and in the west, the south, and up the Amazon tributaries. Intermarriage and sexual promiscuity among Europeans, Africans, and Indians were commonplace. Brazil joined the European world of the early nineteenth century extremely suddenly following Napoleon's invasion of Portugal in 1807. Guarded by the British Navy, the royal court and ten thousand hangers-on arrived in Rio de Janeiro, where they were to stay from 1808 to 1821.[8]

A new opera house, botanical gardens, and a surge of modernity followed. But the experience also marked out differences between Brazil and its Spanish-speaking neighbors. The ideas of the enlightenment and the American and French revolutions led to violent rebellion against the Spanish crown. In Brazil, by contrast, the king's younger son, Pedro, with his *grito do Ipiranga*—his cry of "Independence or death"—led the colony into independence from Portugal in 1822. This launched the long anomalous period of the Brazilian Empire, finally concluded by an army mutiny in 1889. One year earlier, Brazil had belatedly abolished slavery, an indication of the social conservatism of the empire.

In the early years of the twentieth century, the era in which Lula's parents were growing up, Brazil's politics were dominated by coffee and milk—the states of São Paulo, with its powerful coffee growers, and Minas Gerais, with its dairy farmers. The northeast was in thrall to the *coroneis*—reactionary local landowners who may or may not have once been colonels in the militia. In the south, along the border with Uruguay and Argentina, European immigration and a cowboy tradition had led to a certain impatience with the sloth and corruption of the federal government in Rio de Janeiro. Politics was elitist, subtle, and personal, and habits of accommodation and the exchange of favors persisted from the imperial era.

Brazil was still overwhelmingly agricultural, but in the big cities of the central south there was the start of modern capitalism and an industrial working class. Francisco Matarazzo, an entrepreneur, opened his first textile factory in São Paulo in 1904, and thirty years later the combined revenues of his businesses represented 87.5 percent of the income of the state. The Brazilian Communist Party was founded in 1922, and the federation of São Paulo industrialists six years later.

What changed Brazil more profoundly than the end of the empire in 1889 was the revolution that brought Getúlio Vargas to power in 1930.

Vargas had been the state president of Rio Grande do Sul and had run in a federal presidential election that year as the candidate of the Liberal Alliance. His father and maternal uncle had been commanders on opposite sides in a brutal statewide civil war, and he inherited a ruthless streak. He had backing from Minas Gerais and the northeastern state of Paraíba in the 1930 election. But there was no secret vote, and elections were fixed through a carving up of spoils among state political machines. After the 1930 election, the outgoing president, Washington Luís, claimed that his candidate, Julio Prestes—the state president of São Paulo, so a Paulista like himself—had won by a two-to-one majority.

The country was ripe for a revolution. Stocks had crashed in 1929, and in the same year there had been a crisis of overproduction of coffee, the key export earner—output had almost doubled in five years, outstripping demand. Foreign capital fled Brazil. The government's gold reserves, healthy at the end of World War I, had dropped to zero by the end of 1930. And over the previous decade there had been bubbling dissent and minirevolts among young army officers, the phenomenon of *tenentismo*.

Launched in Rio Grande do Sul on 3 October after careful planning, the insurrection was successful relatively quickly. Vargas was in the Catete, the presidential palace in Rio, by 31 October. He was greeted by tumultuous crowds. A canny, introverted man with a fatherly smile, he was to be the key figure in Brazilian politics until his suicide in 1954. He defeated a rebellion in São Paulo in 1932 and an attempted communist coup in 1935, and he was imprisoned for a few hours in a nearly successful putsch by the Integralistas, the Brazilian fascists, in 1938. Having introduced a personal dictatorship with his fascist-style Estado Novo in 1937, he brought Brazil into World War II on the side of the Allies in 1942.[9]

Two key elements of the Vargas era, which resurfaced when Vargas was democratically elected president in 1951, were the incorporation of the growing working class and significant gestures of economic nationalism within a context of industrialization. Fascist ideology, which in Europe had done little for organized workers except to destroy their autonomous unions, was reinterpreted by the Estado Novo in Brazil to give unionized workers a stake in society. The approach was paternalist and clientelistic, with much power vested in the Ministry of Labor and not much freedom for workers' elections. Strikes were outlawed under the 1937 Constitution. But with a minimum wage in some industries, and attempts to provide pensions and social protection, it seemed like progress for poor people who were moving from the countryside into a free-for-all industrial society.

The biggest symbols of economic nationalism were in steel and oil. Late in 1940, when the United States was still trying to keep the Americas out of World War II, it authorized its Export-Import Bank to loan twenty million dollars for the construction of a steel plant in Volta Redonda; it was already known that Brazil had substantial reserves of iron ore. In December 1951, after he returned as president, Vargas sent the Brazilian Congress a bill to set up a national oil corporation, Petrobrás, which would have a monopoly on extraction and new refineries. The Petrobrás question became a major unifying force among Vargas supporters over the next two years—the popular slogan was "The oil is ours"—before the bill became law. At the same time, it discouraged foreign investment in other sectors, as well as in petroleum.[10]

From 1930 to 1945, Getúlio Vargas had been a dictator. But in the early months of 1945, the illogicality of Brazil's political situation caused the Estado Novo to crack, and calls for democracy, freedom, and elections became unanswerable. The military had become politicized and was now opposed to Vargas. In October, when there was doubt as to whether Vargas would permit elections, and the appointment of Vargas's brother Benjamim as police chief enraged his now wide range of opponents, the generals overthrew Vargas. Eurico Dutra, who had been Getúlio's defense minister, was elected president. Vargas, who was elected senator by the Partido Social Democrático (PSD), one of the two parties he founded—he showed more affection for the Partido Trabalhista Brasileira (PTB), set up by his supporters in the Labor Ministry and controlled unions—retired to his home in São Borja, in the southernmost state of Rio Grande do Sul. In October 1950, however, he was elected president by nearly a majority, backed by the PTB and PSD.

Getúlio's final government was not a success, and it stimulated more military plotting. Although the Korean War had resulted in a boom in primary products, the government kept chopping and changing its economic policy, inflation grew, and there was serious corruption, some of it linked to thugs in the presidential bodyguard. The murder of an air force major, Rubem Vaz, killed in an attempt on the life of a noisy anti-Vargas journalist, Carlos Lacerda, led to a military ultimatum. On 24 August 1954, Getúlio committed suicide rather than be forced out of office for a second time. There was a nationwide outpouring of emotion at the death of a man rebranded as "the father of the poor."

Plots and counterplots punctuated the next couple of years. There were two temporary presidents, Café Filho and Carlos Luz. Only a "pro-legality coup" by Henrique Lott, a minister of war who refused to be sacked, enabled Juscelino Kubitschek and his running mate from the PTB, João Goulart, to assume the offices to which they had been elected.

All of this may have seemed rather remote to a street boy like Lula, still only ten years of age when Kubitschek became president at the end of January 1956. But the next five years, with the optimism and showmanship of the new president, marked the consciousness of all Brazilians and were certainly influential for a young teenager. Dubbed "the country of tomorrow" in the 1940s by Stefan Zweig, an Austrian writer who ended his days in Brazil, the strategy of "goals" and the breakneck building of a new capital, Brasília, did suggest that the country could escape its stagnation, poverty, and backwardness. Kubitschek and those around him were advocates of the doctrine of development, *desenvolvimento*, even if this led to high rates of inflation and a row with the International Monetary Fund (IMF).

But for Lula's family, now in Vila Carioca in São Paulo, life was still tough. They lived in a room behind a bar belonging to an uncle. There was no chair for the doctor who came to see Frei Chico, then known as Ziza, when he had pneumonia. The road outside was unpaved, often a sea of mud. People around were very poor. Though Lindu was washing clothes and Lula was shining shoes, the family could not afford meat. Lula borrowed a jacket to enter a cinema, then a requirement, and when his friend Cláudio asked for it back, Lula was not allowed in.

The family moved several times, gradually acquiring more furniture. Lula worked for a dry cleaner and life looked up. He worked six months in an office, and then in a factory that made screws—the Fábrica de Parafusos Marte. It was here that he worked as part of his course in SENAI, when he trained as a lathe operator.

SENAI, Serviço Nacional de Aprendizagem Industrial, was a national industrial training program originally launched under Vargas. It became increasingly important in the São Paulo area with the arrival of automakers and other new industries in the spurt of industrialization promoted by Kubitschek. The program was quite hard for a teenager to get into, and Lula took the entrance exam twice. The first time, the only vacancy was for a welder, which did not attract him. Because his educational attainment became an issue more than thirty years later, when he first started campaigning for the presidency, it is worth stating that the entrance requirement was equivalent to that of a good high school.

Interviewed by Denise Paraná in the 1990s, Lula said that his SENAI time was the happiest period of his boyhood.[11] His mother was exceedingly proud of him; they had come a long way together, from Vila Carioca to Ipiranga, when he went to take the test. His two-year SENAI training was what is sometimes described as a sandwich course, involving linked classes and practical experience, and also some physical education.

He spent five months in classes, six months in the factory, and had a month's holiday. All this time he was being paid, at a rate of half the minimum salary. He was the first member of his family to have a trade or profession that required training, and he was able to contribute money regularly to the household. "I feel that my mother's pride was the same that I feel when a son of mine goes to university," he remarked later.[12] This was the culmination of his formal education.

Lula was properly fed, and he was able to play soccer in lunch breaks at the factory and afford entertainment. One of his means of relaxation at the time was to go swimming in lakes around Vila Carioca. Other northeasterners were working at the factory, and as a youngster he was treated with affection. He was taken under the wing of an older man, a black lathe operator named Barbosa, who shared his refreshments with him, taught him on the job, and was a kindly father figure. Altogether he stayed at the screw factory for three and a half years, moving on in 1964, a baleful year in Brazilian history.

Although life had been getting more pleasant for Lula, the optimism of the Kubitschek years in Brazil as a whole had turned sour. Whether Kubitschek had achieved his intended fifty years of progress by the time he left office after the inauguration of Brasília in 1960 is a matter for debate. But there certainly had been remarkable growth, with a combination of import substitution for the internal market, foreign capital, and national planning. Special executive groups were set up to stimulate the auto industry, shipbuilding, road building, production of agricultural, railway, and heavy industrial machinery and equipment, iron ore exports, and warehousing. Between 1957 and 1961, gross national product grew by 8.2 percent a year, and real income per capita by 5.1 percent.[13]

Growth was particularly striking in road building, where more than 10,000 miles were built; in the electricity supply, where 1.65 million kilowatts came online, much of it through hydropower; and in the auto industry, where production rose to 170,000 car and truck units a year, and international companies such as Volkswagen and Mercedes-Benz opened factories.

But there were substantial costs, both economic and political. Inflation soared in the last eighteen months of Kubitschek's term, when talks with the IMF had broken down; 1960 saw a record payments deficit; and by early 1961, three times the amount of cruzeiro money was in circulation as at the end of 1955. The dash to build the new capital of Brasília, inaugurated in 1960 after work had started only four years earlier, was inflationary and involved substantial corruption. Construction firms made fortunes. That the city, with its sensational modern architecture, was a symbol of a new more developed Brazil did not disarm conservative critics.

Kubitschek passed on the presidency to a maverick from São Paulo, Jânio Quadros, who suddenly resigned in August 1961.[14] He had been supported by the conservative, anti-Vargista party, the União Democrático Nacional, and had won 48 percent of the vote. But his departure opened a worrying prospect for conservative groups, and especially those in the military who had been plotting on and off against Vargas and his legacy since 1945, because the vice president was João Goulart of the PTB, known as Jango to his supporters. Although he was a landowner in Rio

Grande do Sul, he had always run on a populist platform of economic nationalism and benefits for organized labor.

Initially, Goulart was not allowed full powers, but an experiment in parliamentarism was swept away in January 1963, when in a referendum the people voted five to one to return to an executive presidency. Goulart by now was calling for basic reforms—tax reforms to hit the rich, land reform, and the nationalization of foreign-owned utilities such as the Canadian-owned Rio Light in Rio de Janeiro. While inflation rose, ineffective price controls were introduced. Social malaise was growing, with pro- and anti-Goulart demonstrations, and the president seemed to dither.

Finally the crisis came to a head in March and April 1964. At a Rio rally on 13 March, organized by the trade unions that were part of the PTB machine, Goulart expropriated private oil refineries and decreed that underused landed estates close to roads, railways, or federal irrigation projects could be taken over by the state. He said that he was planning to introduce rent controls, to give the vote to illiterates and servicemen, and to change the Constitution. After a hostile demonstration, and a naval mutiny, which Goulart tried to resolve by sacking his navy minister, the army launched a coup, backed by governors in Minas Gerais, São Paulo, and the city-state of Guanabara, formerly Rio de Janeiro.

The coup was all over in three days, by 2 April, with little bloodshed although, in a warning of what was to come, there were allegations that opponents had been tortured in the northeast.[15] It had received discreet help from the U.S. government, which, like Brazilian conservatives, was concerned about the possible spread of the Cuban revolution to the rest of Latin America. Many congressmen, union leaders, artists, and journalists were deprived of their political rights by the regime; a process of "cleansing" (called Operação Limpeza), with military police inquiries, was launched by the hard-line defense minister, General Costa e Silva.

The military was to rule Brazil for the next two decades and, as we shall see, Lula played a major part in getting them back to their barracks. The military dictatorship was the context in which Lula was to develop as a trade unionist and become a national figure.

Meanwhile, Lula himself, still a teenager in 1964, was trying to get on in the world as a lathe operator. He left the Fábrica de Parafusos Marte because it refused to raise his wages to the level of older men, even though he had worked there as long. In 1965, therefore, when the economic squeeze was biting, Lula found himself out of work for eight months. His brothers were also unemployed, and Dona Lindu's household was under strain. Lula would leave the house at 6 A.M., trudging around to the factories to see if any of them were taking on workers. Sometimes the staff would say there were no jobs. Sometimes they would take away Lula's professional card, hang on to it for a while, and then say that there was nothing available. His dreams of being well paid and working for one of the big automaking firms seemed far from reality.

The family moved around frequently, and several of the poor-quality houses they lived in flooded. There was not much to eat—just rice and potatoes cooked in oil, but no chicken or meat. Lula found the experience of unemployment profoundly depressing; he had no workplace friends or money for modest pleasures.

After what seemed a long time, he found a job in another factory, Fábrica Independência, where he was employed as a lathe turner on the night shift. He could sleep a little on the job, waking up before the boss arrived. He earned enough to buy a secondhand bicycle. It was here that he lost the little finger of his left hand in an accident. A screw broke on a machine, and a heavy press fell, smashing the finger.[16] It was painful, and he had to wait some hours before the factory manager arrived at 6 A.M. and took him to a doctor. The loss of the little finger gave him a psychological complex for months but won him compensation of 350,000 cruzeiros, a fair sum at the time; he used it to buy furniture for his mother and to help her buy a little piece of land.

Safety arrangements in the new factories springing up in the São Paulo area left much to be desired, and many mechanics and lathe operators suffered industrial injuries. Other members of Lula's family were also victims of the largely unregulated rapid industrialization. One Volkswagen manager told the correspondent of a German newspaper that he preferred employing the uneducated northeasterners of Brazil, and that the car output in São Paulo was higher than with German workers in Wolfsburg.[17]

At Independência, where the firm offered a flagon of wine with the thirteenth month's salary, Lula had his first experience of getting completely drunk. He and his fellow workers drained the flagon in a nearby bar and chased it with a number of beers. Fortunately, Lula had a short walk home. After eleven more months at this factory he went to another, Fris-Moldu-Car, where he was sacked after a minor act of rebellion. The boss there wanted him to work on a Saturday. But he wanted to go on a picnic to Santos with his brothers. So Lula refused to work that Saturday, went on the picnic, and lost his job.

At both Independência and Fris-Moldu-Car, Lula had the experience of participating in metalworkers' strikes. The military regime of Humberto Castelo Branco was following the tight anti-inflationary policy of its finance minister, Roberto Campos.[18] This squeezed the income of workers and, although there was a crackdown on communists, leftists, and other opponents of the military takeover, unions had to respond to the desire of ordinary members to maintain their earnings.

But in the late 1960s, while the military regime was tightening its grip on power with Institutional Act number 5—after its friends proved incapable of winning elections in 1967—Lula's situation improved. Following his brother Frei Chico, who was already working there, he got a job in Aços Villares, a large engineering firm. The firm had a policy of not employing relatives, but because the personnel department had not figured out that José Ferreira da Silva and Luiz Inácio da Silva were brothers, he got the job.

Lula was embarrassed on his first day because, short of money before he got his first paycheck, he could not afford to buy lunch. He had to walk for an hour and a half or two hours to get to work because he had no money for the bus. He also had to work the night shift.

At this time Lula seemed to be a typical young working man—fanatical about soccer, not greatly interested in politics or trade unions, beginning to date girls. His first serious girlfriend was a pretty girl of Japanese origin—there was a large Japanese community around São Paulo—but she lost out to his interest in soccer. Although close to much of his family, he was completely out of touch with his father.

Even an apolitical worker, however, was neither immune to the labor unrest of the late 1960s nor totally unaware of the heightened tension in the country in 1968–69. As an ordinary worker, Lula had observed a number of strikes. Some were violent. When he was fifteen, he was advised not to go to work one day because the factory was being picketed. His sister Maria was one of two thousand strikers locked into a jute factory by management but rescued by fellow workers. Lula himself went on strike at the Metalúrgica Independência.

Lula's brother Frei Chico had become increasingly active in the metalworkers' union. Although Frei Chico did not join the Communist Party (the PCB) until the early 1970s, he was angry at the unbridled capitalism unleashed by the military regime, with metalworkers' wages dropping by a third, accompanied by longer shifts and more Saturday work. In 1968–69, he threw himself into the campaign for higher wages, spoke up at meetings, and began to serve in various union offices. Lula, who attended one or two of these meetings, thought that his brother was too much of an activist. Behind the scenes the PCB did what it could to stimulate unrest, although Catholic anticommunism in the context of the Cold War, police arrests, and government repression all obstructed the party.

In December 1968 the regime, which had already removed the mandates of congressional representatives who might oppose it, decreed the fifth Institutional Act (AI-5). Institutional Acts were the decree-laws of the regime that substituted for a democratic constitution. Castelo Branco had handed the presidency over to Artur Costa e Silva in February 1967, following the collapse of his policy for a more suave military regime, which had envisaged continuing elections. Costa e Silva represented the hard-line anticommunist elements who opted for a much more frank dictatorship.

The excuse for AI-5 was a provocative invasion of Brasília University by the hard-liners, which was matched by an incendiary speech by an opposition deputy and journalist, Marcio Moreira Alves, who denounced the army as a bunch of torturers and executioners, and urged the girlfriends of young officers and cadets to boycott them. AI-5 unleashed more censorship, waves of arrests, and repression.[19] Leaders of the student movement such as José Dirceu, later to be a key organizer for the PT, were thrown in jail.

While the student movement in the United States was protesting the Vietnam war and that in France was protesting the presidency of de Gaulle, in Brazil the military regime and more parochial student concerns had led to a clandestine mobilization. But after AI-5, many leftists and Marxists who had managed to escape arrest—such as the young sociologist and future president Fernando Henrique Cardoso—went into exile. At the same time, inspired by urban and rural guerrilla movements elsewhere in Latin America, small cells, mostly of young men and women, decided to take up arms against the dictatorship.

The year 1969 was important for Lula. He married. He took a post in his union, the Sindicato dos Metalúrgicos. And apolitical though he was, a dramatic incident—the kidnapping of the U.S. ambassador—showed him and all Brazilians that the military regime was not impregnable.

Lula's marriage and union involvement began almost simultaneously. He had known Maria de Lourdes Ribeiro, a textile worker, for some years simply as a friend and neighbor. She was dark and pretty, and she had come from Ipatinga, a town in the interior of São Paulo state, near the Minas border. Lula and his family found themselves living next to Lourdes, her three brothers, and her parents when they moved to a house in Jardim Patente, in greater São Paulo. Lula became friendly with Maria's brothers, especially Jacinto, and they all went to dances together.

Lula realized that he was becoming attracted to Lourdes, but he was very shy. He asked Jacinto how he should approach her and whether he ought to talk to her parents first. Jacinto said he should talk directly to her. At a weekend dance, after he had drunk four brandies and several dances had gone by, he summoned the courage to say that he loved her.

While Lula was falling in love, he was also becoming an active trade unionist, almost against his will. In September 1968 he signed up as a member of the Sindicato dos Metalúrgicos de São Bernardo. São Bernardo was an industrial suburb of São Paulo with several motor and engineering factories. It was part of the industrial and working-class belt that was known as the ABCD region—along with Santo André, São Caetano, and Diadema. This region, and São Bernardo in particular, were to be the center of Lula's activity over the next fifteen years and his springboard to national prominence.

On 24 April 1969 Lula assumed a position as an alternate or substitute member of his union's executive. Just over a month later, on 25 May, he married Lourdes in a happy occasion, surrounded by their extended families. They went away in a horse-drawn carriage and had a brief honeymoon at a beautiful spot, Poços de Caldas.

But the wedding nearly did not happen, because Lourdes was anxious about Lula's enhanced status in the union. She was employed by a small textile firm, and the managers put pressure on her when they learned that her fiancé was to be a union official; to them (a sign of the oppressive atmosphere of the time), active unionists were probably communists, and union prominence would bring trouble from the police. Lourdes was not political, or especially conservative, but it was common knowledge that leftists and active unionists were being persecuted.

In fact, Lula himself had needed much persuasion to join the winning slate in the union elections. His general feeling was that the union was a waste of time, union meetings were occupied with trivial disputes and power struggles, and the real capacity of the union was limited to modest social assistance. The person who persuaded him to allow his name to be included in the slate of candidates was his brother, Frei Chico, who also got the metalworkers' leadership to talk to him.

It was Frei Chico, not Lula, who had originally been invited to run for the directorate of the union. But Frei Chico had by then moved on from Villares, where he spent less than a year, and had joined a firm of two hundred employees called Carraço, which made vehicle bodies. There was already a union man, older than Frei Chico, from the small company; if Lula's brother was successful in the election, it would debar the current union official because the rule prohibited more than one member of the executive from the same business. Frei Chico did not want to exclude the older man so, even before Lula had joined the union, he suggested his name as a candidate in union elections. Frei Chico knew the union's leadership well—Afonso Monteiro da Cruz, the president, Mário Ladeia, the secretary-general, and Paulo Vidal, the second secretary, who would shortly become president. Frei Chico said he knew someone good at Villares, a big firm, who was his brother. The leadership asked what he was like. According to Denise Paraná, Frei Chico replied, "He's young, he doesn't like the union, and he doesn't know anything . . . but who knows? He might agree to take a part."[20]

It says a lot for the status of Frei Chico, and possibly the weakness of the metalworkers' union, that this lukewarm recommendation should lead to a siege of Lula by the union hierarchy. Frei Chico, who understood Lula well, had noticed that whether Lula was playing soccer or at work, he had a natural gift for leadership. The principal figures in the union all tried to persuade him, encouraging him to attend courses and meetings. Lula held out for a long time, telling them that all he wanted to do was to get on with his life. Lourdes's worries did not make his choice any easier; like him, she dreamed first of a small house of their own, backed up by steady wages. But by the end of 1968 the die was cast. Lula talked it over with Lourdes and disarmed her concern.

With the support of the leadership, therefore, Lula went on to be elected one of a union directorate of twenty-four. From 1968 to 1972, Lula still worked at Villares, and when fellow workers brought him questions he could not answer, he would stop by the union offices at night to speak to lawyers and others who might solve their problems. It was a humdrum, undramatic apprenticeship in union affairs, far removed from heroics on the national stage.

Yet Brazilian heroics burst into international consciousness on 4 September 1969, when a group of urban guerrillas succeeded in abducting the U.S. ambassador, Charles Burke Elbrick. The world's media suddenly became aware that Brazil's military government, a close ally of the United States, was not all-powerful. It faced armed opposition. In fact, following Costa e Silva's incapacitation by a stroke, Brazil was temporarily being ruled by that standby of other South American countries, a military junta.

What was more embarrassing was that the government, with all its soldiers, police spies, and capacity for torture, was unable to find and release Elbrick. It had to make a deal. It agreed to free an eclectic group of leftists—including José Dirceu, then a student leader, who had been arrested in São Paulo—in return for the ambassador's release. A famous photograph of thirteen handcuffed political prisoners was taken at Rio's Galeão airport, as they posed in front of the Hercules plane that would fly them to Mexico. When a policeman yelled, "Smile, you sons of bitches," they all glowered at the camera. Many of those involved in the kidnapping and many among those released in consequence would play a part in the growth of the prodemocracy movement and the debates that led to the foundation of the PT.

It is worth pausing at this stage to consider what sort of a person Lula was at age twenty-four, married, and on the brink of his true career. Had one met him then, he would have seemed like thousands of other young men—soccer-mad, relatively unambitious, close to his extended family. In matters of personal belief, his Catholicism would have seemed more important than any other political or ideological allegiance, of which he had virtually none. He was physically strong and shared the pride in survival of many of those born in the northeast, who see themselves as the truest Brazilians.

But there was much more to his experience. His family support network was vital in helping him and the other da Silvas to keep going through periods of hunger and poverty. His mother had faith in him. The absence of a father he disliked was—if the psychology of other successful men is anything to go by—another spur. His brother Frei Chico, who did not hesitate to call him a "vagabond" during one of his spells of unemployment, liked and promoted him.

The insecurity of poverty, and the poverty of Brazil during the era in which he was growing up, were also a crucial context. It was part of that "biography" that was to enable him to empathize with other Brazilians, and for millions to empathize with him, when he came to run for the presidency. He had genuinely known hunger. He had been a shoeshine boy and had had to sell peanuts on the streets as a child. He had lived in small, poor shacks that were not rain-proof and were liable to flood. Money was hard to get and vulnerable to the constant devaluation caused by rampant inflation. Educational advancement, without the lucky SENAI break, would have been out of reach.

At the same time, for the da Silvas as for the country, there was an enormous desire for progress. The excitement of the Brasília boom had come and gone. But when the da Silvas and other *retirantes* (internal migrants) had come down from the northeast to the central south, they had wanted to partake in a richer, more developed Brazil. Lula had longed for the "monkey-suit" of a well-paid engineer in an auto factory. The positivist national slogan, "Ordem e Progresso"—order and progress—influenced all parts of what was still a conservative society. It infected the anticommunist ideology of the military takeover of 1964, whose officers were also fed up with politicians' populism, bureaucratic muddle, and outdated systems from telephones to public finance.

And Brazil was doing things. The onward march to megalopolis of São Paulo, with its factories and skyscrapers, was symbolic. In 1970, amid national rejoicing, Brazil would win the World Cup in soccer. A better future seemed achievable.

Yet Lula had learned about the dark side of what military apologists would call the Brazilian economic miracle: poor safety in factories, depression of living standards, and an environment in which those who stood up for the rights of workers were spied on and arrested, and could lose their own rights. He himself had lost two jobs when trying to stand up for his own rights.

He had also been drawn into trade unionism in a way that was not exactly democratic, but which mirrored an enduring element in the country's politics and society. It reflected a widespread tradition of patronage and the significance of family connections. He had been invited to become a member of a union executive before he was even a union member, before any election, because he was Frei Chico's brother, and he was put on the winning ticket.

His own take on the military regime at this stage was much hazier and less confrontational than Frei Chico's. It was a world away from the leftist ideologies of the middle-class students and their professors, wrapped up in arcane Marxist disputes, moving toward different schools of armed revolution. To most Brazilians, a little fearful of the military regime and keen to keep their heads down and go about their business, the small guerrilla groups seemed eccentric if not threatening. In 1969, Lula's attitude and the anxieties of his new bride, Lourdes, were probably typical of a large chunk of Brazilian opinion. His own political education had hardly begun.

2 STRIKE LEADER

Both Lula and his mother cried when the newlyweds departed for their honeymoon. Lula and Lourdes seem to have been very happy together. Lula had been her first boyfriend. With a loan from the Villares firm's social fund, they were able to get their own two-room house in Vila das Mercês, close to Dona Lindu. Lourdes, who was working at a firm in Ipiranga, kept their home spotless. Lula's sister Maria and her husband, who was then out of work, stayed with them. But tragedy was about to strike the young couple.

Lourdes became pregnant. In her seventh month, in 1971, she started vomiting seriously. Initially the doctors said this was normal. She was then taken to the Hospital Model, in São Paulo, where she was diagnosed with hepatitis. The doctor in charge was an inexperienced trainee. Lula visited her and found her crying out in pain, with no nurse or doctor to attend to her.

On a Monday, he received a call to take clothing for mother and baby, as a cesarean birth had been scheduled. But when he arrived at the hospital, he was told that both mother and baby—a little boy—had died.[1] Naturally, he was distraught. He would not permit a postmortem autopsy. Perhaps surprisingly, his father, Aristides, came up from Santos for the funeral; his mother stayed away.

The loss of his wife and baby, when he was only twenty-five, had a huge impact on Lula. It was a life-changing event. He was bitter about the hospital and its lack of care. This made him realize the importance of social assistance work for the union, his first portfolio as a full-time official. He felt that health services for the millions of Brazil's poor were utterly inadequate and second-rate.

Personally, he was depressed. For at least six months he would not go out. He did not want to meet people. Every Sunday he would place flowers on the grave. Many years later, the deaths of his first wife and baby still brought tears to his eyes. Dona Lindu, worried about him, asked another child to move out so that Lula could live with her for a while and she could keep an eye on him. In fact, he lived with her for three years.

When he did come out of the worst of his depression, he reacted. He took out a different girl every weekend. It was a phase that lasted three years. But he also became more serious with one, Miriam Cordeiro, who was working as a nurse in a clinic. Lula had gotten to know her from regularly taking twin girls, the children of the brother-in-law of his sister Maria, to the clinic for treatment.[2] He took her out, the relationship became sexual, and when she was three months pregnant, she told Maria and Lula that she was expecting a baby. Lula was delighted.

The baby girl was born healthy and named Lurian—a combination of the names of her parents—but Lula soon broke up with her mother because he had met someone else. Miriam tried to cut off all contact between her child and Lula. In a dirty political trick in 1989, when Lula was running for the presidency the first time against Fernando Collor, Miriam was paid to go on television to say that Lula had wanted her to have an abortion. Lula's family says that this was rubbish.[3]

It was while he was still with Miriam that he first heard about the woman who was to become his second wife, Marisa Letícia Casa. Coming back late, up to midnight, after seeing Miriam, he would often take a taxi home. He got to know an elderly cab driver who told him how his son had been killed in a fight in the square. His daughter-in-law was pretty and was bringing up their little boy with his help.

Then, by chance, Lula met Marisa at his union office, where she had come in to get a form witnessed. Lula liked to talk to people when he was doing his social assistance duties—it was one of his skills as a union

organizer—and he had given instructions to colleagues that he would
personally attend to any good-looking widows who came in. As he drew
her out in conversation, he realized that she was the daughter-in-law of
the taxi driver.[4]

Very quickly, he fell in love with Marisa, who was working as a school
secretary in São Bernardo. Lula's determination was shown when he
persuaded Marisa to send away a former boyfriend—a Volkswagen
worker—who then stalked them for a while. Lula insisted on staying put
at her house early one evening, when the former boyfriend was due to
visit her, until she told the man it was all over between them. She
warned Lula that she would not live with him until they married. So,
after knowing each other for only five months in a whirlwind romance,
Lula and Marisa had a civil wedding. Lula became the adoptive father
of her three-year-old boy, Marcos.

Marisa was popular with Lula's family. She was the eleventh child in
a family of twelve, of Italian ancestry. She had been working since the
age of nine as a nanny and a packer in a candy factory, before getting her
position in a school.[5]

Although the couple were happy, Marisa's former in-laws were not.
They felt they had lost both a grandson and a daughter. It was not until
more than a year later that the couples were reconciled, when Lula and
Marisa invited them to be *padrinhos*, or godparents, of their first son
together, Fábio. It was an example, in family terms, of a talent for accommodation that Lula would demonstrate in wider fields.

His marriage to Marisa in 1974 provided real stability in his personal
life, and they went on to have three children together. It also coincided
with significant advances in his status and reputation in his union.

Lula had managed to recruit three hundred workers at Villares into
the metalworkers' union; but he had needed some persuading to let his
name go onto the slate of the controlling faction for the union elections
in 1972. The man who did the persuading was Paulo Vidal, who effectively ran the union. He asked Lula to stand for election as a first secretary in the so-called Green Slate. It won with more than 70 percent of the
vote, and Lula became a full-time union official, responsible for a new
social security department. He took various courses and he remained

shy of public speaking; his favorite paper remained the sporting *Gazeta Esportiva.*[6]

Vidal was a controversial figure. He was egocentric and a good orator. He was conservative in his political attitudes, and accused perhaps unfairly of fingering some communists to the dictatorship's police. When ten Ford workers came to see Lula in late 1973, suggesting they go on strike, Vidal discouraged them, warning that they could be caught by the dictatorship's National Security Law, and even tortured. But in union circles he was regarded as more progressive, organizing the first national metalworkers' congress in 1974 and seeking to modernize the union.

Shortly after that, the factory in which Vidal had worked moved, making him ineligible to preside over a union based in the municipality of São Bernardo. Vidal therefore put forward Lula as candidate for president in the 1975 elections, with himself as secretary. This controlling faction was challenged by a leftist slate, supported by the illegal and persecuted Brazilian Communist Party (PCB).

Lula had various indirect contacts with the communists, but only one formal meeting with one of its leaders, Emílio Maria de Bonfante, whom he talked to on a bench in the square in front of the mother church of São Bernardo. He strongly disliked the atmosphere of subterfuge and paranoia in which the communists worked, telling his brother Frei Chico frankly that he would not be a party to secret meetings. He wanted to act in the open.

He also learned that what he liked about the union was the sense of solidarity with workers, not its bureaucratic technicalities. Shortly before the 1975 elections, Vidal had called a massive rally, threatening a loss of medical benefits to those who failed to turn up; many assumed that they were going to be called out on strike, but Vidal made what Lula called a "Vaseline" speech and handed over the chair to one of the union's lawyers. It was another example of Vidal's lack of courage, consistency, and empathy. Nonetheless, the slate including Lula as president and Vidal as secretary was elected with 92 percent of the vote. Lula suspected that Vidal was hoping to continue to pull the strings in the union.[7]

Lula took up his post on Saturday, 19 April 1975, at a big ceremony. There were ten thousand people present—workers; Paulo Egydio Martins, the governor of São Paulo; Dona Lindu; and Marisa, who was pregnant with their first baby, Fábio. Lula was very nervous when he spoke, using a text written for him with terms he would not normally employ. But his balanced approach, reflecting Catholic social teaching, gave a clear insight into the thinking of a man who was still not thirty years old and had been given sudden responsibility.

He argued that the moment through which Brazilians were living was "one of the blackest for the individual and collective destinies of the human being." On one side, in the Soviet bloc, the people were crushed by the state, enslaved by Marxist ideology, and restricted in their freedom to think and demonstrate. But on the other, in the West, the people were enslaved by the economic power of capitalism, exploited by other men, deprived of the dignity of labor, affected by greed, and joined to mad production rhythms. Implicitly he rejected both the capitalist model being pursued by the military regime and any communist alternative to which the regime's divided revolutionary opponents adhered.

By the end of the year, however, Lula himself was faced with one of his blackest moments. In October, as president of the São Bernardo metalworkers, he had gone to a world Toyota congress in Tokyo. It was his first international outing, and he did not enjoy it. He had little money, knew no one, and disliked Japanese food. While in Japan, he was telephoned by a lawyer for the metalworkers' federation, who told him that his brother Frei Chico had been imprisoned on 4 October. Frei Chico, who was by then a member of the PCB, had been elected vice president of the metalworkers of Santo André only the week before. He had been eating lunch at a bar near his home with one of Lula's predecessors as president of the São Bernardo union when he was picked up by members of the feared DOI-Codi, a military intelligence outfit in São Paulo.[8]

This arrest was part of a much bigger anticommunist sweep throughout Brazil but carried out with particular viciousness in São Paulo, which was a center for the most ruthless security thugs who were only partly under the control of the military presidents. A major scandal erupted over the murder there of a well-known journalist, Vladimir Herzog.

The sweep aimed to destabilize the regime's more respectable opponents in the tolerated Brazilian Democratic Movement (Movimento Democrático Brasileiro, MDB) by showing that some of its parliamentarians had links with the underground communists. The MDB had done well in elections in 1974, particularly in the big cities. It was also a strike against President Ernesto Geisel, who had launched a strategy of *distensão*—or relaxation—aiming to take some of the sting out of the dictatorship.[9]

The lawyer who telephoned Lula in Tokyo warned him to stay away, as he risked being arrested if he returned to Brazil. Subsequently, the security services tortured Frei Chico to get him to state that Lula had been passing a letter to Luís Carlos Prestes, the veteran leader of the PCB, now in exile. It was nonsense. Lula had made clear that although he was biologically related to Frei Chico, he had nothing to do with the Communist Party.

Lula dismissed the lawyer's caution and decided to fly home at once. He was greeted at the São Paulo airport by union colleagues and advisers. No attempt was made to arrest him. The following day he went to the prison to try and find out what had happened to Frei Chico and also to Osvaldo Rodrigues Cavinato, another party member who had been working at the São Bernardo union, and who had been tricked into going with security men who had told him they were taking his father to the hospital. At that time it was risky to inquire about political prisoners, and Lula was insulted when he tried.

Frei Chico, who had been picked up with an incriminating document from a European communist party, was beaten, tied up, and tortured on the "dragon's chair." The soldiers who tortured him were very young and were paid extra for their work. The interrogators faked a confession, but Frei Chico totally denied the story that Lula had been a messenger for the party. After seventy-eight days in prison, Frei Chico and sixty-four others were released, and only nine were sentenced; confessions obtained by torture were rejected by the court.

A number who had been arrested in the sweep died, and Lula and the family were worried about Frei Chico's fate. But more significant was the radicalizing effect on Lula himself. He asked himself: What was the logic of arresting a worker simply because he was against social injustice? Frei Chico, the father of a family, had been working since he was ten years old. What possible order or ideology could justify the arrest and torture of men like him? Lula was simply revolted. At the same time, he lost most sense of personal fear.

But Lula also concluded that the approach of the PCB was all wrong, as was the nonconfrontational approach of his union. Although the communists might want social justice, they were crippled by their conspiratorial methods and their obsessive secrecy. Furthermore, his own union was letting down its members by opting out of any serious effort to improve wages and working conditions, and settling for a quiet life. Although the national security laws sought to outlaw strikes, other more militant groups were finding the courage to push against wage restrictions.

While the political scene was restrictive, the economic picture was more helpful to workers in the advanced industries around São Paulo. Foreign money had been pouring in to Brazil, offsetting deficits on the current account, buoyed up by talk—promoted by the military—of an "economic miracle." In fact, with tight controls on wages and the political system, annual growth in the gross national product from 1969 to 1974 had been running at 11 percent, with the lowest levels of inflation since the 1950s. Although occasionally hitting 9 percent, the average growth from 1973 to 1981 was only 5.6 percent a year.[10]

But there was a particular spurt in investment in Brazil after the oil shock of 1973, when petrodollars were sloshing around international markets. In conjunction with conservative economic management by the military, Brazil was able to take on new foreign bank loans. The fact that the country was building dangerous and ultimately unsustainable levels of debt was sometimes brushed aside.

The military regimes were not homogenous. There were running battles inside them over political and economic policy, and zigzags almost month to month. Each military president followed a slightly different line, with different cabinets. General Garrastazu Médici (1969–74) had pursued a tough anticommunist strategy with nationalist flourishes such as the attempt to "occupy" Amazonia with a vast road network and incentives for poor northeastern colonists to migrate there. He was followed by General Ernesto Geisel (1974–79), a political general and a technocrat, whose brother Orlando had been Médici's defense minister.[11] He and General Golbery do Couto e Silva, the head of the Serviço Nacional de Informações (SNI), the intelligence service,[12] were resolved to manage a gradual opening-up of the political system, but at their timing and under their control.

Broadly speaking, the frictions over political stance were between, on the one hand, the so-called *linha dura*, the hard-line anticommunists, who believed in ruthless suppression of supposed enemies, with censorship and torture, and were prepared to rule for a long time, and, on the other hand, military men who saw the takeover in 1964 as a temporary aberration from the gentler, accommodating, and constitutional political traditions of Brazil. The latter wanted a clean-up of the system—*limpeza* or *saneamento* were the words used in Portuguese. They supported the post-1964 device of "military police inquiries" (Inquéritos Policias Militares, IPMs), which led to the stripping of rights from politicians, civil servants, union leaders, intellectuals, and artists, but they looked forward to going back to the barracks when the clean-up was complete.

Although the military had been a factor in Brazilian politics since the overthrow of the empire in 1889, it had usually been in the background. The difficulties of governing Brazil could expose weaknesses in the high command and put at risk its status and privileges. In 1964, Castelo Branco had been one of those who had been in favor of a temporary takeover, but clear signs of opposition to the military whenever elections were permitted and small but embarrassing guerrilla activities had played into the hands of the *linha dura*.

Uniting both factions was an ideology—the doctrine of national security. This had been developed, with some encouragement by the U.S. military, in the officers' own "university" in Rio de Janeiro, the Escola Superior de Guerra (ESG).[13] The doctrine held that Brazil was threatened, both internally and externally, by totalitarian, revolutionary communism. This might be Soviet communism, the Cuban communism of Fidel Castro, Maoism, or the ideas of the Italian Marxist Antonio Gramsci.

What was more important was that a mortal threat was perceived to the religious and social traditions of Brazil. It justified the overthrow of Brazilian democracy, censorship, and restrictions on free association and labor movements. Parallel ideas were influencing the officer class in Argentina and Chile also.

There was also a more ambitious side to the teaching of the ESG. This was that Brazil must become a great power. It tapped into the positivist strain in the country's history, its pride in its size and extensive resources. This teaching led to some hyperbolic propaganda and use of the soccer successes in the World Cup to boost the nation's self-image.[14] The concept of the national security state was, therefore, all-embracing.

São Paulo, where Brazil's Second Army was based, was a stronghold of the *linha dura*. Since July 1969, the Second Army had been orchestrating "Operação Bandeirantes," attempting to deal with the divided but visible urban guerrillas, and setting up the vicious DOI-Codi as its instrument.[15] There had been a series of small guerrilla actions, including the theft of weapons from the fourth infantry regiment by Captain Carlos Lamarca in January 1969, a raid on the safe of the corrupt former São Paulo governor Adhemar de Barros, and the "execution" of a businessman who had helped finance Operação Bandeirantes, Henning Boilesen.[16]

The dragnet that picked up Frei Chico led also to the murder of Vladimir Herzog, the head of journalism at TV Cultura, by agents of DOI-Codi; journalists and Catholic church groups, skeptical of the official claim that he had committed suicide, organized large demonstrations, and President Geisel flew to São Paulo, where the commander of the Second Army promised that there would be no more such suicides.

Herzog had died in October 1975. But in January 1976 there was another death at Codi in São Paulo, of Manuel Fiel Filho, a worker. Geisel saw this as a challenge to his authority over the army, as well as undermining his strategy of political relaxation by fueling more disgust throughout the country. He dismissed the commander of the Second Army, General Ednardo d'Ávila Melo. Later, he fired the army minister, Sílvio Frota, and the head of his own military cabinet, Hugo de Abreu, for standing in the way of the strategy. The election in 1976 of a new U.S.

president, Jimmy Carter, was not irrelevant. Carter was talking the language of human rights, and South American dictatorships were losing favor in Washington.

Just as there were political frictions within the military regimes, so there were economic divergences. Again it was not easy to generalize, and the economic partisans did not match the different political factions. The issues were various. There were those who were concerned to control inflation, a bugbear of the professional middle class since the 1940s. There were those who were keen to see more international investment in Brazil and an opening up of the economy, which still had high protectionist tariffs. There were those who still saw a strong case for state leadership in the economy—a continuance of the Vargas approach to nationalization and the Kubitschek emphasis on development.

The military regimes relied heavily on economic technocrats, and these debates were often a continuation of those that had taken place prior to 1964. But there were differences. Whereas there had been a strong push from the leftist parties before 1964 on income inequality, land reform, and unemployment, these matters received less attention under the military; income inequality increased dramatically. Also, by the late 1970s the import substitution model for Brazil, which had led to the local manufacture of cars and other goods that had formerly been imported, was losing its power as an engine to drive the economy.

The impact of the 1973 Yom Kippur war, and its resulting oil shock, was delayed for Brazil. But by 1975, the year when Lula assumed the presidency of his union, the Geisel government was forced to react. Reis Velloso, the planning minister, prepared a second national development plan, to cover the five-year period through 1979. It aimed to reduce the nation's dependence on imported energy and promoted a national program to produce sugar-based ethanol to substitute for gasoline in vehicles; it led to a deal with West Germany, criticized by the United States, to build nuclear power stations; and it paid for two massive hydroelectric projects at Itaipú, on the Paraguay border, and Tucuruí, in Amazonia. These and other infrastructure investments, for instance in steel capacity, were largely funded by foreign loans to state or parastatal agencies.

Although Brazil's economy had raced ahead in the "miracle" years and was still growing, at a more reasonable pace, under Geisel, the reality for workers was that most were suffering from a wage freeze. The pressure was intolerable at a time of so-called boom, when government propaganda was telling everyone how great it was to be Brazilian. The official minimum salary (*salário mínimo,* set by a law going back to Vargas) was not keeping pace with the cost to buy the minimum food ration, which had been laid down in 1938. Whereas in 1970 it would have taken 105 hours and 13 minutes per month to earn enough to buy basic nutrition for one adult, by 1974 the time taken was 163 hours and 32 minutes.[17]

Also increasing visibly, even though statistical evidence was unreliable for people living in poverty and on the margins of the cash economy, was social inequality. The newsmagazine *IstoÉ* estimated in 1979 that 50 percent of the poorest Brazilians had had 14.91 percent of the gross national product in 1970, but only 11.6 percent in 1976; the 20 percent who were richest had enjoyed 62.24 percent in 1970, and 67.0 percent in 1976. A very unequal society was getting more so.[18]

It was against this difficult and complex background that Lula began work as a union president. Vidal had achieved something significant in running a first congress of the metalworkers of São Bernardo in 1974. This had opened up discussion of wages and the hiring and firing practices of engineering firms. Several agents of the dictatorship, thinly disguised as factory workers, had managed to get into the meeting. In all, around 250 had attended.

Lula, now the president, made a practice of visiting factory gates and engaging in discussion with the workers. He also shared decision making with members of the union executive, thereby limiting Vidal's influence. He made alliances with a number of leaders of other unions, such as Olívio Dutra of the bank workers of Porto Alegre, and Jacó Bittar of the petroleum workers of Campinas—both of whom helped establish the PT in the 1980s. Together these and others who were to create what was called the "new unionism" liaised to obtain more autonomy for the workers. In theory interunion cooperation was illegal, and the corporatist labor laws that the dictatorship had inherited from the Vargas era were still in place.

But by 1976 Lula and his union were in a position to begin flexing their muscles. Union representatives were recruiting more members. In a salary campaign that year, São Bernardo appealed to the labor court, the Tribunal Superior de Trabalho, to prevent a deal agreed on by the employers, the Federação dos Metalúrgicos de São Paulo, from being extended to all engineering workers. Much to the irritation of the employers, the court accepted at least part of the union's case—limiting the deal to unorganized workers, guaranteeing that young men called up to do military service would get their jobs back, and providing more security for pregnant women. When Lula held a second union congress (attended by the governor of São Paulo, 250 workers, and more police and army spies), militants spoke out against the lack of freedom.

Lula, who discovered that he was rather good with people and in the rough-and-tumble of union politics, also managed to cut Vidal down to size. Toward the end of 1976, the Ford motor company decided to reduce its medical services for staff. Lula told a journalist that he would not hold meetings inside the factory, in case management tried to influence the workforce to accept its plans. Vidal told another journalist exactly the opposite. This conflict became public, and Lula got the executive to approve a new rule—that only he, or in his absence the vice president, was entitled to speak on behalf of the union. Vidal, as secretary, lost his standing.

Lula took trouble to maintain contact with his members, not only by meeting them at the factory gate. He also gave a lift to the union's newsletter, *Tribúna Metalúrgica*, by encouraging a cartoon figure, João Ferrador. This Bolshy worker caught the fancy of members, and his sly and ill-humored comments on life and the workplace made trade unionists see their organization as more human, down-to-earth, and sympathetic.

In 1977, Lula, who was still fixated on the rights and incomes of workers and not much interested in national politics, found a cause that energized him. It enabled him to mobilize support not only among the metalworkers, but more widely across the union movement. It made him a national figure.

An economics professor, Eduardo Matarazzo Suplicy, wrote an analysis of a World Bank study in the economics section of the *Folha de São*

Paulo that showed that the military government had been manipulating Brazil's inflation figures. The Fundação Getúlio Vargas (FGV), a semiofficial institution, had defined the rate of inflation in 1973 as having been 22.5 percent, but the military government had announced that it was 12.6 percent. The issue was serious, because the *salário mínimo*—the official minimum wage—was adjusted once a year on the basis of the FGV index; with strikes prohibited by the military, the labor court (Justiça do Trabalho) simply passed on the inflation increase to all workers. Lula commissioned a study that showed that, with the passage of more than three years, the cumulative loss as a result amounted to 34.1 percent of the value of the minimum salary.[19]

Lula decided to fight, but was initially cautious as to the means. More than forty thousand workers signed a petition for the reinstatement of the lost earnings; crowded meetings were held in factories and the industrial areas, and thirteen unions were drawn into the campaign. The sense of grievance gained momentum. President Geisel refused to see the union leaders, but four of his key ministers—finance, planning, industry and commerce, and labor—spent three and half fruitless hours in discussion with them.

When Lula ran again as president of the São Bernardo metalworkers in February 1978, with a slate of fourteen directors, he won 97.3 percent of the tally and twenty-five thousand votes.[20] At the union presidential inauguration ceremony for his second term, Lula told a large crowd that it was time to end the exploitation by employers. More privately, he got his union executive to agree to a switch from a welfare approach to a riskier, more confrontational strategy aimed at boosting the workers' wages. He had acquired more skill and confidence, at a time when both police spies and leftist groups with their own agendas were seeking to infiltrate and influence the union.

In July that year he attended the fourth congress of the Confederação Nacional dos Trabalhadores da Indústria, where he was a highlight of the meeting and strengthened his contacts with the *autênticos*—other union leaders trying to build a free labor movement. There was a burgeoning excitement that trade unionists could create a new kind of movement, more responsive and democratic, and that in the process they could remake Brazil.

At this congress the *autênticos* adopted a wide-ranging charter of principles. It called for a secret, free, and direct vote (one of the ways in which the military had emasculated Congress and the presidential "elections" was by use of an indirect voting system); a new constitution; amnesty for exiles and those who had lost their political rights; human rights guarantees; a new wage policy; the right to strike; and union representatives and works committees inside factories. Political opposition to the military system was growing, with Geisel forced to close Congress; a Trotskyite group, Convergência Socialista, was challenging the PCB for militant support in the industrial belt.

But Lula gave absolute priority to the salary needs of his members, and in 1978 he had his hands full because this was the year of the first great strike wave by metalworkers. It began on 12 May, with a strike at Scania, and it ran on until 23 December. Almost every day a new strike broke out in another factory—Lula described it as a kind of fever among the workforce.[21] The strike wave does not seem to have been directly stimulated or organized by Lula in the beginning, but he and his executive were soon in the thick of it, trying to make deals for the workers involved.

It paid the union leadership to make the authorities think that the strikes were totally spontaneous. They were all, of course, technically illegal under the dictatorship and members of the executive could have been arrested. Because the flare-ups were all over the place and unpredictable, it was more difficult for the police and government to crack down on them. Lula telephoned the new, more liberal commander of the Second Army to give the unionists' side of the story. General Dilermando Gomes Monteiro then told journalists that the strikers were peaceful, there was no evidence of subversive foreign interference, and it was impossible for soldiers or police to force people to work.

The workers also invented innovative tactics—for example, going to work but not doing anything at their benches or machines, or, in the final strike of the year at Resil (a firm that made extinguishers), surrounding the building with a picket of five hundred men sitting down, so that those who had been hired to replace the strikers could not enter.[22]

The actual deals that were struck varied—the Scania workers got a 20 percent increase in real terms, others only 15 percent. But their success changed attitudes in the São Paulo working class. Furthermore, the agreements had been reached by direct negotiation between union and employers, without diktats from the Vargista labor court.

There was an informal, popular quality to these strikes. Lula and his colleagues made many of the decisions in a bar in São Bernardo run by Tia Rosa, "Aunt" Rosa, like Lula a northeasterner. They were a group of friends, not union bureaucrats. Marisa too was involved insofar as her family commitments allowed, and for Lula it was a twenty-four-hour, seven-day-a-week occupation.

Lula was disappointed that employees in one of the biggest factories, Volkswagen, never went out on strike as a whole. He criticized the disorganization of his own union, the irresponsibility of far-left students who rabble-roused in factories where they had much less to lose than other workers, the lack of clarity about the objects of a strike, and the disregard of risk. But he was immensely proud of what the hitherto downtrodden workers had achieved, he was tireless himself, and he had become a media figure with fans in unexpected places.[23] The union executive became more professional: its members gave up their own factory jobs to work full-time for the union.

Family commitments inevitably took second place. Just when the first strike broke out at Scania, Lula received a letter from Dona Mocinha that told him that his father, Aristides, had died. Aristides, retired, was living alone and was a shadow of the man who had terrorized his children. He suffered the physical consequences of alcoholism and wasted what money he had on prostitutes. Lula asked his brothers to attend to a funeral, but when they got to Santos they found that Aristides had been buried twelve days earlier as a pauper. Lula's father had had little influence on his career, except that he respected his mother the more for the way she responded to his father's treatment of her, and he was determined to have more to show for his own life.

In July, after the first wave of strikes had been settled, Lula and Marisa had their second son, Sandro Luís. There was no question of paternity leave. Lula was actually fourteen hundred miles away, at a conference of petroleum workers in Salvador, when the baby was born. Lula, Marisa, and their three children were now living together in a small house in Jardim Lavínia, São Bernardo do Campo. It had been bought two years earlier with a loan from the state housing bank. Marisa found it hard to adjust to Lula's heavy travel schedule. The following year she started going to the strike meetings herself.

The strike wave in 1978 had a number of wider consequences, in addition to giving a new direction to the Brazilian labor movement. It was not possible to classify it as a result of foreign intervention by Castroites or by the Brazilian leftist exiles who had been forced abroad after the overthrow of Goulart in 1964. It was not connected to the small groups of armed insurrectionists, now largely killed or rounded up by the military regime. It could not be blamed on agitation by Catholic radicals, members of the communist movement (which had now split into pro-Soviet and pro-Chinese wings), or Trotskyites—although all these had contributed. It was predominantly a home-grown, rather unideological rebellion against the compression of wages in the advanced manufacturing sector.[24]

For this reason it was seen as a threat by employers and their allies in the military government. It challenged the high rates of return on capital in the early years of the Brazilian "miracle," which had led to an influx of foreign money. The fruits of growth had not been shared with labor because unions had been decapitated and strikes prohibited. Employers and the government had been caught off guard by the sudden upsurge of labor unrest that started at Scania. They resolved to act differently in the future, mobilizing police and other agencies of force. At the same time, the excitement among workers was infectious and beyond the capacity of Lula and other leaders to control.

What happened in 1979 was a great deal rougher. Whereas in 1978 more than 539,000 workers had participated in 24 strikes, the following year more than 3.2 million workers, more than a quarter of them metalworkers in the auto and engineering industries, participated in 113 strikes. The labor struggles, which involved sharp repression by the government and temporary closure of the São Bernardo metalworkers' union, also interweaved with political developments. On 15 March 1979, in a flamboyant ceremony in Brasília, General Geisel handed over the presidency to the last of the military presidents, João Baptista de Oliveira Figueiredo.

In an extraordinarily ambitious move, Lula had hoped to roll out a general strike to coincide with the handover. It was an example of his own growing confidence, boosted by media interest in what was nicknamed the "trade union republic" of the ABC districts around São Paulo; he himself had now grown a beard to add to his moustache.[25]

In fact, three days before the change of president, Lula and other union leaders reached a good agreement with the employers' organization in São Paulo, FIESP. This would have given increases of 63 percent to the poorest metalworkers, and 44 percent to the higher paid. But when Lula tried to convince his members to support the deal at a large meeting in a soccer stadium—he stood on a table in the middle and those nearest to him had to pass his message outward, as there were no loudspeakers—they shouted him down. "Strike, strike, strike," they cried. It was an awkward moment for Lula. "So, we are on strike," he replied. He warned that it might last a long time.

Employers and state authorities were still unable to produce a coordinated response. The regional labor court (Tribunal Regional do Trabalho)—an instrument of the corporatist labor system—awarded an increase of 44 percent, but declared the strike illegal. FIESP, the employers, offered considerably more. Armed military police broke up a small cordon round the Pirelli factory, and police threw tear gas at workers outside the Volkswagen factory.

Although paid advertisements on radio stations urged the strikers to return to work, the strike stayed solid. Lula told meetings that the whole future of the working class depended on success. His rhetoric was exalted. "We will give our life, if necessary," he said.[26] By 21 March, Lula and two other union leaders had a private meeting with a new minister of labor, Murilo Macedo, and eight employers in São Paulo. Although Lula authorized one of his aides to make an agreement, he did not try to sell it to a mass meeting, which insisted on a continuance of the strike. Cleverly, he asked for a vote of confidence in the executive, but he returned home feeling devastated, and others called him a traitor.[27]

After that the conflict sharpened. Authorities shut down the São Bernardo union. Lula moved in with his father-in-law. The Catholic Church launched a relief fund for the families of strikers, and put churches at the disposal of the union for meetings. Not permitted to use the Vila Euclides soccer stadium, twenty thousand metalworkers gathered in the Samuel Sabatini square in São Bernardo, also known as the Paço Municipal. They were met by one thousand shock troops, more than a hundred armored cars, and a vehicle firing sand and colored water. The workers stayed put.

The shock troops threw tear gas canisters, which the strikers threw back at them. The mayor and a colonel asked for calm and trust in the authorities. The workers sang the national anthem. They called out Lula's name. The colonel telephoned the head of the military police, and obtained permission to withdraw his forces. The bishop of São Bernardo, Dom Cláudio Hummes, led the gathering in the Lord's prayer, and the crowd dispersed. Dismissed as unimportant by the government, it was a moral victory for the strike and encouraged opposition politicians to criticize the state intervention in the union.

The 1979 strike had not always seen Lula at his best. At one point he was directly warned by the general commanding the Second Army that if he turned up at meetings he would be arrested. He went missing for a few days, and other strike leaders tried to represent him. When a delegation went looking for him he was found at home, playing with his children, and a left-wing actress, Lélia Abramo, told him that he had to turn up at the next assembly and resume his leadership.

The strikes spread beyond São Paulo and beyond the metalworkers. The unions could not afford any strike pay, and there was real hardship. The metalworkers' strike was not called off until 12 May, two months after it had begun. Most of the workers got an increase of 63 percent, with a discount of 50 percent for the days they had not worked, and their promise to put in extra hours in compensation. A mass meeting, at which tears were shed, accepted the agreement and gave unanimous backing to Lula and his executive.[28]

There was no let-up in conflict in the rest of 1979. One auto firm would fire a worker so that another could take him on at lower pay. The Ministry of Labor intervened in bank workers' unions in Rio de Janeiro, São Paulo, and Porto Alegre. When the metalworkers of São Paulo decided in September to go on strike, over the opposition of their president, Joaquim dos Santos Andrade, they were met with violence. Troops broke up picket lines, churches were invaded to disperse union meetings, and strikers were persecuted in their home districts. In one factory gate confrontation, a Catholic union leader was shot dead, strengthening the church's support for workers' rights.

The salary campaign of 1980 for the São Bernardo metalworkers was more bitter still. The perception among the government and employers that Lula was in any sense tractable or nonpolitical had vanished. There was a feeling on both sides that the union movement was challenging the state and the regime. At the same time, the Figueiredo government, launched by Geisel with the hope that it would complete a return to democracy, was running into difficulty. In August 1979, the government had agreed to a political amnesty, and celebrated exiles, such as Leonel Brizola, Goulart's brother-in-law, Miguel Arraes, former governor of Pernambuco, and Luís Carlos Prestes, veteran leader of the pro-Soviet PCB, had returned within a couple of months.

But Figueiredo's hope that he would disarm the opposition by conceding an amnesty backfired. Instead the opposition wanted more, and quickly. Army critics of democratization exploited the situation. The Machiavellian General Golbery, who was trying to manipulate a controlled relaxation from the intelligence service, was dismissed. Hardliners were getting into positions of power, and right-wingers were organizing provocative acts of terrorism to destabilize the process. The economy was running into trouble.

In 1979, Lula was already in advanced planning for a PT, a workers' party, whose birth is described in the next chapter.[29] Its formal act of foundation took place on 10 February 1980. As a labor leader, Lula saw an increase in wages as only one of the demands a union should make. He wanted a forty-hour workweek and freedom for workers to elect their representatives in factories. He was fighting for job security. He sought the right to strike, free collective bargaining, and an end to the corporatist labor legislation. Having built alliances among metalworkers' unions in various cities, and with other types of workers, he wanted an end to the divisive union structure that had been imposed by Getúlio Vargas and maintained by subsequent governments.

He also realized that, in the kind of struggle in which the metalworkers were engaged, they needed a new kind of organization. In the previous two years, they had depended too much on him and a handful of other leaders. Hence the union introduced a system of decentralization, a pyramid in which an executive related to a commission of 450 people elected in factory meetings, who were responsible for factory-level coordination. It meant that, if the union was closed by state intervention and its leaders were arrested, a strike could be maintained.

On 1 April 1980, the metalworkers of São Bernardo went on strike again. The previous day, sixty thousand of them had gathered in the soccer stadium of Vila Euclides, backing the strike and singing Brazil's hymn of independence. Nonviolence was a crucial tactic, and one reason for the sturdy support of the Catholic Church. Although the government was all set to declare the strike illegal and occupy the union offices, the union's lawyer, Almir Pazzianoto, succeeded in persuading the regional labor court (the Tribunal Regional do Trabalho) that it was incompetent to decide the legality of the strike.

On 2 April, Pazzianoto addressed another vast crowd at the Vila Euclides to explain the court's decision, thinking it would enable Lula to call off the strike. But at that point two army helicopters, with eight armed soldiers in each, began flying low over the stadium for twenty minutes, in a blatant attempt to intimidate. Lula's adopted son Marcos, then six years old, hung on to his mother's skirt while Lula called on the unionists to stay calm. An elderly right-wing general had taken over the Second Army and ordered up the helicopters. But the effect was to make the strikers more determined to carry on.

The atmosphere was difficult for militants. A new government incomes policy provided for cost of living increases for workers and made it hard for firms to pass on higher wage awards in higher prices. At the same time, a recession was impending and jobs were becoming scarcer. In neighboring São Caetano, on 9 April, a mass meeting of metalworkers chaired by Lula's communist brother, Frei Chico, voted to return to work. Frei Chico said that the men were going back anyway.

On 14 April, the regional labor court changed its mind and declared the strike illegal. Five days later, Lula, twelve other union leaders, and some lawyers, including the president of the Catholic Commission for Justice and Peace, were arrested. They were held under the regime's National Security Law. The strike went on, coordinated by the improved and decentralized organization of the union.

Although the military occupied much of São Bernardo, dragging unionists from churches, the Catholic Church defended the legitimacy of a strike that the government had labeled "political." The hierarchy was vocal in support, with Cardinal Evaristo Arns and Bishops Mauro Morelli and Cláudio Hummes speaking out.[30] Volunteers provided food and money for the strikers, and there were weekly lines outside churches as the strikers' families came to collect food and money.

Lula was relatively well treated in prison. When he had a toothache, Romeu Tuma, the director-general of DOPS, the political police that detained him,[31] arranged for him to see a dentist. Marisa visited him in jail with the children, and Fabio Luís, then five years old, said, "Mommy, my father is in Tuma's Hotel."[32] When Lula learned that his beloved mother, Dona Lindu, had been taken to the hospital with cancer of the uterus, he was allowed to visit her. When she died on 12 May, he was allowed to attend the burial.

Lula and the other union prisoners were given preventative detention and went on a hunger strike in protest. Outside, the real strike went on. But strikers were trickling back to work, and on 11 May the strike was called off. On 20 May, after thirty-one days in prison, Lula was released along with the other unionists. When he got home, he set free his caged birds in an act of solidarity. In 1979, some had attacked him as a traitor for being willing to give up the strike too soon. In 1980, he resolved to stick it out to the end.

Less than a week after his release, on 26 May, Lula assumed leadership of the national executive of the Partido dos Trabalhadores, the PT, and a new chapter in his life opened. State intervention in his union ended, the workers went back to work, and Lula finished his second term as president of the São Bernardo metalworkers. His authority within the union was demonstrated afresh.

Much to everyone's surprise, he chose Jair Meneghelli, a thirty-four-year-old worker from the tool shop at Ford, to be the presidential candidate on "his" union slate. Meneghelli was little known in the union and, like Lula when he was first involved in union affairs, was more interested in soccer than the details of wage negotiation or the labor movement. He was up against knowledgeable and well-known candidates backed by the PCB and by the MR-8, one of the formerly armed antimilitary groups. The MR-8 ran a smear campaign, alleging that Lula's group had made off with the union's strike fund.

Meneghelli had not wanted to be a candidate and, in a press conference with representatives of both slates, Lula answered questions on his behalf. But when the results were declared he had won overwhelmingly, with more than twenty-seven thousand votes, or 89 percent. It was an extraordinary testimony to Lula's popularity.

The real importance of the industrial campaigns spearheaded by the São Bernardo metalworkers from 1977 to 1980 was in the raising of consciousness, rather than in the raising of wages. Many in the São Paulo industrial belt had come, like Lula, from a rural background in the northeast or other areas. Politically and socially they were often naïve, and many lacked formal education. The succession of strikes over these years, with their discussions, mass meetings, and personal hardship, provided a tough and practical schooling. It put them in touch with Catholic radicals, students, and those politicians who were opposed to the military regime.

The "new unionism" of these years, led by better-paid workers in the more advanced industries, was honed in the face of constant repression and the presence of police spies at meetings. The workers involved felt they had to rely on themselves alone. They wanted their own representatives. They wanted to break out of the narrow compartmentalism imposed by the corporatist labor structure, in which union leaders known as *pelegos* were in the pay of the bosses and the government. They recognized that freedom for themselves and their own bargaining could come only in the context of a freer, more democratic Brazil.

By 1980, there was a growing alliance between the more assertive unions, the Catholic grassroots movement that had originated in the 1960s but had taken on a new life in reaction to the dictatorship, the church hierarchy, and professionals and politicians. Labor unrest had spread widely. In that year there were strikes by primary and secondary teachers in Minas Gerais and the northeast. More remarkably, 240,000 sugar workers, underpaid on the cane plantations in Pernambuco but now seen by the regime as providing a source of biofuel, went on strike. They had often been intimidated in the past but in this year forty-two rural unions got together, efficiently coordinated by the Catholic land pastorate (Pastoral da Terra da Igreja Católica), to organize a strike. It showed the range and capacity of labor solidarity.

The self-confidence of increasing numbers of workers, as the military regime looked to control the timing and nature of its own demise, was paralleled by the ferment of other types of social movement in the cities and the countryside. There was a do-it-yourself and democratic spirit to many of these, although ideological conflicts between Marxists and Catholic radicals were not far from the surface.

In the shantytowns or *favelas* of the big cities, the residents were getting together in local organizations to demand basic services—drinking water, sanitation, electricity, child daycare, and schools. There were thirteen hundred of these associations in greater São Paulo, and one per week was being formed in the state of Rio de Janeiro in 1980. In 1978, organized *favelados* managed to collect 1.5 million signatures on a petition calling for a price freeze on basic foods.

In the countryside, where the church's Comissão Pastoral da Terra had been formed in 1975 to improve the lot of laborers, dissatisfaction was growing with the conservatism of CONTAG, the Confederação Nacional dos Trabalhadores na Agricultura. CONTAG was the old grouping of rural unions. Calls for land reform, which had been championed by peasant leagues in the run-up to the 1964 coup—and were a major reason why the takeover had been supported by rural landowners—were bubbling up again. In 1979 and 1980, there were successful land occupations in the states of Rio Grande do Sul, Santa Catarina, and São Paulo; these led to expropriation of a few properties and their transfer to the landless.

Although some of these social movements were purely secular, many were influenced by the Catholic Church. Since the 1960s, the church had stimulated a network of grassroots communities (Comunidades Eclesias de Base, CEBs) that were involved in social action as well as practical Christianity. They were regarded with suspicion by the military governments, and Dom Helder Camara, a prominent supporter and the archbishop of Recife, was seen as a crypto-communist. But the CEBs, like the Brazilian bishops, had been influenced by the social teaching of Pope John XXIII and the Second Vatican Council. Some too were persuaded by liberation theology that it was the duty of Christians to end exploitation of man by man.

The forthright position of the Catholic bishops in favor of human rights and against growing income inequality under the military dovetailed with the local action by the grassroots CEBs. Both came publicly to the aid of the metalworkers when they were on strike, and both were contributing to a restlessness for social and political change in many parts of Brazil in the late 1970s.

The period from 1976 to 1980 saw Lula transformed from a shy speaker, drawn gradually into the union movement, into a national figure with thousands of workers hanging on his every word. He loved the oxygen of publicity, the mass meetings, the shouting of his name by enthusiastic crowds. He was unafraid.

But in his own attitudes he was still somewhat naïve, still giving absolute commitment to the working class, specifically to the metalworkers and those like them. He was not well-read, though he had *The Gulag Archipelago* by Alexander Solzhenitsyn, a biography of Gandhi, and John Reed's *Ten Days That Shook the World* on his bookshelves when he was interviewed for *Playboy* in 1979. Asked whom he admired, he listed Tiradentes, the dentist who was executed in an early attempt to win Brazil's independence from Portugal, Gandhi, and Che Guevara; then he suggested Mao Tse-tung and, surprisingly, Adolf Hitler—correcting himself quickly to say that he admired Hitler's dedication, not his ideology. In truth, Lula himself, though influenced by Catholicism and some of the leftists he knew, remained unideological.

He was also sustained by a loyal wife. Marisa had been applauded in the São Paulo cathedral on Sunday, 20 April 1980, when she spoke of her imprisoned husband in a service attended by seven thousand people; Cardinal Evaristo Arns was officiating. She had turned up at the Vila

Euclides when the helicopters tried to terrorize the metalworkers. It was she who telephoned the jail to tell Lula that Dona Lindu had died.

But if Marisa was as involved in the struggle as Lula himself, Dona Lindu thought he was seriously mistaken. He was so busy that she did not see him often. She worried when she saw his photo on the cover of newsmagazines. A relatively simple person herself, she could not imagine where all this was leading, except perhaps into danger. She hoped a guardian angel would watch over him. Frei Chico had been tortured. Might not Lula suffer the same fate? Taking on the government, the police, and the military was risky. It must have been hard for Lula to know of his mother's disapproval. But he had outgrown the limitations of his family background.

3 THE PT, THE WORKERS' PARTY

In all the hubbub at the end of the 1970s, with an amnesty, major strikes, and a sense that the military dictatorship was in its final throes, a different note was sounded. Lula and a group of other more progressive union leaders were calling for a distinctive workers' party—the Partido dos Trabalhadores, the PT. This was a contentious idea and, for many in opposition circles, divisive.

It was divisive because it overtly introduced class-based politics to Brazil. This put off many in the middle class and many traditional politicians and liberal professionals who had been struggling against the military through the tolerated opposition party—the Movimento Democrático Brasileiro, the MDB. For them it was essential to maintain a broad front if the dictatorship was to be banished and a full democracy—something Brazil had never had—was to be achieved. Fernando Henrique Cardoso, then a young sociology professor returning from exile, was among many who took that view.

It was also divisive on the left. The old PCB had split, with the Maoist PCdoB winning credit for tying up tens of thousands of troops in its Araguaia guerrilla campaign, though the PCB retained support in the unions. Trotskyites were also active. Some Marxists were critical of the idea of a PT because it seemed unideological and too concerned with bread-and-butter issues. As one PCB supporter said, there was already one party that struggled for Brazil's working class, and it had been founded as long ago as 1922.[1] The PCB, which had pursued a strategy of infiltration of legal parties since before 1964, was also working for a negotiated transition out of the military regime. The smaller Trotskyite groups were more sympathetic to a PT.

Lula had first brought up the PT question publicly at the conference of oil workers in Bahia in the middle of 1978,[2] but there had been informal discussion in unions in the main industrial centers earlier that year. What was the motivation? Undoubtedly there was a feeling that none of the existing politicians were truly representative of the workers. They had not spotted or campaigned against the erosion of the *salário mínimo*. Workers who had been standing up for their rights did not want to be mere vote banks for bourgeois and opportunist congressmen. Furthermore, the claims of the Marxist groups were bogus; they did not have much support among industrial workers, and atheism was anathema to those from a Catholic tradition.

When Lula went to Brasília to try to get support from MDB congressmen for the strikes and union demands, he found little sympathy. In September 1978 he had gone with a delegation of union leaders to persuade them to vote against a measure of the Geisel government designed to prohibit strikes in essential services including transportation, banking, and petrochemicals. But only two MDB deputies, each of whom had other underground allegiances, gave them a hearing.[3] Lula concluded that the existing Congress was totally aligned with the interests of employers.

At the same time, the union movement was gaining confidence. Between 1960 and 1980, the number of workers in the more advanced industries had almost quadrupled, from 2.9 million to 10.6 million.[4] The strike wave had shown that they were prepared to use their muscle and take risks.

In 1979 the momentum for a new party increased, stimulated by the knowledge that the military regime was preparing new legislation for the formation of parties. The regime was concerned that MDB was overtaking ARENA, the conservative party that supported the regime. The object of the legislation was to create a multiplication of parties, to muddy the waters, and to make it harder for a more democratic system to undo its economic and institutional changes or lead to revenge.

The proposal for a PT was officially launched at a congress of the São Paulo metalworkers in Lins in January 1979. Lula was not the only union figure involved; among others were those who had been working together to coordinate the strikes—people such as Jacó Bittar of the oil workers and Paulo Skromov Matos of the leather workers. Nonetheless, the key movers took care to keep the party political planning separate from the organization of the strikes.[5]

But progress that year was erratic, partly because an informal committee consisting of these enthusiasts circulated a charter of principles at May Day rallies throughout Brazil, which others thought was going too far too fast. Some felt that the metalworkers, or the workers from São Paulo more generally, were hustling the rest of the country. Even Lula, after talking with workers elsewhere, sometimes urged caution.

There were discussions among unionists, intellectuals, and MDB politicians, and provisional PT committees were being set up in some states. These might be based on networks of friends, existing leftist or Catholic groups, or more structured union connections. But by 28 June, Lula was promising to distribute a draft program, suggesting that it would then be for the workers to decide whether to go ahead. Significantly, he widened the concept of "worker" beyond those who were unionized to include all wage earners and those involved in social movements such as the neighborhood associations.

At a large meeting in São Paulo on 18 August organized by politicians on the left of the MDB, Lula argued strongly for an independent workers' party because the union structure, however modernized, could not deliver everything that workers needed. Such a party should welcome politicians from the MDB. The party should not be constructed by unions as institutions, as this could compromise their own work. Union leaders might or might not belong to the PT. Hence the PT was launched on a different trajectory from that of the British Labour Party—founded at the start of the twentieth century as an offshoot of trade unions—and comparable parties such as the German Social Democratic Party.

The final pieces in the jigsaw were put together later in the year. At a meeting in a São Bernardo restaurant on 14 October, around a hundred people, including Lula, decided on a structure for the new party.

Five days later, the government sent to Congress its party reform law, which abolished the two parties, ARENA and MDB, set up the year after the military takeover. The formal foundation of the PT took place in São Paulo in February 1980, at a meeting of three hundred people in an auditorium of the journalists' union named after the murdered Vladimir Herzog. The party adopted a red five-pointed star as its symbol, and Lula's wife, Marisa, sewed an example, using some Italian cloth she had kept by.

The new rules gave parties a year to get organized and required them to hold conventions in at least one-fifth of the municipalities in at least nine states. They also gave advantages to parties that had at least 10 percent of the membership of the Chamber of Deputies and Senate, and that had an inherited structure; state funding was also to be made available, 90 percent on the basis of the number of congressional representatives a party had succeeded in electing.

All this gave considerable assistance to the conservative PDS (Partido Democrático Social), the heir to ARENA, and to the PMDB (Partido do Movimento Democrático Brasileiro), a continuation of the MDB. The PT, which acquired a small number of leftist deputies from the São Paulo state assembly, never had significant support from the existing Congress, which had not been freely elected. The other new "opposition" party was the PDT (Partido Democrático Trabalhista), formed by Leonel Brizola, who had returned after the amnesty for exiles, but who had failed to recapture the valuable PTB name, which instead was gained by Getúlio's great-niece Yvete Vargas for the party she headed. Over the next couple of years, PT organizers had to fight off constant criticism from those who thought that the PMDB, PT, and PDT ought to work closely together, if not merge outright.

Achieving the required number of party branches and following the new procedures to get registration required a heroic effort by the PT. Money for travel around the country was scarce, and organizers placed a high premium on genuine grassroots participation. Sectarianism was a constant risk, though Lula, perhaps naïvely, hoped that workers would elect their representatives based on merit rather than label. On 22 October, the party requested provisional registration from the Supreme

Electoral Tribunal, showing that it had regional commissions in eighteen states and municipal commissions in 647 municipalities in thirteen states.[6] The PT was the last of the parties to get registration, yet by June 1981 it was claiming some two hundred thousand members.

The PT was the creation of a group of people who had been radicalized by their experiences fighting for union rights in the late 1970s. It was not a creation of Lula alone, though he was a symbolic, charismatic figure. It was part of a much wider context of the struggle for democracy and socioeconomic progress in the dying days of the military regime.

The end of the 1970s and beginning of the 1980s were a turbulent time in Brazil. The attempt by the military regime to secure itself a soft exit was under constant threat from its own right-wingers, who wanted no backsliding from a *linha dura*; from a wide range of opponents in civil society, who were hoping to build, for the first time, a truly democratic state; and from events that were often outside the government's control. An aggressive strike movement led to violent police repression, especially in 1980. And Brazil's systemic internal inflation and increased dependence on external loans meant that the economy could suffer unpredictable shocks.

A major campaign was under way to grant amnesty to the politicians, artists, and intellectuals who had lost their civic and political rights. Many had been forced into exile. In August 1979, in President Figueiredo's first year in office, and quite rapidly, Congress granted the amnesty. On one level, it was a response to the campaign and part of the government's strategy for relaxation (*distensão*). On another, it was designed to sow confusion among opponents, as returnees such as Leonel Brizola, Miguel Arraes,[7] and Luís Carlos Prestes sought to resume political careers cut short in 1964.

Right-wing terrorism aimed to destabilize the relaxation strategy and was a challenge both to public security and to the authority of the military regime. Those behind it were torturers and blind anticommunist ideologues, loose cannons lurking in the shadows of the security apparatus. In 1976, ten bomb attacks, for which an "Anticommunist Alliance of Brazil" claimed responsibility, shocked the country; in the same year, the bishop of Nova Iguaçu, in the state of Rio, was kidnapped. Every year from then on until 1981 there were bomb attacks. In 1979, for example, a bomb exploded in a vehicle belonging to one of Lula's colleagues, João Pires de Vasconcelos, the president of the Metalworkers of João Monlevade, in Minas Gerais. It was difficult to guarantee Lula's personal safety.[8]

The culmination took place on the night of 30 April 1981, when two bombs went off at the Riocentro convention center in Rio de Janeiro. There, twenty thousand young people had gone to a concert to listen to musicians linked to the opposition. The explosions had a direct connection to the security apparatus of DOI-Codi, as indicated by the fact that one of the bombs went off prematurely in a car, killing a sergeant and army captain.

This led to a crisis within the regime. General Golbery do Couto e Silva, a Machiavellian figure who had been trying to steer *distensão* through two presidencies, resigned in protest against the loss of control over the security apparatus. President Figueiredo, who himself had commanded the SNI, the national intelligence service, brokered a deal within the system; those responsible for the attacks would not be tried, but the *linha dura* would have to accept that the government was committed to freer elections. In November, therefore, the government produced a package that would govern elections in 1982.

Opposition to the military comprised a broad and often disparate front. There were the liberal professionals, such as lawyers and journalists, whose work had been directly hampered by the dictatorship at its apogee. In September 1980, for example, a letter bomb addressed to the president of the Brazilian lawyers' association (OAB) killed his secretary. University lecturers, such as the future president Fernando Henrique Cardoso—who had had to flee to Europe via Chile—were opposed to the regime. Students, depoliticized in the 1970s at a time of university expansion, were recovering their voice of protest. Artists and writers had been overwhelmingly against the regime from the beginning, and famous musicians such as Gilberto Gil and Chico Buarque had been in exile.

The Catholic Church was, by the end of the 1970s, also largely against the dictatorship. This was not only on ideological grounds, related to human rights abuses and the soaring inequalities between rich and poor.

It was also the product of the church's daily work with Catholic base communities, with workers involved in strikes, and with land conflicts in rural areas. In São Bernardo, an extreme case, priests were working hand in glove with the strike committees.

Several bishops were outspoken in their criticisms—Archbishop Dom Helder Camara in Recife, Dom Cláudio Hummes in São Bernardo, and Dom Adriano Hypolito in Nova Iguaçu. Cardinal Dom Paulo Evaristo Arns, the archbishop of São Paulo, provided leadership in the country's fast-growing industrial and commercial capital. He decried the worsening poverty in São Paulo's periphery of slums.

There was also a significant campaign in the political class for democracy and civic freedom, reflected in the media. Lula, who defined the main division in Brazilian society as being between exploiters and the workers they exploited, had personally supported Cardoso as an MDB candidate in an election in São Paulo in 1978. In 1979, an "opposition" candidate, running against Figueiredo in the electoral college of senators and deputies, which chose the new president, had collected 266 votes to Figueiredo's 335.[9] But MDB politicians were far from united, some being more willing than others to play along with the regime and its rules. Ulysses Guimarães, for example, argued that their duty was to regain the rule of law for Brazil, not to put up candidates for the presidency who were bound not to win.[10]

The resurgence of inflation at the end of the 1970s and the second oil price shock of 1979 added to the unpopularity of the regime and the uncertainties surrounding its departure. The annual inflation rate rose from 40 percent in 1978 to 55 percent in 1979, 90 percent in 1980, and around 100 percent in the two following years. Higher world interest rates and the damage caused by frost and drought to Brazil's agricultural production also hurt the economy.

Hence, although the electoral package had required a two-thirds majority in Congress to change the Constitution under which the military had been operating, President Figueiredo was still taking a risk in permitting general elections in November 1982. State governors and deputy governors would be directly elected for the first time since elections were suspended by the military in 1966.

This was the first test for the PT. Lula, whose initial intention had been to stay out of the election to promote the party nationwide, was running for governor of his adopted state, São Paulo. The previous year he had taken the precaution of changing his name legally to incorporate *Lula*, the nickname by which he was best known, so that it could be more easily recognized on a ballot.[11]

Many of the PT candidates were young and new to politics. The election rules, designed to baffle the less sophisticated and barely literate, required a voter to vote six times—from the presidency down to a seat on the town council—or the vote was treated as null and void.

The election campaign showed up both the strengths and the weaknesses of the PT. It was relatively strong in the industrial belt in and around São Paulo; all told, it elected six out of a possible sixty federal deputies for the state, and nine out of a possible eighty-four deputies in the state legislature. Lula himself came in fourth in the contest for the governorship, with 1.144 million votes, behind both PDS and PTB candidates and Franco Montoro, the PMDB candidate, who won easily with 5.209 million votes.

For Lula it was a personal as well as a political setback. Five years later, in a speech to the PT's fifth national meeting, he reflected ironically on a campaign "in which the least dangerous of us had been condemned to ninety years in prison." Many voters were frightened of candidates who could be stereotyped as jailbirds, and he personally had misunderstood the psychology of working-class voters.

He had promoted himself as "a Brazilian just like you"—a former dye worker and lathe operator and a trade unionist. But workers did not necessarily want someone like themselves as a governor, though they did as a union leader. They expected someone better off, and better educated, as a governor.

Across the whole of Brazil, the PT did poorly. To the great disappointment of its supporters, it did not meet the law's minimum requirement of 5 percent of votes nationally, and 3 percent in each of nine states; this would have entitled it to public funding. Its best efforts were in São Paulo, with 9.9 percent, and the small Amazon state of Acre, with 5.4 percent.

It did appear to be a Paulista party, and the fact that its best-known face was tied down in the São Paulo governorship election meant that Lula could do little to help struggling candidates elsewhere. The main winner was the PMDB, benefiting from an opposition to the military regime that had lasted for nearly two decades. The PDS, successor to the pro-regime ARENA party, did well in the conservative, economically backward, and clientelistic states of the northeast. In a result that indicated that pre-1964 figures still had support, Leonel Brizola won the governorship of Rio de Janeiro for the PDT.

The PT's campaign theme was "work, land, and liberty." It wanted to end the dictatorship, to end hunger, to provide land and better wages for rural workers, to promote better health and less profit from illness, to define access to education and culture as a right, not a class privilege, to promote equality and an end to discrimination, to prevent the stealing of public money, to end the exploitation of public contracts by private companies, and, in a rhetorical flourish, to claim "power to the workers and the people—the workers' struggle is the same all over the world—only socialism will solve our problems once and for all."[12]

Although the PT had been created from a coalition of factions, it ran its election in a centralized way. The same election materials were provided to all its candidates. Those who were elected were expected to turn over 40 percent of their salaries to the party.

There were several features of this first electoral test for the PT that the party took to heart afterward. It became involved in a furious dispute with the PMDB, which saw the PT as a splitter, dividing the antigovernment vote. PMDB leaders, especially in São Paulo, called for the *voto útil*, a useful vote; electors should not waste their votes on parties with little chance of winning.

Lula saw the PMDB as an enemy, describing it as hostile to the working class, as "flour out of the same sack" as the PDS, and as cozying up to the government. He denounced the way in which the media, which had built him up as a hero only three years earlier, were now attacking him. He dismissed as slander the idea that the military government would not let him or Brizola take office if they were elected.[13]

The PT realized that it was bad at public relations with the media and did not appreciate how its propaganda would be seen by others. Strict limits on political advertising meant that only photos and brief biographies appeared on TV; by showing that many PT candidates had been imprisoned by the regime, it inadvertently suggested that they were criminals. It also learned that its capacity to mobilize huge crowds—Lula spoke to as many as one hundred thousand at a rally in the state capital and almost one-third of the population of the small town of Nova Odessa—had little to do with its ability to win their votes. To begin with, it complained that polling organizations were undercounting the PT vote because polling estimates seemed so small compared with the turnout at PT meetings. But the pollsters were right. Lula himself was a celebrity and an exciting speaker, but this did not mean that audiences would vote for him or the new party, or that all the electors were coming to PT rallies.

There were various positives, however. The first related to the performance of Lula himself. In this campaign, in what was to become a running criticism in his early presidential campaigns, he was attacked as too uneducated to be an appropriate governor of the most powerful state in Brazil; the accusation was that he might be all right as a strike leader, but greater sophistication was needed to govern São Paulo. But in fact, in televised discussions among the governorship candidates, Lula debated the issues on terms of equality. A poll taken after the first debate, broadcast on 14 August, showed that the majority of viewers thought that he had won the argument.

The second positive, which the party could not easily interpret, showed that it had an ability to win support outside the unionized workers. Its foothold in Acre, where the PT was winning elections into the twenty-first century, illustrated this wider reach.[14] And, although the organized workers in greater São Paulo were critical to PT's support in the state, the deputies it elected were not all trade unionists and reflected different elements in the party's makeup. For example, Eduardo Matarazzo Suplicy, a former professor and scion of the Matarazzo dynasty, had been fighting corruption from the MDB before joining the PT. Irma Passoni was a Catholic activist who had been an organizer of the popular movement against the rise in the cost of living. Beth Mendes was a film and TV star. José Genoino Neto was a Marxist who had been captured in the Araguaia guerrilla campaign.

Nonetheless, the PT's poor showing in the 1982 elections was a profound blow to activists. Many of them felt that they would do better to return to work in the unions and social movements that had inspired them in the 1970s. The handful of councilors and deputies who had won felt that they had little institutional support from the party.

It was also a personal blow to Lula, who suddenly had a great emptiness in his life. His union was no longer under state intervention and he had handed it over to Meneghelli. He had lost the election, which he had persuaded himself he had a chance of winning. He would wake up in the morning with nothing much to do. In fact, he returned to the Metalworkers' Union of São Bernardo, becoming a director on Meneghelli's executive committee. At the same time, he retained his position as president of the PT's national committee.

The following year, Lula promoted a solidarity strike in the ABC zone that led to another intervention in his union. In July 1983, his old friends the petroleum workers of Campinas launched a strike in protest against a military decree-law that reduced the rights of employees of state enterprises; they shut down the refinery at Paulínia, responsible for a third of the country's gasoline. Lula, who was not even a delegate to the Metalworkers' Congress at Piracicaba, made an off-the-cuff speech urging that the metalworkers should go on strike in solidarity. The congress was suspended, and Lula went off to Campinas in such a hurry to tell the Campinas workers the news that he left Marisa behind. Meneghelli had difficulty taking control of the strike, and once again the Ministry of Labor took over the union.

The conflict rapidly escalated. The government had already taken over the union of petroleum workers of Campinas and Paulínia, throwing out its president, Jacó Bittar, who was also secretary-general of the PT. Workers throughout the country decided to hold a national strike on 21 July, in protest against the government's economic policy and its willingness to negotiate spending cuts with the International Monetary Fund (IMF).

The strike was particularly effective in São Paulo, Rio Grande do Sul, Pernambuco, and Rio de Janeiro, but the government stopped some of the action by mobilizing military police in every state. The repression was violent, with police detaining and beating up workers. Workers in São Bernardo who had tried to take refuge in the cathedral were pulled out by armed police in spite of the protests of Bishop Hummes.

Lula was attacked by some for being irresponsible, and his union did not get its building back for a year. But he argued that, because solidarity strikes were still illegal, it was important that workers should show support for one another if they were to build a strong, autonomous movement. He was also in tune with most of organized labor in criticizing an IMF economic policy that led to cuts in public spending and worsened the recession. The events demonstrated that, even without a prominent role in the union, Lula himself could still sway opinion.

In the PT there was also an organizational development of significance. Lula was rarely interested in organizational matters, but the setting up of the "Articulação of 113"—a pressure group initially composed of 113 people—was designed to bring discipline to the party. It became the dominant faction in the PT into the 1990s, and a key player was José Dirceu, a former student leader who had gone to Cuba after the kidnap exchange and then returned to Brazil in disguise. He fully appreciated the importance of party structuring.

But Lula himself had found a new cause—the campaign for direct elections for the presidency. Some Marxists in the PT thought little of bourgeois democracy, but the Articulação and Lula saw this as a way of mobilizing support. The PT was the first major party to throw its weight behind the campaign and, at a meeting in the Rio governor's mansion on 25 June 1983—just prior to Lula's solidarity struggle alongside the petroleum workers—Lula, Leonel Brizola, and Franco Montoro agreed to work together for "Diretas Já," direct elections now. Significantly, this brought the PMDB, the PDT, and the PT together. Huge demonstrations took place in the main cities in 1984—eight hundred thousand in Candelária, in the center of Rio de Janeiro, and 1.4 million in the valley of Anhangabaú, São Paulo.

Brazil had not seen anything like it. Newspapers such as the Globo group, based in Rio, and *Folha de São Paulo*, both of which had attacked Lula in 1982, backed the movement. Lula, breathing the oxygen of publicity again, was a star speaker at rallies. Any speaker who seemed at all hesitant in backing direct elections for the presidency was booed.

The constitutional amendment, put forward by a young PMDB congressman from Mato Grosso, Dante de Oliveira, was due to be voted on 25 April 1984.[15] Such was the tension in the country that President Figueiredo declared a state of emergency in Brasília and neighboring municipalities of Goiás six days in advance of the scheduled vote; TV stations were prohibited from covering the voting; and six thousand troops occupied the heart of the city on the day of the vote. The troops were led by General Newton Cruz, mounted on a white horse, who tried to stop motorists from honking their horns to show their support for *Diretas Já*.

The constitutional amendment needed a two-thirds majority, which it just failed to reach. Although 298 deputies voted in favor, with only 65 against and 3 abstentions, the amendment's passage was stymied by the absence of 112 parliamentarians. In effect, the absentees won. This meant that the regime's attempt to keep the transfer to a civilian president within a system of indirect election, which it had a better chance to control, had succeeded.

This was to overlook the wily skills of the Brazilian political class, however. Although Lula and the PT were strongly critical of this class— its elasticity of principle, its elite proclivities, and its self-enrichment—its sense of public opinion had survived the two decades of dictatorship. Elected politicians realized that it was time for a change. The PMDB put together a "Democratic Alliance" with a breakaway group of progovernment congressmen and launched a campaign to elect the PMDB governor of Minas Gerais, Tancredo Neves, as president. The formerly progovernment José Sarney, now in the PMDB, was his running mate. Once again there were huge public demonstrations.

While the PCdoB joined the pro-Tancredo demonstrations, the PT leadership was adamant: there had to be direct elections, there had to be a constitutional convention, and this was just a "conservative transition."

Lula was vitriolic. He said that the election of Tancredo would not mean the end of the dictatorship and the military regime. There would still be an authoritarian regime, which would try to persuade Brazilians to forget the crimes of the previous twenty years. PT members were consulted directly. They were asked to vote on three options—whether their deputies should support Tancredo against the "fascist" Paulo Maluf,[16] whether they should back Tancredo after reaching an agreement on a program of interest to workers, or whether they should boycott the process.

Although only 7 percent of party members took part in the internal referendum, they voted overwhelmingly to boycott the process. In January 1985, however, Tancredo and Sarney were elected by Congress with 480 votes; three out of the eight PT deputies, including the film actress Beth Mendes, voted for them and had to leave the party. Tancredo, a subtle politician, appointed an old friend of Lula as his minister of labor. He was Almir Pazzianoto, a labor lawyer who had represented the São Bernardo Metalworkers. In a tragedy that moved the country, however, Tancredo was taken to the hospital on the eve of his inauguration, and he died on 21 April. He was succeeded as president by José Sarney.

In May, the Congress finally reestablished direct elections for the presidency, giving twenty million illiterates the right to vote—something they had not enjoyed prior to 1964—and legalizing all political parties. It also called for a constitutional assembly. Although this was not precisely the format called for by the PT, and Sarney's conduct of the presidency was probably more conservative than Tancredo's would have been had he lived, these measures together meant that the military era was over.

The political changes that led to the establishment of the "New Republic" in 1985 were paralleled by important changes in the economy and the organized labor movement. The early 1980s saw a downturn in the Brazilian economy. In mid-1981, more than nine hundred thousand people lost their jobs in the six major metropolitan areas of Brazil, and by August of that year unemployment in those cities was estimated at two million.[17] The government was also greatly concerned by the growth of Brazil's indebtedness and was encouraging state enterprises to borrow internationally to offset the deficit in the balance of payments. There were constant liquidity crises in 1982 and 1983, and, just after the 1982 elections, the Figueiredo government was forced to start negotiating with the IMF.

Brazil's welfare arrangements for the poor and unemployed were always inadequate and, at a time of recession, there was a risk of social explosion. According to the government's own statistics, around 70 percent of the population had less than the minimum daily calorie intake necessary for human development, and around seventy-one million were defined as undernourished.[18] In 1983, IBGE (Instituto Brasileira de Geografia e Estatística) estimated that hunger and malnutrition were responsible for 40 percent of infant deaths in the country. The armed forces were, in the same year, worried about health standards in even the more developed parts of the country. They were having to rule out as many as 45 percent of those drafted because the young men did not meet minimum requirements for height and weight. The minimum salary was simply not keeping up with the rate of inflation.

It was not surprising, therefore, that a number of the progressive union leaders who had taken part in the strikes at the end of the 1970s and were involved in the creation of the PT felt that they had to strengthen the union movement. It was part of the "return to basics" spirit that affected many after the setback in the 1982 election. In the late 1970s, there had been three tendencies among the more combative unionists. There were the "union oppositions" (oposições sindicais), who focused on factory commissions and action on the local level; a group called Unidade Sindical, close to the PCB, which wanted to take over the old corporatist system and win elections at federation, confederation, state, and national levels; and the autênticos, associated with Lula and São Bernardo, whose focus was on individual employers and firms. Tensions between these positions were exacerbated as the political scene became freer and the autênticos led the process to create the PT.[19]

The first opportunity for a large-scale debate on these issues took place over three days in August 1981 at Praia Grande, São Paulo, where 5,247 delegates from 1,126 unions and professional associations gathered in a National Conference of the Working Class (CONCLAT). Lula persuaded this conference to consider a general strike, but there was division over the election of a commission to carry on the work of CONCLAT. Lula's group, promoting a confrontational form of unionism, had only a minority of seats on this commission. In August 1983, following the national strike, which the Unidade Sindical had opposed, the *autênticos* held a convention in São Bernardo and set up the Central Unica dos Trabalhadores, CUT, the United Workers' Organization. It involved 5,059 delegates from 665 unions and 247 other labor organizations. Three months later, the opposing group, with 4,254 delegates from 1,258 unions, federations, and confederations, set up their own CONCLAT—Coordenação Nacional de Classe Trabalhadora.

This was a definitive split. Over the next two years, however, the CUT gradually overtook CONCLAT, as its members got better plant-level deals. By the time the New Republic had arrived and Almir Pazzianotto was in the Labor Ministry, he indirectly helped CUT by a hands-off style, encouraging employers and local unions to negotiate their own agreements. Although the CONCLAT group tried to take a more militant stance and renamed itself the Confederação Geral dos Trabalhadores, it lacked the practical experience in industrial action that had been acquired by the metalworkers, bank workers, and petroleum workers. It did not have the same capacity to deliver improved wages and benefits.

Although there was no requirement for CUT leaders to join the PT, a number did so in the mid-1980s. But for most of them, their union work still took priority. Jacó Bittar, for example, gave up his role as secretary-general of the PT in order to compete for leadership of the petroleum workers. For the "new unionists" labor autonomy was crucial; they rejected Vargas corporatism and the manipulation of the PTB and PCB prior to 1964. Lula said at the time that it was difficult to divide their effort and attention between the party and the unions.

The CUT made steady progress in the 1980s, and union leaders who had been involved with Unidade Sindical, the PCB, and PMDB began to join. It secured recruits in the service industries—more important in Rio de Janeiro than in São Paulo—and among the rural unions, for instance in the northeast.

The CUT was part of a more democratic, pluralistic society that the PT wanted to see. The PT was still espousing socialist goals and had Leninists in its ranks at senior levels. But it sought to reflect and accept other important social movements. One of the most influential, as the 1980s wore on, was the landless movement—Movimento dos Trabalhadores Rurais sem Terra, MST.[20]

The MST shared certain roots with the new labor movement and the PT. It too was a product of the downside of the "economic miracle" of the dictatorship, but in the countryside rather than the cities. The export model of the regime and its grandiose programs had led to the wiping out of small farms and the establishment of huge soy and cattle ranches; others had been dispossessed by big hydroelectric projects, such as Itaipú and Tucuruí. Hundreds of thousands had become landless.[21] Although many had gone to the cities to look for work in the *favelas,* a great number of others preferred to stay on the land. They looked at the unoccupied lands owned by Brazil's landowners and companies[22] and thought they should take it. One of the promises of the Goulart government, which had been cut down by the 1964 coup, was agrarian reform. By the 1980s, it had become topical and possible.

Historians of the MST identify its first meeting as taking place in Medianeira, near the confluence of the Iguaçu and Paraná rivers, in July 1982. A few years earlier, some ten thousand families had been forced off their land nearby to make way for the giant Brazilian-Paraguayan dam project at Itaipú. Occupations had begun in the south and by the early 1980s were spreading to São Paulo and the rest of the country. Landowners reacted with hired gunmen; state authorities, as the dictatorship broke down, did not always know what to do. In September 1983, a thousand days after an MST camp at Encruzilhada Natalino had been set up to demand land in Rio Grande do Sul, a newly elected governor awarded it to them. In January 1985, the founding congress of the MST took place in Curitiba.[23]

The movement, like the strike wave, had a grassroots quality. It had its leaders and ideologists, notably João Pedro Stédile. It was much encouraged by the Catholic Church, whose Pastoral Land Commission (Commissão Pastoral de Terra) had been set up originally to mediate land conflicts in the Amazon. It became interested in education, the possibilities of less ecologically damaging types of agriculture, and the nature of government in Brazil. It had radical, socialist, and alternative qualities.

But rather like the PT and the new unionists, the MST remained firmly independent, confrontational for its rights, not optimistic that the New Republic would give it much help in the countryside, skeptical about the old rural unions, but willing to work with allies. It attracted considerable media attention, some hostile. It added to the feeling of social euphoria, optimism, and ferment that was engulfing Brazil with the demise of the dictatorship. Lula was sympathetic, but the MST would not let him come too close.

While some in the PT leadership had turned back to their industrial work after the 1982 elections, activists around the country were getting on with building party branches and membership. The PT was a new kind of party, more democratic, more attuned to those who had been excluded from the system in the past. It was attractive, becoming more national in scope, and it did much better in the mayoral elections of 1985, when it succeeded in winning its first state capital, electing Maria Luiza Fontenelle as mayor of Fortaleza in Maranhão. Once again it had a spat with the PMDB in São Paulo, where the 20 percent obtained by Eduardo Suplicy for the PT was blamed for the defeat of the up-and-coming Fernando Henrique Cardoso by ex-president Jânio Quadros, who was running on a right-wing platform.

Late in 1985, in an interview with *Folha de São Paulo*, Lula got into trouble by expressing doubts as to whether the PT could win power by means of elections. He said that the party was trying to play by the rules of the game, but Congress was a means, not an end. If it was impossible for the working class to win that way, "I take the responsibility to say that the working class would have to find another way." If the PT did succeed and the right attempted to retain power by force, the PT could legitimately resort to arms, as had been claimed by the American colonies in the eighteenth century. This led to a damaging headline: "Lula Admits Armed Struggle to Guarantee Power."

Lula tried to undo the impact, both with the press and in the polls, but it was followed by two other incidents that were used to attack the party.

One involved a raid on a Banco do Brasil branch in Salvador by militants of a communist faction who also belonged to the PT, and were rapidly expelled; the other involved deaths and shootings among striking cane cutters in rural São Paulo, where the military police alleged that some shots had come from a car occupied by the PT deputy, José Genoino.

The truth was that democracy in Brazil, after the military handover, was still nervous and insecure. The powerful Rio-based Globo media group, strong in TV and the press, had supported the military and was not shy about attacking Lula. Lula responded, complaining that his party got no fair coverage from what he denounced as a private monopoly.

Part of the problem for Lula and his party was their vagueness about what they meant by socialism in modern Brazil. This was four years before the fall of the Berlin Wall, when state communism in eastern Europe had already lost favor elsewhere. In the same late 1985 interview in *Folha,* Lula said that he felt that the great challenge for socialism was to see a society in which everyone produced for the benefit of everyone else but individual creativity was not restricted. This should be a society that did not curtail freedom of the spirit or the desire of a citizen to progress in life. Lula thought that to define socialism merely in terms of education, health, and work was too narrow.

Nonetheless, the PT's nationwide status received more recognition in the congressional elections of 1986, when the PT elected sixteen deputies to a Congress that also had to write a new Constitution. This election was a triumph for Lula, who received more votes in São Paulo— 651,763—than any other deputy in the country. Several other leaders, such as the PT president, Olívio Dutra of the bank workers of Rio Grande do Sul, were elected at the same time. But Lula was the leader of the parliamentary group.

The PT, more cohesive than any other political party, played a significant role in the constitutional assembly. But for Lula personally it was not a satisfying experience. His own motivation had come from mass meetings and working with groups of friends. The detailed deals in Brasília and the atmosphere of the largely elitist congressmen who looked down on or feared the former lathe operator were both uncongenial. And Lula's wife and family were still in São Bernardo.

The constitutional assembly operated with a majority bloc, formed of politicians from many parties, known as the Centrão, the big Center. By comparison with the lack of party discipline showed by the other parties, wheeling and dealing on particular issues at the behest of individuals, the PT showed remarkable consistency. Its congressional representatives focused particularly on labor and agrarian issues, but participated across the board.

Lula himself, though he took part in 95 percent of the votes, did not play a prominent role in the Congress or the constitutional assembly. He voted in favor of limits on private property; for the legalization of abortion (which was a brave move, in view of his close links with the Catholic Church); for guarantees of employment and a forty-hour workweek; for a voting age of sixteen; for an upper limit of 12 percent on interest rates;[24] for legalization of the illegal gambling game that was popular in poorer districts, *jogo de bicho;* and for the expropriation of productive land.[25] As for the system of government, although Lula had spoken up for a parliamentary system, he ended up voting for an executive presidency; he was voting for the agreed party line, and it was an example of his willingness to accept party discipline. In contrast to other presidential systems, the president could only be elected for one term.

Lula did not hide his discontent with the parliamentary routine. He said that speeches often settled nothing and deputies did not listen to what others were saying; that there was too much egotism, and votes went one way or another as a result of personal vanity; that some two hundred deputies never even turned up at debates, while drawing salaries; and that he himself, who had addressed mass meetings, found it irksome to speak to five other deputies in an almost empty chamber. In June 1987, he seriously considered resigning his seat but was dissuaded on the ground that this would look bad if he was to run for the presidency.

In Brasília he stuck to old habits, liking to play soccer during his lunch hour. But he also began to worry that he was putting on weight. There were too many embassy dinners and meals with friends in *churrascarias,* steakhouses where different meats keep being brought to your table. Encouraged by another PT deputy and a fellow union leader from São

Paulo, Luís Gushiken, Lula began to take daily walks, stopped smoking and drinking, and became a fan of a macrobiotic diet of fruit and vegetables. He went to the gym in the Congress Club. In May 1988, he was rushed to hospital with a burst appendix, and in the course of that year he lost twenty-two pounds.

In fact, in December 1987 the PT's national meeting had decided to support Lula as its presidential candidate, arguing that to win the government through elections was the right strategic approach for the "struggle for socialism in Brazil." It opened the door to alliances with other left-wing parties. It firmly damped down any idea that the PT was in the business of armed revolution, a smear that the Globo press had been promoting.

Nonetheless the PT, in its concern for labor rights and progressive values, was still unhappy with the new Constitution, which came into effect in 1988. Members criticized it for paying insufficient attention to land reform and allowing the elite and the army to retain too much power. Lula said that he would not sign it, and the PT was attacked for being undemocratic. In the end, Lula and the other PT deputies did sign it.

The transition out of the military regime was, in reality, a gradual decade-long process interrupted by political and economic hiccups. The early 1980s had seen a recession. The second half, under President Sarney, saw a succession of efforts to bring Brazil's inflationary and debt-ridden economy under control. Indexation of wages and a series of mini-devaluations resulted in a sharp rise of inflation in 1985. On 28 February 1986, Sarney went on television to announce a shock treatment— his Cruzado Plan.

The plan, introduced by a decree-law in the fashion of the military regimes, introduced a price freeze, a wage freeze (which included an increase of 8 percent in an average salary over the previous six months, and an increase of 15 percent in the official minimum salary), and the introduction of a new currency, on the basis of one new cruzado for every thousand of the old devalued cruzeiros. The idea was to kill inertial inflation, and for most of 1986 it worked. Furthermore, industrial production started rising again and a consumer boom was under way. By the second half of the year, however, the surplus in the current account went into decline, with a sharp reduction in foreign investment in Brazil, and by the end of 1986 inflation had revived. The plan assisted salaried workers more than others, and although the government tried to introduce a modified Cruzado 2 Plan, it had little effect.

Sarney tried three different ministers of finance and three different stabilization programs before he handed over the presidency to the directly elected President Collor, but none of them were truly successful and, after the initial excitement of the Cruzado Plan, he lost political support. Under the transitional rules, it was for the Congress elected in November 1986 to determine the length of his term; he had already served as president for more than a year by the time of that election and was kept to the five years laid down in the new Constitution. He would have to hand over the presidency in March 1990.

Lula, forty-four years old in 1989, appeared to be a strong candidate in the October presidential elections of that year. He was a nationally known figure, standing out for his radicalism and proven experience among the twenty-one candidates who wanted to run in the first round. Brazil was going through a flourish of democracy in its first taste of direct elections, and the opportunities for alliances and voter confusion were considerable.

Lula was buoyed by the fact that the PT had done well in the mayoral elections of 1988, and the country was fed up with the Sarney government. A number of friends and colleagues had won *prefeituras*, mayoralties, in late 1988, including Olívio Dutra in Porto Alegre—who started a world-renowned experiment in participatory budgeting there—Jacó Bittar in Campinas, and Maurício Soares, who wrote Lula's first speech for the Metalworkers Union, in São Bernardo. Celso Daniel, who later was murdered under sinister circumstances in January 2002, was elected in Santo André, the industrial suburb adjoining São Bernardo.

The most satisfying victory was in São Paulo itself, where Luiza Erundina, a former primary school teacher whom the city's PT had preferred to a candidate backed by Lula, defeated Paulo Maluf, a former "bionic" or indirectly elected governor of São Paulo. Maluf, who had been indirectly elected during the military era, summed up all that the PT hated about the reactionary right. Erundina was helped by public reaction to the tragic death of three workers at the Volta Redonda steelworks, killed when soldiers invaded the premises to break up a strike.

Also, for the first time, the argument for the *voto útil*, the useful vote, worked in the PT's favor. A group of modern-minded, economically liberal politicians who had opposed the dictatorship had broken away from the PMDB to set up the Partido Social Democrático Brasileiro, the PSDB. Like the PT, its heartbeat was in São Paulo, and it included a range of talents such as Fernando Henrique Cardoso, the future president; Mário Covas, who was to be governor; and José Serra, a minister of health for Cardoso who was defeated by Lula for the presidency in 2002 but elected mayor of the city in 2004 and governor of the state in 2006. In 1988, Serra ran for the *prefeitura* on behalf of the PSDB, and came in fourth. Erundina, using the wasted vote argument against Serra, was able to defeat Maluf with only 30 percent of the vote.

The deaths in Volta Redonda and the failed economic plans gave many Brazilians a feeling that it was time to sweep away the detritus of the dictatorship and to make a new start. Underlying social realities justified a drastic change. According to IBGE, the number of workers earning less than the minimum salary had risen from 25.7 percent in 1987 to 29.1 percent a year later; the proportion of school students who had completed their first level of education in 1988 was only 57 percent, the lowest level in seven years.

Early in 1989 Lula made a number of overseas trips to give himself more international experience and improve the gravitas of his candidacy. He met social democratic leaders in Europe; in Latin America, reflecting his supporters' sympathy for the left, he visited Nicaragua, Fidel Castro in Cuba, and a Chile that was breaking away from the inheritance of the Pinochet dictatorship. In the mass of presidential hopefuls, he seemed one of the strongest, along with Leonel Brizola for the PDT, Ulysses Guimarães for the PMDB, and Maluf for the PDS. He was backed by a leftist coalition that included the PCdoB and the Partido Socialista Brasileira, the party of Miguel Arraes: it was dubbed the Frente Brasil Popular. He chose as his running mate a lawyer from Rio Grande do Sul who had been a PSDB senator, José Paulo Bisol.

His overseas trips left him skeptical of claims that revolutionary leftists could achieve the good life for their peoples. In Cuba he noted that the Castro regime had not solved housing problems. In Nicaragua, the Sandinistas, under severe economic pressure from the United States and about to be voted out of office, were managing an economy that was visibly crumbling.

At the same time, he was friendly to leftist leaders and, in a challenge to Brazilian conservatives, he told an audience in the United States that he would default on his country's overseas debt. "Either give us the rings or you will lose your fingers," he put it in his earthy way.[26]

The conservative candidate he had to beat was a forty-year-old newcomer to national politics, Fernando Collor de Mello. He came from a political family in the northeast, had edited a paper in Maceió, in the small state of Alagoas, and had been elected its governor in 1986. He was good-looking, ran a fiercely critical campaign against the Sarney government, and won the endorsement of the powerful Globo media group. But he belonged to a tiny, virtually new party, the Partido de Renovação Nacional, PRN, and therefore had to create a nationwide coalition from scratch. His path was not made easier by the existence of Paulo Maluf, as a candidate of the hard right, and the hostility of Sarney, who was promoting a successor, Silvia Santos, whose candidacy was disqualified only late in the year on the ground that his party was, in reality, moribund.[27]

Lula's campaign did not really take off until he benefited from free television advertising. This showed that he was attracting big crowds, and it broke a boycott of his campaign by large media groups. At one point he was scoring only 2.5 percent in the polls and thought seriously of pulling out. He quarreled with his press advisers, led by Ricardo Kotsch, who had started by covering the strikes as a neutral journalist in the 1970s but had fallen under the spell of Lula and the PT. The campaign was amateurish and short of money and technical support such as telephones. Lula was flying around the country in commercial planes, which were not always on schedule, while Collor had his own private jets.[28]

There were two main lines in the PT manifesto—a call for Brazil to stop paying its international debt, and a call for agrarian reform. These were radical if not socialist campaign commitments. Lula argued that if Brazil had not paid twelve billion dollars in interest on its debt in 1988, there would have been enough money to end illiteracy. With the MST stepping up its land occupations around the country, land reform had become a hot topic. But each of these issues frightened the middle class and conservative forces, and arguably served to mobilize conservatives more than Lula's own supporters.

The election rapidly became dirty. In April, the *Jornal do Brasil* published an article drawing attention to the existence of Lula's illegitimate daughter, Lurian Cordeiro da Silva, by then fifteen years old, the product of his relationship with Miriam Cordeiro. It claimed that he had tried to disown her. This personal attack developed as the year went on, with false allegations that Lula had wanted Miriam to have an abortion—still a matter of horror to Catholic Brazilians—and evidence that Miriam was in the pay of Collor's machine.[29] Lurian attempted suicide. Late in the campaign, Lula was severely depressed and disoriented by these allegations and Lurian's suicide attempt, which affected his appearance in a TV debate. Collor also claimed that Lula would confiscate savings accounts and commandeer rooms in middle-class homes for the homeless.

Although Lula loved campaigning, shaking hands, listening to the grievances of street vendors, and addressing mass meetings, he was also a sentimental family man. He liked Marisa's chicken and polenta, and a beer or *cachaça* at home in São Bernardo with friends. His family was still young—Fábio Luís nearly fifteen, Luís Cláudio coming up to eleven, and Sandro Luís still a toddler of three. Fábio Luís, later to be known as Lulinha, came in second in a mock presidential election at his school.[30] From the chaos of his own childhood, Lula had created a fortress of domestic security, which the Collor camp had brutally bombarded.

There was also a vicious side battle going on between Lula and Leonel Brizola, the hero of the pre-1964 left who had been a popular governor in Rio de Janeiro. The PDT man had backing in Rio and the southern state of Rio Grande do Sul, where Brizola, Jango Goulart, and Getúlio Vargas had originated. Against this, Lula was relying on his nucleus in São Paulo and with the labor movement, and his nordestino credentials in northeast Brazil. Brizola attacked Bisol, Lula's vice presidential candidate, saying that he had used his status as a senator to get a $150,000 loan to buy a ranch in Minas Gerais. What was really at stake was which of the two left-wing candidates would get into the second round; the new Constitution required an absolute majority to win outright in the first round, and with so many candidates, this was unlikely.

On 15 November, Collor came in comfortably ahead, with 30.5 percent of the votes. Lula, with 17.2 percent, had only five hundred thousand votes more than Brizola. But he had got through the first round in second place, holding open house for journalists at his home after the poll. The second round, a runoff between the top two candidates from the first round, was due to take place on 17 December. In the meantime, both candidates were involved in a hectic, exhausting period of electioneering, high on rallies and rhetoric. Lula accused Collor's landowning family of killing their rural workers by paying barely the minimum salary, continued to speak out against the big agricultural estates (*latifúndios*), and warned that he would merge the separate military ministries into a single Ministry of Defense. Collor said that Lula was preaching armed struggle and wanted to come to power through bloodshed.

This, the first direct presidential election over two rounds, showed the importance of alliance building. Conservative Brazil, genuinely scared of Lula and the PT, pulled together behind the little-known and inexperienced Collor. His good looks appealed to some women, and many others were put off by the image of a bearded strike leader. At the same time, Lula's campaign managers tried to soften his image with an optimistic jingle—"Lula-lá, brilha uma estrela. Lula-lá, cresce a esperança!" ("Lula, a star is shining. Lula, hope is growing.")

Politically, the Lula campaign was not as clever in its alliance building; although the PSDB and parts of the PMDB came on board, Brizola and the PDT were rather half-hearted, and Lula made an error in failing to win over Ulysses Guimarães, the standard-bearer of parliamentary opposition to the military, who had come in a surprisingly poor seventh in the first round. Progressive Catholic clergy continued to make clear their support for the PT candidate. A moment Lula savored in retrospect was when Fernando Henrique Cardoso of the PSDB, who was to beat Lula twice for the presidency in the 1990s, appeared on a platform to support him in the second round.

In fact, the pollsters suggested that Collor really pulled ahead of Lula only in the last few days of the second-round campaign. But there had been a number of incidents that showed the difficulties Lula faced. The momentous fall of the Berlin Wall, on 10 November, put a question mark against the kind of state socialism that many of his supporters had preached in the past. On the day before the election, police in São Paulo rescued from kidnapping a prominent businessman, Abílio Diniz, the boss of the Pão de Açúcar supermarket group. The kidnappers were an international group, claiming to raise funds for guerrillas in Nicaragua, but the police and some media alleged that they had links with the PT, that PT material had been found with them, and that they had used a safe house rented by a priest linked with the PT.

On the same day that Diniz was released, Lula had the unwelcome experience of being booed by a soccer crowd at the Morumbi stadium in São Paulo. Still a great soccer fan, he had gone to watch the final between Vasco, a Rio team, and São Paulo. On the way in, he admitted to sports reporters that, as a fan of Corintians—a very old Paulista team and traditional rival of São Paulo—he would be hoping that Vasco won. The news got out and Lula was booed—he was told insultingly that he should enlist in the national literacy campaign, Mobral—and he left at halftime. The next day, Collor won the election by 42.75 percent to 37.86 percent. Lula had raised his vote over the last month from 11.6 million to 31 million, but it was not enough.

Given where Lula had started in life, it was, however, a huge achievement. Lula had also managed to keep his feet on the ground, to maintain his family life, to be himself. When journalists visited his home in São Bernardo at the time of the first round, they were struck by the normality of it all and the sense of an extended family, as the mother of Marisa's murdered first husband came around.[31] "Lula's house breathes the typical atmosphere of the rising middle class," commented a reporter from *Folha de São Paulo*, with video games and Batman stickers as evidence of his sons' presence.

4 PERSISTENT CANDIDATE
FOR THE PRESIDENCY

Lula had come surprisingly close to winning the 1989 election, but it was Fernando Collor de Mello who took office in March 1990. He was the first directly elected president of the new democracy, but he was an oddity. In spite of an advertising blitz, he was less well known and with a shorter track record than many of the candidates he defeated. He was a conservative who had run on an antigovernment platform.

Because his party was tiny, he was totally dependent on makeshift alliances in Congress. Many of his confidants, notably Paulo César de Cavalcanti de Farias, his campaign manager, known as P. C. Farias, and Zélia Cardoso de Mello, his finance minister, had come with him from the small state of Alagoas. Farias, whose businesses had gone into receivership in 1983, and who had been charged with fraud, forgery, and tax evasion two years later, was not a figure to inspire confidence when handling money.

Collor in his campaign had promised deregulation, the selling-off of state enterprises, and an opening to external investment. He sold these ideas, the currency of President Ronald Reagan and Prime Minister Margaret Thatcher as the Berlin Wall fell, as part of the overdue modernization of Brazil. They went along with his youthful sense of style and his jogging: they would bring Brazil up to date with a bang.

But the immediate crisis he faced was hyperinflation. Inflation was running at 81 percent a month. He immediately introduced a surprise stabilization plan. Overnight deposits and current and savings accounts with more than the equivalent of U.S. $1,300 were frozen for eighteen months; a new currency, the new cruzeiro, replaced the cruzado; a one-time tax was levied on dealings in stock shares, gold, and financial titles; prices and salaries were frozen; the prices of public utilities were raised—gas went up by 57.8 percent, electricity by 32 percent; three hundred sixty thousand civil servants and public employees were dismissed; and privatizations and a gradual liberalization of the economy were promised.

The result was a drastic decrease in the amount of money circulating in the economy, a decline of 7.8 percent in the gross national product in the second three months of 1990, a sharp reduction in inflation to single digits monthly, and a strike wave. But by the second half of the year, inflation was rising again. The trouble was that shock tactics and a recession brought their own reaction.

The problem was illustrated in São Paulo, where the Metalworkers of São Bernardo and Diadema were involved in a campaign to make up for the erosion of their wages by inflation. On 30 May, they negotiated an increase of 166.9 percent with FIESP, the employers' organization; this was to make up for inflation of 94.3 percent in March and 44.8 percent in April. By July, the employers were offering 51–59 percent. In November, they were offering increases of 160 percent.[1] The inflationary dragon was not slain.

Collor's team introduced a second anti-inflationary package in February 1991, which included an attempt to cut the spending of state enterprises and social ministries such as health and education. But by May, before it was possible to see whether this package had worked any better, Collor had fired Zélia Cardoso and his economic team. They had become deeply unpopular for their authoritarian habits and for reportedly "stealing" people's savings. The new team, led by Marcílio Marques Moreira, who had been ambassador in Washington, promised that there would be no more shock tactics.

Meanwhile, Lula joked, "Wasn't it I who was going to steal people's savings?"[2] In spite of his disappointment, he returned to building the PT. He was elected as a federal deputy in late 1990, with a large vote, but never took his seat. He had decided that Congress was not his scene. Instead, he worked as the paid president of the PT, traveling around the country, speaking for party candidates.

The reality was arduous, not all large crowds in soccer stadiums. An Australian writer saw Lula talking to a small crowd in the rain in Recife, standing on the back of a truck and then dashing away with a satchel over his head, and decided that he was like the "battlers" he knew from his own country.[3] One of Lula's most striking characteristics was his staying power and determination.

In June 1990, at the party meeting where Lula resumed the presidency, the PT produced a long statement explaining its commitment to socialism. Lula was somewhat uncomfortable, as after his defeat he had decided that he might need alliances on the center and right. But it had never been clear what the party meant by socialism. Ideologically, the PT had been from the start, and remained, a broad coalition—unionists, intellectuals, people from social movements, Catholic radicals, socialists, and Marxists of different persuasions. Different factions ran for internal elections, although the moderate Articulação, led by Dirceu and Genoino and close to Lula, was in the driver's seat.

What was clear was that the PT had a growing coherence, and was in part defined by its enemies. A business leader had warned that eight hundred thousand businessmen would leave the country if Lula won in 1989; the fast-growing evangelical churches opposed a party that seemed so close to the Catholic Church; MST land invasions had let Collor allege that no middle-class home was safe, while Lula said that he would never back down on agrarian reform.

The PT's resolution gave an absolute value to its commitment to plural democracy and argued that the "real existing socialism" of the collapsed Soviet bloc was not democratic. The party had supported Solidarity in Poland and the demonstrators in Tienanmen Square in Beijing. But it had also attacked U.S. imperialism, which had threatened Cuba and Grenada. It would always be on the side of the oppressed— workers, women, and the poor. It regarded capitalism as an obstacle to democracy, which would not be achieved until capitalism was overcome. It was vehement in its opposition to capitalism:

It is capitalist oppression that results in the absolute misery of more than a third of humanity. That is what imposes new forms of slavery on Latin America, which has reduced the income per capita by 6.5 percent in recent years, forcing various countries back to the levels of twenty years ago. It is the capitalist system—founded, in the last analysis, on the exploitation of man by man and the brutal commercialization of human life—that is responsible for frightful crimes against democracy and human rights, from the gas chambers of Hitler to the recent genocides in South Africa, coming to our own sadly celebrated torture chambers. It is Brazilian capitalism, with its predatory dynamic, that is responsible for the hunger of millions, for illiteracy, for social exclusion, and for the violence that is spreading through all parts of national life.[4]

But what would PT socialism look like in Brazil? The resolution argued for social ownership of the means of production, which should not be confused with state ownership; this could involve individual, cooperative, or state ownership, which society itself should decide on democratically. There should be a new organization of work, and workers' councils in every factory. The party was not ashamed to call for a utopia.

If there was still a certain fuzziness about the PT's program—and ideology had never been Lula's strongest point[5]—it was bolstered by exciting and different experiments by activists on the ground. In Amazonia, Chico Mendes was promoting extractive reserves for rubber tappers, which would allow people to make a living while conserving the forest ecology. In Porto Alegre, in a development that attracted activists and local government experts from around the world, a PT council was introducing a process of "participative budgeting." The local authority was demystifying the city's budget, throwing it open to citizens to argue over priorities. This was what the party meant by a commitment to democracy, and its ideas had been nurtured by links with other social movements.

Lula wanted to consolidate the PT manifesto into something closer to a plan for a government. Imitating the Labour Party in the United Kingdom—which itself was merely following a practice of the Conservatives when they had been in opposition—Lula decided to establish a "shadow cabinet." It could audit the programs of the Collor government and produce counterproposals.

One of the loose ends from the 1988 Constitution was a promise to hold a referendum on the future organization of Brazil's government: Should Brazil have an executive presidency, a parliamentary system, or even, in a throwback to the nineteenth century, a resurrected monarchy? Lula, although not a fan of Congress, was a supporter of parliamentarism.

By the 1990s, Lula's international experience was wider, and the PT was a member of the Socialist International. In Britain, he had met Labour Party people who were struggling against the Conservative governments that had been in office since 1979, and there were superficial parallels between the two situations. But Lula's shadow cabinet, which in the first six months met five times and produced policies on education and the northeast, did not seem a headline-grabbing initiative.

What was grabbing headlines, in 1991 and 1992, was the sensational corruption surrounding the Collor government. There was a great deal of it, exposed in the press and by a Parliamentary Commission of Inquiry (Comissão Parlamentar de Inquérito) in which PT congressmen José Dirceu and Eduardo Suplicy took the lead. In different ways it had involved Zélia Cardoso, who had taken bribes from transportation companies to break the price freeze, and Rosane Collor, the president's wife, who had been abusing the Legião Brasileira de Assistencia, the traditional charity of the first lady.

But absolutely central to the sleaze surrounding the clique from Alagoas was P. C. Farias. Elections in Brazil, in the new democratic era in which illiterates could vote, required snazzy and expensive marketing—top-quality TV ads, pop musicians and celebrities at party rallies, and money for posters, travel, public relations, and nationwide offices. The challenge for Farias, who was Collor's campaign manager and treasurer, was to create a national figure from a relative unknown. To do this, he needed to exploit the fear of Lula in the business community and to collect payments in advance.

Farias raised far more in campaign contributions than he needed to get Collor elected. He started using the surplus money for himself, establishing overseas accounts and a private jet firm in Brazil. At the same time, he and Collor were in each other's pockets, with P. C. providing money for the president's family. After rather a slow start, the parliamentary commission began to collect damning evidence linking the two; a breakdown of family solidarity, with the president's brother Pedro providing further information, exposed some of the rackets. By the middle of 1992, the press was in full cry, and crowds as huge as those for the *Diretas Já* campaign were calling for the president's impeachment.

At the end of September, the Congress achieved more than the two-thirds majority needed—voting by 441 to 38 to impeach the president. Collor departed, to be succeeded by Itamar Franco, his vice president from the PMDB. Although between U.S. $300 million and $1 billion, purloined by P. C. Farias (who was murdered in 1996 alongside his lover), was never recovered, it looked as though Brazilian democracy had struck a blow for ethics. At the same time, Collor was being punished for his economic policy, his freezes and his privatizations of state-owned firms such as VASP, the São Paulo airline. In both ways it seemed a triumph for the PT's advocacy.

Itamar Franco inherited a difficult situation, and Lula and the PT opposed the new government. But at the same time, the president tried to broaden his administration. He recruited Fernando Henrique Cardoso, the sociologist who was the coming man in the PSDB, to be his foreign minister. He persuaded Luíza Erundina, the former PT mayor of São Paulo, to run his Ministry for the Administration; although there were calls for Erundina to be expelled from the party, Lula saw to it that she was only suspended. The involvement of Cardoso in the government was a setback for Lula, who had been discussing with him a combined PT-PSDB campaign for parliamentarism.

On a personal level, Lula and Itamar maintained good relations. Lula handed him a national plan to improve nutrition and deal with hunger that had been prepared by the PT shadow cabinet. This was a forerunner of Lula's Fome Zero—Zero Hunger—plan of 2002. He persuaded Itamar to appoint a well-known sociologist, Herbert de Souza, to chair a national council for food security.

The PT saw itself as on the way to power, and Ricardo Kotscho was preparing a plan for a government that would last ten years. At the start of 1993, the PT succeeded in getting fifty-two of its candidates elected as mayors, some in significant state capitals such as Belo Horizonte and Porto Alegre. Lula had a private meeting with twenty-five bankers and industrialists in São Paulo on 1 March to show that he was not the rabble-rousing striker of the past, but a man with whom they could do business. He was demonstrating a genius for straddling the views of the left and the reality of the Brazilian economic establishment.

He was also out of touch with his party on the constitutional issue of presidentialism versus parliamentarism. He was in favor of a parliamentary system, as was the PSDB, but the PT was against it. The tradition of a strong executive president dated back to Getúlio Vargas in Brazil and was commonplace throughout the Americas, and the checks and balances of a parliamentary system—let alone the exoticism of a revived monarchy—were unattractive to most Brazilians. In the plebiscite on 21 April 1993, two-thirds voted to maintain a republic, while a narrower majority, 55 percent, wanted an executive presidency.[6] Lula, who was on a bus from Garanhuns to São Paulo—retracing his own migration as part of his first Caravan of Citizenship—did not vote at all.

The Caravan of Citizenship reflected Lula's ongoing campaign for the presidency, a focus on the needs of the poor, and his continued resentment that the political class was not really in touch with the needs of the real Brazil. It was a populist tactic that highlighted his own career, a year ahead of another presidential election. It also gave him something to do. In spite of his achievements, he was still out of office, in opposition and to some degree frustrated.

The caravan, or campaign bus tour, from Garanhuns, which took Lula once more to Vicente de Carvalho, was the first of fourteen. Altogether Lula traveled to 350 cities and towns in twenty-three states, in separate campaign bus tours usually lasting a fortnight each. He spoke off the cuff to groups small and large. Talking to two hundred businessmen in Rondonia in September, he denounced congressmen, saying that at least three hundred were crooks—an allegation remembered against him during his own administration.[7]

But Lula was still up against considerable media bias. A reporter from *Veja*, a newsweekly, had been told to ridicule the campaign bus tours in her coverage—even after she had a lengthy exclusive interview with Lula. Kotscho, as Lula's press secretary, wrote a furious article in reply, titled, "*Veja* and the Marketing of Infamy."[8]

In 1993 and until well into 1994, it looked as though Lula had every chance of winning his second presidential election. The impeachment of Collor suggested that the public wanted a cleaner Brazil; even Paulo Maluf, running a successful campaign to become mayor of São Paulo with the aid of a skilled publicist, Duda Mendonça,[9] had disowned Collor. The Itamar Franco government was not strong. But then something unexpected happened. The new finance minister, Fernando Henrique Cardoso, introduced an economic plan and yet another new currency that seemed to work.

Cardoso, born in 1931, came from a political and military middle-class family with progressive tendencies. His great-grandfather had been governor of Goiás, involved in the emancipation of the slaves and the proclamation of the republic. His father, Lêonidas, had taken part in several rebellions since the 1920s, became a general, and was a PTB deputy close to the Brazilian Communist Party. Fernando Henrique was an academic-turned-politician, a sociology professor whose PSDB represented a liberal, modernizing reaction to the dictatorship that had forced him into exile. The PSDB itself was a breakaway from the PMDB, formed during the debates on the Constitution in 1988 and initiated by a talented group from São Paulo. They were nicknamed "toucans" (*tucanos*) for their bright, birdlike party colors.

Cardoso had been elected senator for São Paulo. He was delighted to be made minister of foreign affairs by Itamar Franco, but was not keen to take on finance. But the president phoned him in May 1993, when he was on a working trip to New York, and made him an offer he could not refuse. The previous minister, Eliseu Resende, was accused of favoring an engineering firm he had been working for before; inflation was running at around 30 percent a month. Cardoso decided that the only way to break out of the cycle of disasters that had gone back at least to the Sarney era was to tap some of the best brains available. Interestingly,

Lula himself had been advocating a government composed of the best talents when Itamar succeeded Collor.

Within a few months of taking office, Cardoso had gathered around him a group that included Edmar Bacha; André Lara Resende, who was responsible for renegotiating Brazil's excessive overseas debt; Pedro Malan, who took on the presidency of the Banco Central; and Pérsio Arida, who headed the state development bank, BNDES. Gustavo Franco was put in charge of exchange rates at the central bank. Some of these men had been involved in the failed Cruzado Plan and had learned certain lessons. They were determined that a new stabilization plan and a new currency should be introduced in stages, with public knowledge and, ideally, public support. One of the first moves would be to introduce a new indexation unit, equal to the U.S. dollar, in February 1994.

Already in June 1993, Cardoso—or FHC as he had been dubbed—had introduced an immediate action plan. This cut public spending by U.S. $6 billion, increased tax collection and punished evasion, and required the heavily indebted Brazilian states to start paying off their debts to the federal government. In December he put forward a proposal to Congress that had two aspects—a tax adjustment and the introduction of the new URV (Unidade Real de Valor) index, equal to the U.S. dollar.

The tax changes included an overall increase of 5 percent; the creation of a Social Emergency Fund, which would take 15 percent of all taxes to smooth the changes and pay civil servants; and further cuts in public investments, staff, and state enterprises worth U.S. $7 billion. The URV, translated into cruzeiros, would fluctuate every day with the exchange rate of the dollar; official prices and contracts would be fixed in URV, and the government encouraged private firms and individuals to do the same.

By May and June 1994, more and more prices were being set in URV. FHC and his team were ready on 1 July to introduce the new currency, the real. It was equal to one URV, or one U.S. dollar—or 2,750 units of the former cruzeiro currency. Unlike Collor, the finance minister did not attempt to freeze prices, although many shops and supermarkets took advantage of the currency change to hike prices. Instead, the government used its public relations to persuade people to boycott shops that were profiteering, and restricted credit in the economy.

After so many crises and so much disappointment, Brazilians warmed to a plan and a currency that actually worked. From annual rates of 2,104 percent in 1993 and 2,407 percent in 1994, the inflation rate fell dramatically to 68 percent in 1995 and 9.3 percent in 1996.[10] Industrial production and public consumption rose. There was also an important increase in the purchasing power of low-income groups, which had particularly suffered from high monthly inflation.

The political fallout from the real was equally dramatic. Lula and the PT initially discounted its effects, seeing only the public expenditure cuts and thinking it was no more likely to succeed than its predecessors. Lula, who had been pleased that the PSDB had joined him for the second round in 1989, had been hoping for an alliance with FHC's party in the 1994 election. The left had become more powerful in the party, however, was distrustful of alliances with ideological dissimilars, and had frightened off the political marketing genius Duda Mendonça, whom Lula had tried to recruit for his second campaign. Up until the end of 1993, the PT had anticipated that Lula would be running against the hated right-winger, Paulo Maluf, and Lula was well ahead in the polls until the middle of 1994.

But FHC was ambitious. He pretended, when he took on the poisoned chalice of finance in 1993, that his only interest was in solving the country's economic crisis. His wife, Ruth, opposed his becoming a presidential candidate. But he moved up the introduction of the real so that this preceded the 1994 election, and well before the currency came in it was clear that he would be running for the presidency. Other circumstances helped him. Itamar Franco did not find a favorite son to succeed him. Antonio Carlos Magalhães, the astute boss from Bahia of the conservative PFL (Partido Federal Liberal), had already picked out Cardoso as a man his party could support. Marco Maciel, a gangling but shrewd northeasterner from the PFL, who was nicknamed "the map of Chile," became Cardoso's running mate.

Lula, still leading FHC in opinion polls by 40 points to 17 in June, on the eve of the real's introduction, was slow to realize that an earthquake was about to bury him. He made fun of Cardoso riding a horse with a leather hat in the northeast, and said that working women did not have time to shop for bargains or boycott stores that priced their goods too high in reais (the plural of *real* in Portuguese). He refused Cardoso's challenge to debate the real.

Cardoso's successor as minister of finance, Rubens Ricupero, was recorded at the end of an interview, when he thought he was off-air, saying that he had no scruple in hiding bad news. He was forced to resign, but even that was insufficient to derail the well-financed and skillful Cardoso campaign. A vague hint from Lula that Cardoso might be an atheist—a line that had been toxic to a previous FHC campaign—made no difference. Neither did a PT attack on Marco Maciel, alleging that he had been financed by P. C. Farias.

When the election took place at the start of October 1994, Cardoso won in the first round, with twice the support Lula received. He got 54.3 percent, or 34.3 million votes, to Lula's 27 percent, or 17.1 million. It was a crushing defeat of Lula, inconceivable two years earlier. It was overwhelmingly the result of the tangible success of the Real Plan and the public's belief that Brazil had at last acquired a solid currency, as valuable as the dollar. Although Cardoso had talked of privatizations, and financial aid for the poorest families to offset an otherwise conservative economic stance, it was the real that caused the election upset. His five-fingered salute—the fingers represented his commitments to employment, health, education, security, and agriculture—was less a manifesto than a contrast to the balled fist of a striker.

Lula had doggedly toured the country with the same leftist alliance that had been behind him in 1989, and the same running mate, José Paulo Bisol. His final big rally, as before, was in Rio. He had done his best to neutralize businessmen. He had been photographed with that icon of reconciliation, Nelson Mandela. It would have been understandable if he had been depressed or had decided to pull out of politics altogether following his stunning defeat.

In fact, he thought hard about the lessons from this second presidential defeat. Unlike FHC, he was not an intellectual. But he was amazingly intuitive. For some fifteen years he had been working with a group of friends and colleagues; he knew Brazil well, and the political game that had emerged from the dictatorship; he had a good memory for faces, names, and individuals. He had taken to heart a cynical remark by Celso Furtado, an economist and grand old man of the Brazilian left. At a lunch in Paris, discussing party structures, Furtado told him, "You should never give up on your radicals. They give vitality to the party and, more important, show you the path you shouldn't follow."[11]

By nature, particularly as he was getting older—and Lula was nearly fifty in his second presidential election—he was a conciliator, a man who floated above factions, someone who wanted to reach out to the whole Brazilian family. His own conclusion was that Brazil did not want a worker as president; it wanted a middle-class president. Furthermore, in the complex labyrinth of Brazilian politics, he had to make alliances where he could, without the limitations imposed by PT purists.

Although there were four parties that were larger than the rest—the PT, PSDB, PMDB, and PFL—there were at least a half-dozen others that had strength in particular localities, with particular leaders, and with defined constituencies, and there were more besides. In a federal country of large geographical extent, where pork-barrel politics was traditional and ideological baggage was light, there was insufficient pressure to create the two-party structure familiar in Anglo-Saxon countries. Indeed, the two-party structure that had been imposed by the military was rejected as antidemocratic. Furthermore, a statewide electoral system without local constituencies worked against accountability to voters, as did the fickleness of prominent politicians who made hopping from party to party seem respectable.

Above all, the system of two-round voting, for the presidency and governors, required leaders and parties to look ahead. It was difficult to win an absolute majority in a first round with many candidates. Rivals in the first round would have to reconcile their differences to assure a victory in the second.

Lula noted that his own vote in 1994 was a great deal larger than that of his party; where necessary, he should break free from party constraints. Although he may have continued to believe that there were three hundred crooks in Congress, they were crooks he would have to work with to get himself or a PT government into office. As different issues came up, PT senators and deputies were voting with or against different allies; in the states, especially where it had elected governors or mayors, the PT was already enmeshed in alliances, even if these were based on the left.[12]

Although the alliance issue caused continuing ructions within the PT, it was unavoidable. A major party, the PMDB, shared some antidictatorship history with the PT, as did the younger PSDB. But the PMDB was actually a collection of regional and personal fiefdoms, not a coherent formation; there was always a slight friction between those PMDB chiefs who wanted to be close to the government in power in Brasília—usually the majority—and those who saw more advantages in opposing it. And many of the tiny parties, the *partidos nanicos*, were openly for sale.

In the 1990s, after his first defeat by FHC, Lula frankly embraced the need for alliances, even apparently unsuitable ones. It was to haunt him after he was elected president in 2002. It may well be that his sympathy for the parliamentary option in the referendum derived from his insight that the Brazilian system requires alliances. In his own personality he had always been, in the unions and in his attitude to the social movements, an alliance man.

Although Lula was to criticize FHC for the amount of time he spent outside Brazil as president, he too liked traveling and was a quick learner. He met everyone who was anyone—the pope, Nelson Mandela, Bill Clinton, Fidel Castro, and the other Latin American leaders. He had first met the pope in 1980, during John Paul II's visit to Brazil, shortly after he was released from prison.

The mid-1990s was a curious time for Brazil in international affairs, with promises of a new international order after the Cold War that were quickly disappointed. The first Gulf War, the bloody breakup of Yugoslavia, and the genocide in Rwanda called into question humanitarian hopes for a world built on human rights and the United Nations. The power of China and the European Union seemed to grow; the desperate state of much of Africa, even after the end of apartheid, was a reminder that developing countries that failed left their peoples at the back of every line.

There was only one superpower, the United States, and there was one prevailing economic philosophy—the globalization of free-flowing capital and the "Washington consensus." The Peronists in Argentina, traditionally economic nationalists, were converted into privatizers and free-traders under Carlos Menem. The Chilean left, thankful to be rid of the Pinochet dictatorship, had largely turned its back on the radicalism of Salvador Allende, the socialist president martyred in 1973. Farther away, the communist Chinese had adopted private enterprise with gusto, India's finance minister, Manmohan Singh, was tearing down the "license raj" of planning and red tape, and the African National Congress had junked most of its socialism on winning the first democratic elections in South Africa in 1994.

Moderate Anglo-Americans on the center-left were trying to make free enterprise do more for social welfare, but felt they had to live with the Washington consensus. In the United States, where Bill Clinton was president from 1993 to 2001, the Democrats were involved in a rightward strategy of "triangulation," looking for a vote-winning midpoint between traditional conservatives and radicals. In the United Kingdom, where Labour had been forced into opposition just as the big strike wave was making Lula a household name in Brazil, Tony Blair was more dramatic. Elected leader in 1994, he persuaded his party to dump its constitutional Clause 4 commitment to nationalization; instead he encouraged his outriders to promote a "New Labour" and a "Middle Way" that would be more friendly to business and the middle class.

Lula was to some degree caught between the ideological militancy of many of his followers and the neoliberal world order. He was not himself an ex-communist or Marxist, but he was fiercely critical of the "social democracy" of the PSDB. He sought to focus on issues on which he himself felt strongly—hunger, poverty, the global terms of trade (which he thought penalized Brazil and other developing countries), and maintaining national economic sovereignty.

But increasingly Brazil was exposed to the ebbs and flows of international finance. A formula had been devised to assess the "Brazil risk" (*risco Brasil*) for outside lenders and investors; while developing countries were being rebranded as emerging markets with lots of opportunity, it was still the case that U.S. and European investors could withdraw their money instantly for reasons that might not have much to do with Brazil.[13]

Irritatingly for Lula and the PT, Cardoso came to the presidency with considerable goodwill—outside Brazil, where he was known as a prominent sociologist,[14] as well as inside the country. Alain Touraine, a fellow sociologist and friend in France, hailed his election as a victory of the future over the past, which would enable Brazil to take advantage of the positives in globalization.

Several times Lula rejected presidential overtures by FHC, seeking his support. FHC frequently treated Lula with respect as a former ally who had taken a different path—though the academician could not resist lecturing Lula as if he were a refractory student. On one of Lula's visits to the presidential palace in Brasília, FHC even went so far as to say that one day it would be Lula's own. Cardoso still felt nostalgia for that moment in the late 1970s when they were both together in the struggle against the military, and had a sense that their division was unnatural.

But Lula and the PT were adamantly opposed to much that Cardoso was doing. The fight began when Cardoso took office—it was only the second time in Brazilian history that one elected president handed power to another in public[15]—and a PT deputy put forward a proposal to raise the monthly minimum salary to one hundred reais.[16] Cardoso vetoed the raise, the union movement began to mobilize in favor, and the issue got mixed up with the Mexican devaluation crisis of early 1995, when large quantities of hot money left Brazil and the government bravely avoided devaluing the real. Nonetheless, the unions got their increase in the minimum salary.

Lula attacked the government for being in the pockets of its conservative PFL allies. He also criticized its plans to open up the domestic economy to international investors. Soon after taking office, and less than seven years after the democratic Constitution of 1988, Cardoso proposed five constitutional amendments. These aimed to redefine what was a "Brazilian" company, to reform the national welfare and pensions system, and, most controversially, to end the state oil and petroleum monopoly of Petrobrás.

The military governments had permitted Petrobrás to bring in foreign partners for risk contracts for exploration. But it was symptomatic of a strain of economic nationalism that ran through the 1988 Constitution, and a reflection of the enormous symbolism of Petrobrás dating back to the days of Getúlio, that the fuel monopoly had actually been written into the new constitution. Lula's old allies among the petroleum workers went on strike to try and save it, but without success. Cardoso sent troops into the refineries, and the unionists returned to work after a month.

There were other significant privatizations during the Cardoso era, notably of Telebrás, the inefficient state telecommunications monopoly. As in other developing countries, it had often been costly and slow to get phone lines installed in Brazil; in the era of e-mail and mobile phones, the public quickly latched on to cheap, newly available products. Although they were able to attack possible corruption or profiteering in the process of such privatizations, the PT and unions were in danger of looking outdated as younger generations of consumers grasped new opportunities. A fundamental difficulty for the PT was that the real remained popular, especially among low-income groups that no longer had to scrabble for money each month as inflation destroyed its value.

In 1995, Lula handed over the presidency of the PT. José Dirceu, the former revolutionary and organization man who continued to arouse suspicion on the right, was elected in his place. He defeated a more left-wing opponent and consolidated party control in the hands of a moderate coalition. Lula himself remained dedicated to his continuing campaign for the national presidency.

The 1988 Constitution prohibited a second term for a president, a governor, or a mayor. But in June 1997, Congress passed a constitutional amendment, after much discussion, horse-trading, and the transfer of funds to some congressmen. This permitted a president and these other elected executives to stand for two terms. To no one's surprise, Fernando Henrique Cardoso agreed to run again for the presidency in 1998.

The mid-1990s saw further personal attacks on Lula. Though they were not as hurtful as the use of Lurian against him by Collor, and not particularly damaging, they were not pleasant. He was criticized for living in a house in São Bernardo paid for by a friend, Roberto Teixeira;

he was exposed by the *Folha de São Paulo* for accepting a pension arising from his imprisonment by the dictatorship.

Although the PT was now a regular part of the political system, from Brasília to town councils, it continued to gain nourishment from its links with the social movements that practiced participative democracy. Democracy in Brazil was still young. Although there were frictions between the grass roots and its elected representatives, the PT encapsulated an aspiration that Brazil could build a different kind of democracy. This was all the more attractive as a soulless globalization seemed to sweep away industries, family agriculture, and a sense of security.

The PT's government of Porto Alegre was held up as an example of how things could be done differently. Porto Alegre, the state capital of Rio Grande do Sul, with more than a million people, was by national standards relatively well off, with high literacy levels; the state itself had a substantial population of German and Italian descent, and a radical reputation. In the nineteenth century, Garibaldi had fought for it, Getúlio had launched his 1930 revolution as its governor, and, in 1964, Governor Brizola was pushing for agrarian reform there as the military launched its coup.

Capturing power in Porto Alegre in the mid-1980s, the PT resolved to share it with local communities, especially the poor, by means of a series of public meetings to set the budget. The process was inspired partly by the democratic way in which the CUT union movement dealt with its own finances, partly by the ideas of the educationist Paulo Freire, who linked learning by doing to a deeper public ownership of democracy, and partly by a recognition that the exercise of financial choice is the key power in politics.

Over some two decades, the PT ran Porto Alegre and refined its system of participative budgeting. There was an annual cycle of three types of meeting, regional and thematic plenaries, forums of delegates from the sixteen regions of the city, and meetings of a budget council. The process was real, and involved feedback on performance: the budget, arduously agreed, then went to the mayor for approval by the town council. Whereas only 3,700 local people had been involved in debates in 1991, the number had risen to some 40,000 a decade later. The PT itself benefited, with party membership in the city rising from 8,817 in 1990 to 24,033 by early 2001.[17]

The process had measurable social benefits, especially in poorer neighborhoods, with the building of fifty schools, improvements to the housing stock, and a rise in coverage of the sewer system from 46 percent to 86 percent of the city in just over a decade. The educational and empowering aspects of the process had additional benefits: the city was able to insist that Carrefour, the French supermarket chain, employ young people and make space for forty local shops; there was even a significant drop in school truancy.

Although the PT had other exemplary areas of regional support, for instance in Acre in Amazonia and in Santo André in the ABCD industrial belt around São Paulo, Porto Alegre attracted the most international attention. It was partly for this reason that in 2001, during Cardoso's second term, it became the site of the first World Social Forum, set up to coincide with and confront the ideas of the World Economic Forum in Davos, Switzerland. This provided an occasion for debate among antiglobalization activists, the exploration of green, localist, and socialist ideas, and alternatives to the World Trade Organization. Lula was cheered at these events until 2005, by which time he had been president for three years and was booed.[18]

If Porto Alegre illustrated how the PT was trying to develop the practice of democracy, the MST, the landless movement, was trying its own radical solutions in the countryside. The case for agrarian reform had been acknowledged, but not acted on, for decades before the MST came into existence. On a moral level, there was the original grab by the Portuguese of lands used by the Indians, who did not have a European concept of property ownership. This was followed by a pattern of occupation by force, and forging of land titles, which put much land ownership in question. Speculation and drastic land clearing for soy, citrus, and cattle raising had expelled many land workers and small farmers in the late twentieth century. Modernization was leading to concentrations of wealth and of land in the countryside.

Against these trends the MST launched a series of occupations. In May 1986, it was able to hold the first national meeting of its settlers, to which seventy-six settlements from eleven states sent delegates. In 1989, Lula held his most successful rally outside the cities, attended by forty thousand people, in the MST settlement of Encruzilhada Natalino in Rio Grande do Sul. The MST moved away from its original tutelage by the Catholic Church. In addition to fighting landowners and state organizations, it started pressing for proper educational and health services at its camps, and became interested in organic, small-scale agriculture. It was idealistic, experimenting in collective living and its own forms of direct democracy.

The struggle in the countryside was brutal, with landowners hiring gunmen (*pistoleiros*) to defend their property, and deaths and scuffles. One of the worst atrocities took place in Pará in April 1996, when at least nineteen MST settlers, including a number of the movement's local leaders, were killed by state police working in conjunction with landowners.[19] The place, known as Eldorado de Carajás, was not far from Marabá on the Trans-Amazonica highway built by the military, but it was no Eldorado. It was an area of land conflict, influenced by the big CVRD iron concession at Carajás, and four years later, no military policeman had been brought to justice.

Cardoso's neoliberal enthusiasm tended to increase rural friction. While Brazil was earning some U.S. $5 billion from soy exports in 1999—and the soy frontier in Mato Grosso was spearheading deforestation—it was spending U.S. $7.5 billion on importing traditional Brazilian food crops such as rice, beans, and corn.[20] Multinationals were getting a grip on the seed business and food processing, and an area four times the size of the United Kingdom was brought into agricultural use, mostly savannah and tropical forest, between 1992 and 1998.[21] All this coincided with a sharp decline in the agricultural labor force, and critics felt that Cardoso did not seem to care.

Lula, by contrast, inveighed against the inhumane aspects of market forces and the loss of economic sovereignty by Brazil. But he knew he faced a tough fight against Cardoso for the presidential election of 1998. FHC had become a darling of businessmen in the developed world and, although the trade deficit had moved up from U.S $3.4 billion in 1995 to $6.5 billion in 1998, Brazil was swimming in external investment.

The annual net numbers for foreign direct investment had risen from U.S. $9.6 billion in 1996 to $26.3 billion in 1998.

Cardoso was feted internationally not only for his privatizations and willingness to challenge labor, but also for the solidity of the real and his Lei Fiscal (fiscal law), which, put simply, required the state not to spend more money than it could raise in taxes. He dismissed his critics as fools, and frankly said that all that he had said and written as a radical young sociologist should be forgotten.

In 1998, Lula ran for the presidency with the veteran Leonel Brizola as his running mate. Once again there was an international financial crisis, with Brazil and other Latin American states obtaining support from the IMF and the G7, and a loss of U.S. $30 billion from Brazil's reserves by 30 September. The crisis had begun in southeast Asia in 1997, spreading with a Russian default in 1998. The São Paulo stock exchange, BOVESPA, was moving up and down like a yo-yo, rising 18.6 percent in one day when it was announced that IMF help was on its way.

Lula set up an "above party" advisory council, asked Cardoso to recall Congress, and urged higher taxes on large fortunes, and taxes on financial speculation. He compared the government's approach to that of Brazil's coach in the World Cup soccer tournament in Paris, whom he blamed for failing to substitute an off-form player, Ronaldo, because his uniform was sponsored by a multinational. He tried to build new segments of support and, talking to representatives of the Protestant evangelical churches in Belem, said he would give priority to "genuine causes of the faith." A "Cry of the Excluded" on 7 September, coinciding with the national independence day—the first emperor's cry for Brazilian independence at Ipiranga, near São Paulo, was on 7 September—became a demonstration of the marginalized and the churches in favor of Lula's candidacy.

But it was hard for Lula to shift public opinion. FHC's line in television commercials was that the choice was himself or chaos, and Lula's effort to blame him for the crisis did not work. Instead, the public regarded the father of the real as a port in a storm. By 6 September, the polls were giving Cardoso a lead of 47 percent to 23 percent for Lula, and Lula was facing the prospect of being knocked out in the first round.

This is exactly what happened. Cardoso won with 35,923,259 votes to Lula's 21,470,442; the PT won only three governorships—in Rio Grande do Sul (with Olívio Dutra), in Mato Grosso do Sul, and in Acre.

Where did this leave Lula, after his third presidential defeat? He was just short of his fifty-third birthday, on 27 October. Arguably, he had done better in his first campaign, which had forced Collor to a second round, than in either of his contests against Cardoso. In a more settled democracy, his party would almost certainly have wished to replace him, to give another candidate a chance.

But in spite of the achievements of the new democracy, for which Lula, the PT, the unions, and the social movements could join in taking credit, Brazilian democracy was still in a state of development. Lula was a more important vote-winner than the PT. The PT was never going to be more than one of the chief political parties, and its structure assumed the persistence of factions within it. The evolution of Brazilian society, with the significance of television, advertising, and image, meant that the candidate counted for more than his party.

In this context, Lula was, apart from President Cardoso, the best-known politician in Brazil. He had been a household name for twenty years and, unlike anyone else, had made it his business to visit every corner of the country. All Brazilians felt they knew him as a fellow human being. He also represented something, however vague: greater social equality and an end to extreme poverty; a better kind of plural democracy; a Brazil that defended its own economic interest, alongside other developing countries.

In spite of his own pertinacity, his love of the limelight, and the support of his wife and family in whatever choice he made, it would have been surprising if Lula had not suffered a moment of doubt in October 1998. Shortly after his defeat, he did discuss with close confidants the possibility that the PT and Brazilian left might put up a different candidate in 2002.[22] He encouraged Tarso Genro from Rio Grande do Sul; José Genoino, the one-time guerrilla; Eduardo Suplicy, one of the PT intellectuals from São Paulo; and Crístovam Buarque, who was to become governor of Brasília, to tour the country and see if any of them could win the necessary backing. But the answer came back that Lula was still the best bet, and in a PT primary election against Suplicy, he won 70 percent of the vote.

Lula was a man who held certain beliefs, and his record stood for itself. But there is little doubt that he was a victim of what Brazilians call the *mosca azul*—the blue fly of ambition. In deciding that he would mount a fourth challenge for the presidency, due in 2002, he vowed that he would do so on his own terms. He simply *had* to win next time. He needed a breakthrough to gain a substantial part of the 70 percent of voters who had rejected him three times already. He would make whatever compromises were necessary—in alliances, in program, in the way he presented himself. There seemed no alternative. If idealists on the left still saw him as some kind of utopian socialist, this was their illusion.

Cardoso's second government was not a great success, and by the end of it the president, his party, and his anointed successor—José Serra, who had been minister of health—were not popular. Crime and unemployment rose. Financial crises persisted. The first was precipitated in January 1999 when Itamar Franco, the former president who was now a PMDB governor of Minas Gerais, said that his state would suspend debt payments to the federal government, causing a crash in Brazil's international credit.

This triggered a devaluation of the real and a shift to a floating regime for the currency. FHC appointed Armínio Fraga, a wealthy former academic and colleague of the international speculator George Soros, as head of the Banco Central.

Lula was caustic about this appointment, and the CUT, in an official statement rejecting Fraga as a symbol of the excesses of neoliberalism, said that it was like putting a fox in charge of the chicken coop. Lula rejected approaches from Cardoso to join him in a national response to the economic crisis. Some in the PT tried to launch impeachment proceedings against the president. In May 2001, adding to the sense that the economy was not being well managed, there were power cuts and electricity had to be rationed.

Over the border in Argentina, in the first years of the new century, there was an economic and social implosion; presidents changed at high speed, there was a default on debt, bankrupt factories were occupied by the workers, the middle class was pauperized. The default on sovereign debt by an interim Peronist government, in December 2001, caused particular drama. Inside and outside Brazil there was a great deal of anxiety that Brazil could go the same way, and that if he was elected president, Lula would also default.

By 2002, the year of the next presidential election, however, Lula had amassed a large bank of personal experience and contacts. He had decided that, to win, he had to present a moderate image and break through to the majority of voters who had rejected him three times already. In some ways this was a parallel path to that taken by Tony Blair and "New Labour" in Britain, but the circumstances were different in a complex, multiparty presidential system that was still only fifteen years away from a military dictatorship.[23]

Lula's most daring move was to hand over the publicity and marketing of his campaign to Duda Mendonça. Mendonça, who hailed originally from Bahia, had worked for several individuals and parties since helping to get Collor elected as governor in Alagoas. He was widely regarded as a genius, but the kind of amoral professional who was ready to work with anyone. One of his most celebrated campaigns had succeeded in getting Paulo Maluf elected as mayor of São Paulo in 1992. He sanitized the image of this conservative and widely distrusted man who had been governor of São Paulo state during the military era. He craftily updated a slogan originally used to describe Adhemar de Barros, a Paulista governor of the 1960s, of whom it was said that "he steals but he does."

PT militants had managed to keep Mendonça out of their previous presidential campaigns. In taking a large measure of control in 2002, he used focus groups to assess the strength and weakness of Lula, spent money lavishly on TV advertising and star-studded rallies, and promoted an image of a smart, friendly man of the people—a Lula of peace and love whose time had come. He claimed that he was doing no more than projecting aspects of the candidate that had always been there, but never so clearly presented. A video of Lula's campaign, made by an independent filmmaker, shows the presidential candidate deferring to the marketing man.[24] What was not clear, and became a matter of high drama in 2005, was how this expensive publicity and advertising was being paid for.

After his 1998 defeat, Lula had used the Citizenship Institute and its working groups to chart policy. In the 2002 election, his most attractive social promise was to launch Fome Zero—Zero Hunger—a plan to ensure that no poor family in Brazil should go hungry again. Coming from someone who himself had been hungry as a child, this was a pledge that carried conviction. But in a deliberate attempt to move away from PT radicalism, reaffirmed in the PT national conference of 2001, he wrote "A Letter to the Brazilian People" in June 2002. This stated that he would not default on the national debt, that all contracts would be honored, and that private enterprise would be encouraged. It was a bitter pill for many in the PT, and it did not initially achieve the aim of calming election-based speculation against Brazil's finances. José Dirceu added that the Central Bank would get operational autonomy.[25]

When the MST, the landless movement, occupied a farm belonging to the children of President Cardoso in March 2002, Lula issued a statement backing the president and private property. He did not want his opponents to attack him with the propaganda of expropriation, as Collor's people did in 1989, when they went around threatening householders with imminent occupation by the landless.

Lula took other steps to widen his coalition of support. He recruited as his vice presidential running mate a self-made millionaire businessman, José Alencar. Alencar had left a poor home and large family at the age of fourteen, sleeping in corridors and building a textile business in Minas Gerais through hard work. He was not a prominent politician and was linked with one of the small right-wing parties, the Partido Liberal; he was a Protestant evangelical, and his party was also supported by that religious movement.[26] Lula was therefore sending two signals to the electorate, as someone whose own politics were associated with the poor and with the Catholic Church. He was also undermining a rival, Anthony Garotinho, the governor of Rio de Janeiro, who also had evangelical backing.

The campaign was put in the experienced hands of Luiz Gushiken, one of Lula's longtime union associates, whom he nicknamed "the Chinese" on account of his appearance. The campaign focused on the sixty-two towns and cities with the largest populations, and PT alliances were constructed with whatever parties could be recruited beyond the traditional leftist bloc. These included chunks of the PMDB, parties such as the PTB, which wanted to stay close to power for the jobs and rewards it could bring, and the tiny, personality-based parties that still littered the landscape.[27] Formally, Lula was being supported by his usual four parties in the presidential election, but the alliance in Congress that was elected at the same time comprised nine parties.[28]

Lula was as effective on the trail as ever—speaking to huge crowds, traveling all over Brazil, engaging with people's dreams. He attacked Cardoso for trying to "terrorize electors" when he said that Brazil could fall into the economic abyss of Argentina. He made it clear that he was not keen on the Free Trade Area of the Americas being pushed by President George W. Bush. And he was, for the first time in an election since before the introduction of the real, ahead in the polls. José Serra, one of the Paulista group at the top of the PSDB, had been well regarded as Cardoso's minister of health, but he was not charismatic and FHC had run out of popularity.

The results of the first round, on 1 October, gave Lula 46 percent of the vote and Serra only 32 percent, with a further 29 percent distributed between two other candidates, Ciro Gomes and Anthony Garotinho. But experienced Brazilian politicians saw that it was virtually all over, and people of many persuasions—including Paulo Maluf and Delfim Netto, an economic minister for the military—rallied to what cynics described as Lula's "Noah's Ark." Many in the electorate hoped that Lula would introduce profound change and would end the suffering caused by neoliberalism.

The *Financial Times* of London, in an editorial written at a distance, said that all the signs were that there would be a debt moratorium as called for by the PT in previous elections, and that Lula should calm the market.[29] Antonio Palocci, the program coordinator for a Lula government and about to be named finance minister, said that a Lula government would maintain Cardoso's stance on taxation, however; at once

Brazilian bonds rose by 5.85 percent, the stock exchange jumped by 6.34 percent, and the so-called *risco Brasil* fell by 8.66 percent.

In fact Lula had been consistent, following his letter to the Brazilian people. Cardoso, concerned about market speculation that drove down the real as the election campaign got going, had called in the three leading contenders—Lula, Serra, and Ciro Gomes—in August. The outgoing president encouraged them to agree publicly to maintain the current IMF program, whoever won.

After Lula came in ahead at the end of the first round, the world adjusted to his impending victory. Journalists reported that although Washington was not eager to see a Lula presidency, President Bush hoped that it would be a great deal more friendly than the Chávez presidency in Venezuela and would put a brake on leftist anti-Americanism.

In the second round, at the end of October, Lula won at last. He got 52,788,428 votes to Serra's 33,366,430—or 61.3 percent to 38.7 percent. It was definitive. His supporters' excitement was enormous. There was still trepidation among the rich. Lula still faced prejudice and snobbery.[30] The second round had taken place on 27 October, his fifty-seventh birthday. The first round, on 6 October, had coincided with the date his father had wrongly registered as his birth date.

5 OVERVIEW OF THE FIRST TERM

Lula's election victory brought euphoria to all those who had backed him from the beginning. When the second round of voting confirmed his victory, the wealthy center of São Paulo, the Avenida Paulista, erupted in the red flags of the PT. When he accepted the presidential sash from Cardoso in early 2003, there was a carnival in Brasília; the poor, workers, students, and members of the social movements crowded the area around Congress—the Praça dos Tres Poderes—in a show of unity and celebration.

It was not the man who had had secret meetings of reassurance with businessmen, or the man who had cut a middle-class figure in smart suits and ties with a Windsor knot who was acknowledged. It was "the worker president"—*o presidente operário*. A group of seventeen da Silva relations from the area around Garanhuns came to Brasília to party and to witness the miracle. Many were still poor. If Abe Lincoln had symbolized to Americans in the nineteenth century that it was possible to debate your way from log cabin to White House, the story of Lula, the migrant from a broken home who had lost a finger in a factory accident, seemed equally incredible and inspiring.

For Lula and Marisa this was a dream come true. His victory, on the fourth attempt, had come on his fifty-seventh birthday. In the fickle, self-seeking, and often corrupt world of Brazilian politics, he represented commitment and pertinacity. He had played a big part in the establishment of democracy, in obtaining better conditions for workers and an autonomous union movement, and in the creation of an ethical, democratic labor party, the PT. His win promised maturity for Brazil's new republic, and a serious attempt to challenge the social inequality and ingrained conservatism of his country. Now, at last, he was president. What would he do?

His first acts and appointments were designed to calm those worried about the economy, while also signaling to his supporters that change was on the way. The last year of Cardoso's government had seen another speculative attack, inflation of 20 percent, and a situation so damaging to the public sector that Cardoso's minister of education could not afford an airline ticket to Washington.[1]

In Lula's first major press conference, he announced the Fome Zero program, designed to banish hunger from Brazil. But his two key appointments, following the line he had taken in his Letter to the Brazilian People, were of Antonio Palocci as minister of finance, and Henrique Meirelles, previously an international banker with BankBoston, to run the Central Bank. Palocci had been a PT mayor of the town of Ribeirão Preto, in São Paulo state.[2] A Trotskyite in his youth and a medical doctor, he came from a middle-class family. Meirelles had just been elected as a PSDB deputy for Goiás.

These two made it clear that there would be no debt cancellation or renegotiation. Instead, they were committed to a more conservative stance with sound currency, high interest rates, an export surplus, and a gradual reduction in the burden of public debt. Brazil would not be Argentina.

At the same time, Lula put his faithful organization man, José Dirceu, in to run the Casa Civil, the presidential office that manages much of the government and party business on behalf of the president. And he signaled that he was serious about social change: Gilberto Gil, the black popular musician who had performed at Lula's rallies, was made minister of culture; Benedita da Silva, also a black Brazilian, was given a social welfare portfolio; Olívio Dutra, the one-time leader of the bank workers who had gone on to become the PT governor of Rio Grande do Sul, was made a minister for cities—where expansion, slums, and crime were creating a combustible mixture of resentment. Crístovam Buarque, who had run the University of Brasília and gone on to be governor of Brasília, was put in charge of education; he was a passionate enthusiast for raising the poor standards of state schooling, and an admirer of Paulo Freire, the iconoclastic Brazilian reformer.

But Lula's government comprised two different coalitions, frequently in conflict, so that an opponent could say that he was closer to leading a fractious nongovernmental organization than a government.[3] There were divisions within the PT, which had only 91 of the 513 deputies in the Chamber, and was reliant on its small allies to maintain its majority.[4] And there were divisions with and among the allies.

Within the PT, the main tendencies in conflict were those of left and right. On the left were those who harked back to the kind of socialism that they had espoused in the 1960s, with strong government leadership in the economy, rejection of the IMF and foreign bankers, and serious income redistribution. On the right were those such as Palocci who had decided to make peace with international capitalism, and who believed that there was no way that Brazil could divorce itself from the world economy and that the best route forward was to manipulate the system in favor of the poor and national development.

There were personal rivalries between Dirceu and Palocci, although both belonged to the Campo Majoritario, the moderate controlling bloc in the PT that was the successor to the Articulação. As Palocci's policies calmed the international markets and growth resumed, his strength in the government increased. By the third quarter of 2004, the country's gross national product (GNP) was growing by an annual rate of 6.1 percent, the fastest jump in eight years; industrial employment was rising by an annual rate of 5.9 percent—the highest in thirteen years; and exports of $95 billion in 2004 were a record. Dirceu's power was also clipped when Lula made Aldo Rebelo, from his communist ally the PCdoB, a political coordinator.

But within the first year of the government some leftist members of the PT were expelled from the party in a fight over welfare and pension reform that was part of the legislative overhang from Cardoso. Previdencia Social, the basic pension system, which also provided support for rural workers, went back to the Vargas era and was linked to the minimum salary. It gave enormous privileges to civil servants, retired judges, and retired military officers. It was structurally unsound as the Brazilian population began to age, and it was loading a growing deficit onto the state finances. Cardoso had sought to change the system, and the Lula government enacted a reform in 2003 that raised the retirement age of officials to sixty, and could be seen as involving partial privatization.[5]

This was fiercely criticized by a small group of leftist deputies and senators, who felt that the PT was betraying the poor and its basic commitments. There were major demonstrations in Brasília against the legislation. The most prominent of those expelled was Senator Heloísa Helena, who became one of the most effective critics of the administration when it ran into its corruption crisis in 2005; she ran for the presidency in 2006.

Although only a half-dozen elected PT members of Congress were expelled from the party, they objected to a whole raft of government policies and decided to set up a new party—PSOL, Partido de Socialismo e Liberdade. By December 2004, they had obtained the 438,000 signatures they needed to get their party registered. It was a warning to Lula, who had faced down the left in both the PT and the unions before, that he would have difficulty in retaining his image as a radical.

In fact, rather as in Britain, where some of the cheerleaders for the "New Labour" government of Tony Blair had been Marxists in their youth,[6] a handful of the key players around Lula had come from this background and had accepted a capitalist compromise as they had grown older. Few espoused a "third way" ideology, although José Genoino, as president of the PT, came close when he said that both the neoliberal and the traditional socialist state had failed: "The PT is post-communist and post–social democrat."[7] But this leadership group was now rather distant from the anticapitalist and antiglobalization ideas of the campaigners in the MST and World Social Forum.

Much of Lula's time in his first term was spent oiling the wheels of political alliances and trying to reach out to the nonpolitical. His conciliatory skills brought old enemies, such as the former president José Sarney, about whom he had said extremely rude things in the past, into his congressional majority. Sarney was part of the progovernment wing of the PMDB.

Faithful also to the principles of inclusion that underpinned his own and PT's thinking, Lula set up various commissions on social policy and development, designed to bring in more stakeholders.[8] For instance, his Economic and Social Development Council had around eighty members, drawn from politics, business, and the wider society. It was the same spirit that had led him to establish the Citizenship Institute as a think tank that went beyond the PT as a party. Some who participated in these commissions felt that they were a waste of time; others thought that they were getting closer to the government.

By the end of his second year in office, 2004, Lula's government faced its first electoral test, with elections for mayors. These were traditionally settled by personal as much as political factors, but the Cardoso government had suffered an antigovernment swing in its midterm elections, and Lula and the PT could have expected the same. The 2004 polls, however, showed the PT gaining ground in the smaller towns. It won the state capital of Belo Horizonte in Minas Gerais, and Aracajú, Recife, and Fortaleza in the northeast, but lost São Paulo, Porto Alegre, and Belem. It was not a bad result.

Both São Paulo and Porto Alegre had been emblematic for the PT, and it was significant of the willingness of the party to strike deals and bury old hatchets that it was willing to accept the support of Paulo Maluf in the second-round runoff in São Paulo. Nonetheless, its glamorous mayor there, the PT's Marta Suplicy, the divorced former wife of the PT senator Eduardo Suplicy, was beaten by the PSDB's José Serra, the PSDB presidential candidate defeated by Lula. São Paulo had a special place in the history of both the PT and the PSDB.

In Congress, the government majority, though attacked by its PSDB and PFL opponents, held together reasonably well for the first half of Lula's term. As with previous administrations Lula relied considerably on "provisional measures" (*medidas provisorias*), the executive's tool for enacting legislation prior to congressional approval. Henrique Meirelles, the governor of the Central Bank, was given ministerial status by this procedure.

In late 2004, the government actually obtained PSDB support for a measure approving public-private partnerships to pay for hospitals, schools, and other government works.[9] There was steady turnover in the ministerial team; among those who went were Benedita da Silva, over a financial infraction, and Crístovam Buarque, who had been pushing the bounds of his educational mandate, and who was dismissed over the phone by Lula. Vice President Alencar was temporarily made minister of defense after a row over photos of the dead journalist Vladimir Herzog forced the departure of José Viegas.

It was in February 2005, even before the great corruption scandal of that year engulfed the government, that the administration's control of Congress broke down. The cause was the election of a new president of the Chamber of Deputies, a key position in the management of any legislative program, and constitutionally the third in line to become president of Brazil if the president and vice president were removed. The job is prestigious. Its occupant has a fine mansion by the lake in Brasília, along with a staff there of twenty-one, including three chefs and a nutritionist. There were five candidates this time, and some were spending 400,000–500,000 reais on their campaigns—in excess of $200,000.

The problem was that the PT's own discipline collapsed. The PT candidate favored by Lula and the government was Luiz Eduardo Greenhalgh. But there was also a dissident PT candidate, Virgílio Guimarães, who split the progovernment vote. Of three conservative candidates, the winner turned out to be Severino Cavalcanti, a deputy known as the "king of the lower clergy"—a kind of union organizer for backbenchers. He beat Greenhalgh by 300 votes to 195 in the runoff, with the support of the main opposition parties, the PSDB and PFL.

Cavalcanti, who was seventy-four years old and from Pernambuco, symbolized all that honest democrats distrusted about the ways of Congress. In a long political career, which had started with the anti-Vargas União Democrático Nacional party in 1962, he had managed to belong to seven parties before joining the PP (the Partido Popular of Maluf and the most conservative heirs of the military regimes). That was in 1995. His main campaign plank now was to raise the monthly salaries of deputies from 12,847 to 21,500 reais.[10] When he was unable to implement this blatant appeal to self-interest after he won the election, he used his administrative authority to increase the budget available for deputies to pay their staff by 25 percent. He boasted of the strings he pulled to support people from his hometown of João Alfredo, and employed more relatives than anyone else in the Chamber.[11]

To begin with, Cavalcanti tried to make life difficult for the government. But as the corruption crisis blew up in the course of 2005, Lula found himself working with Cavalcanti to try and put a brake on the headlong rush of events; Cavalcanti sought to protect Dirceu and others who were in the line of fire. But Lula had to pay dearly for this, in more than just his own and the PT's reputation. Cavalcanti insisted on naming a new cities minister, Márcio Fortes, to replace Lula's old union and PT colleague, Olívio Dutra.

Severino Cavalcanti did not last beyond September 2005. He was caught in the journalistic hue and cry about corruption in Brasília. He was exposed as receiving monthly payments from the operator of a restaurant that served the Chamber of Deputies. Even after he was forced to resign, his man remained in the Cities Ministry, and, when the pressure was building, Lula made it clear that he did not want Cavalcanti to go.

The fact that such an obviously dubious character was in a powerful position in Brasília, at a time when senior figures in the PT were accused of corruption, was negative for the political system as a whole. Who could be trusted? Was it true, as Lula in opposition had once said and Antonio Carlos Magalhães, the grand old man of the PFL in Bahia, now repeated, that a large proportion of Brazil's elected representatives were crooks? Was this one of the factors that held Brazil back to the status of a developing rather than a developed country?

When Severino Cavalcanti was forced out, Lula and the government recognized that they had to exert themselves to put in their own man of confidence as president of the Chamber. Interestingly, they did not turn to a PT deputy, but rather to Aldo Rebelo of the PCdoB, who had been Lula's political coordinator and who had crossed swords with Dirceu.

But Dirceu by this time had lost his ministerial post (as we shall see in a moment) and was under a cloud. In the past, Rebelo, who was from São Paulo, had been regarded as slightly eccentric, but he had won Lula's trust. And although it looked as though some of the traditional pro-Lula parties were breaking away to support a PFL candidate,[12] heavy arm-twisting by the government secured Rebelo's victory.

This was a turning point for the government in its effort to move on from the bigger corruption crisis, which will be described briefly in this chapter and is the subject of a later chapter. After Rebelo became president of the Chamber, Lula's government had an organizer in a key position to limit the damage from the crisis, to prevent too many deputies from losing their political rights in punishment, and to begin to close down the endless bad publicity from parliamentary committees of inquiry.

The crisis of 2005, which severely damaged the PT's standing as an ethical party and led some to call for Lula's impeachment, began with a video. Stills from it appeared in the issue of *Veja*, the newsmagazine, for 18 May 2005.[13] The "exclusive" headline on the cover advertised "the video of corruption in Brasília—an incredible sequence of money leaving the hands of a corruptor for the pocket of the corrupted." The pictures showed Maurício Marinho, the contracts director for the state postal service, Correios, taking a bribe of three thousand reais.

But what Marinho said in this secret recording was far more explosive. He explained that the PTB, one of the nonideological allies of the government,[14] had been able to name the heads of the postal service and of a major electricity utility, Eletronorte, as a political reward. The PTB was then milking bribes from these state enterprises in a systematic fashion; in one case cited by *Veja*, the enterprise was required to produce 400,000 reais (roughly $200,000) a month for the party.[15]

The PTB was no longer the labor-oriented party of Getúlio Vargas. It had fallen into the hands of an opportunist deputy, Roberto Jefferson, who had supported Collor, and whose main strategy was to be close to the government of the day in order to enjoy its perks. It was part of the critique of Lula from the more idealistic members of the PT that he had chosen to recruit his majority from small parties such as the PTB, which were essentially for sale. He had rejected the advice of Dirceu, in the run-up to the 2002 election, to ally instead with the larger, divided PMDB, which at least shared some authentic history of opposition to the military.

Jefferson, a histrionic figure, could see his spoils under threat: Maurício Marinho had been fired as soon as the video became public. Jefferson decided on a preemptive strike. He announced that a large number of deputies had been illicitly put on the government payroll, being paid monthly from undeclared PT or government monies.

This precipitated the scandal of the *mensalão*—the monthly paycheck.

A parliamentary inquiry commission was appointed to examine Jefferson's claims. Night after night, Brazilians watched TV with amazement as what was known as "the crisis in Brasília" unfolded. It seemed to spread and spread, as journalists, the Federal Police, and parliamentary investigators disclosed information about overseas bank accounts for PT campaign funding, contracts for gambling, and the murky murder of a popular PT mayor of Santo André, Celso Daniel.

The main political casualties came from the top of the PT. They included José Genoino, the party president, who resigned. José Dirceu, regarded as the organizer of the *mensalão*, was forced to resign as minister for the president's Casa Civil, and then, like Jefferson, was deprived of his political rights as a deputy by the Chamber of Deputies. Two party officials also went: Silvio Pereira, the secretary-general, and Delúbio Soares, the PT treasurer. Duda Mendonça, the marketing genius who had made both Maluf and Lula electable, was exposed as a man who had been illegally paid for Lula's presidential campaign in overseas bank accounts.

The scandal hit the PT hardest, but it also affected Lula. Lula's approval ratings went down sharply in the second half of 2005. Inevitably, people asked, how much did he know? If he did know, then he was an accomplice. If he did not, was he not a negligent administrator? A few opponents and the Brazilian association of lawyers (Ordem dos Advogados do Brasil) did consider calling for impeachment, as had occurred with Collor. But there was a lack of evidence affecting Lula directly. There was little enthusiasm for either Alencar or Cavalcanti becoming interim president. Other parties risked damage. This was an issue that was deferred rather than buried.

Always an emotional man, Lula was severely depressed. In August 2005, when the scandal was at its height, a group of his old union friends got together in São Bernardo to give him a good meal and cheer him up. Gijó (Juno Rodrigues Silva), once a member of the Metalworkers' Union executive and now the proprietor of a São Bernardo restaurant, arranged it. His friends wanted to remind him that they still believed in him.

It is virtually impossible to say how much Lula knew. In his union he had cracked down on the occasional item of corruption, and there is little evidence of personal enrichment during his time as president.[16] But he was not the kind of leader who liked detailed administration, which he usually devolved to others, and he knew well enough that pork-barrel politics oiled the Brazilian system. In his public response to the drawn-out crisis he seemed all over the place, variously calling for malefactors to be brought to justice, implying that all Brazilian parties had undeclared accounts, and suggesting that it did not matter very much.[17]

But Lula's government and Lula himself had a different image in 2006 as compared with the start of 2005. They were no longer seen as separate from everything in Brazilian politics that had gone before. The PT itself was no longer a superior, ethical party, although its membership held up, and the Campo Majoritario lost some of its control to left-wingers in internal elections in late 2005. But for poorer voters, the ethics issue was less important than the availability of jobs and the welfare payments of the Bolsa-Família. Such differences in perception became more important in the run-up to the 2006 election.

Lula, with his sometimes ungrammatical speeches and his soccer metaphors—he remained an enthusiastic supporter of the Paulista team, Corintians—came across as a populist nationalist but also a friend to the poor. He inspired two government advertising slogans—"The best thing about Brazil is the Brazilian" and "Brazil—a country for everyone." In an interview with the news agency Reuters in July 2006, when he was asked whether he still considered himself a leftist, he replied firmly, "I was never a leftist."[18]

He used his love of travel and meeting people—his belief in eyeball diplomacy—to try to position Brazil as a strong developing country, in a leadership role in Latin America. He made five trips to Africa, apologizing for slavery in Senegal and gliding lightly over the human rights and corruption records of some of his hosts, such as President Bongo of Gabon, who had ruled his country for thirty-eight years by 2005. Vicentinho, a black PT deputy who had been president of the São Bernardo metalworkers, accompanied Lula on some of these African tours, which had public relations importance at home.

Lula's international campaign to win a permanent seat on the UN Security Council did not succeed during his first term, but the efforts that he and advisers such as Marco Aurélio Garcia made to shake up Brazilian diplomacy had a significant impact. Lula's foreign minister, Celso Amorim, described Lula as *nosso guia* (our guide), which led to ironic laughter among the professionals.

He did, however, give some different emphases to how the national interest should be seen in an era of globalization. He made friends with oil-rich Arab countries. He promoted a number of specific groupings for specific purposes, such as IBSA (India–Brazil–South Africa) and BRICS (Brazil–India–China–South Africa) for the world trade negotiations of the Doha round, and an alliance with India, Germany, and Japan, which with Brazil were all seeking seats on the Security Council. Brazil was active in the G20, the group of twenty key developing countries, and, unlike Hugo Chávez, Lula was careful not to make an enemy of George W. Bush and the United States.

The result of all these endeavors was that Brazil was taken more seriously. Lula, with the leaders of China and India, had been on the edge of G8 meetings of the world's most powerful economies in 2003, 2004, and 2005. By the St. Petersburg meeting of the G8 in July 2006, which he also attended, it was being formally proposed that the G8 should be expanded to G13, to include Brazil, Mexico, India, China, and South Africa; this would recognize the economic and political weight of these countries.[19]

But Lula's own personality shone through much of this international activity. As a contribution to peacekeeping in the long-suffering Caribbean state of Haiti—and incidentally a campaign gesture for the UN Security Council seat—Brazil offered to lead a UN force of blue-helmeted soldiers. But it was a Lula-inspired flourish that subsequently decided to send the Brazilian soccer team on a tour to cheer up the impoverished Haitians.

Lula had strongly criticized the U.S.-led invasion of Iraq in 2003. And when Sérgio Vieira de Mello, the Brazilian-born UN diplomat, was assassinated in Baghdad on 19 August that year when the UN offices were blown up, it was Lula who insisted that his body should be brought back for a state funeral.[20]

There were sometimes gaffes, and many Brazilian journalists reporting his trips were interested only in these.[21] Welcoming President Obasanjo of Nigeria to the Foreign Ministry in Brasília in September 2005, he said "Nigeria and Brazil are the two countries with the greatest population of African descent in the world." As many were quick to point out, there was a big difference between being an African and being of African descent. One of the great difficulties in Brazil, which led to controversy over racial quotas for universities, was defining who was or was not "black."

Lula had an ambition for world power that harked back to the nineteenth-century positivists, the hopes of Vargas, and the statements of the military presidents. "We will make the twenty-first century the Brazilian century," he was quoted as saying in early 2005, before the big corruption scandal broke.[22] It was a claim that propagandists for U.S. power had made in the nineteenth century and had seen realized in the second half of the twentieth.

But not everyone in Latin America was in love with Lula, and important refrains during his first term were Argentina's suspicion of him, his complex relationship with the anti-American radical Hugo Chávez, and the Latin American reaction against Chávez and his ally Evo Morales of Bolivia, which became obvious when conservative candidates won elections in Peru and Mexico in 2006.

It was inevitable that Nestor Kirchner, the Peronist president of Argentina, would look askance at Brazil's desire to be the regional leader of countries with a different political culture, whose language was Spanish. Brazil's much more powerful economy,[23] and its suave response to the speculative attack of 2002–3, took it in the opposite direction from Argentina's debt renunciation. Argentina had done what many PT radicals would have liked but which Lula and Palocci forbade.

In the excitement of Lula's election, it was thought that he and Chávez would be fast friends, in a coalition of the left in South America.

Conservative journalists in Brazil tried to pin support from Cuba and the FARC guerrillas in Colombia on the PT, and to attack Lula for a Chávez connection. But four years later it was obvious that Lula and Chávez sometimes agreed to differ.

Leftists in the PT might see Chávez as the leader they did not have, the Bush administration might hope that Lula would calm Chávez down, but a broad spectrum of Brazilian opinion saw Chávez as a temporarily oil-rich caudillo, whose Bolivarian "revolution" clashed with their own national ambitions. Simón Bolívar had been the great nineteenth-century liberator in the Andes and what is now Colombia and Venezuela. He had never liberated Brazil.

This friction with Chávez, which Brazilian diplomats often sought to play down, was more apparent after his friend Evo Morales, a Bolivian indigenous leader, was elected president of Bolivia in December 2005. His anticapitalist rhetoric was similar to speeches made by Lula in the 1980s. His background was dissimilar, in that he represented an indigenous majority that had been oppressed for five hundred years and coca farmers hostile to a U.S.-backed eradication program.

In May 2006, Morales moved to nationalize oil and gas fields, coming at once into conflict with Petrobrás, the biggest external investor in Bolivian gas; Bolivian gas supplies were now vital to industry in the central south of Brazil. In the middle of 2006, Brazil also warned against meddling with Mercosul, the somewhat ineffective southern regional grouping whose membership included Bolivia only as an associate member.

In fact, Lula was more at home with the center-left administrations of Chile and Uruguay, although Chile made a bilateral trade agreement with the United States, which was further than Brazil wished to go. Just after Lula's own reelection, two more center-left leaders were elected— Daniel Ortega in Nicaragua, and Rafael Correa in Ecuador. Both had been backed by Chávez, but neither was a clone of the Venezuelan.

Lula had made it a foreign policy principle to kill the U.S.-led Free Trade Area of the Americas, and he did not want Latin American countries picked off one by one in bilateral deals. He put a lot of energy instead into trying to make the Doha world trade round a success for developing countries,[24] using his mediatory skills to find a way between U.S. and European agricultural subsidies and the unwillingness of developing countries to lift all protection from their factories and services.

The year 2006 saw a revival in Lula's fortunes. It was not immediately clear why this should be so. As late as January, in a speech to university rectors, he said that "in 2007 I will no longer be here."[25] While the PT began to gear up for his reelection, he himself seems to have been unsure for a month or two. He went on a state visit to Britain in March, hosted by Queen Elizabeth II, although he had told diplomats in Brasília earlier that he would limit his overseas trips if he decided to run for reelection. The sight of the former lathe operator sitting next to the heir to a centuries-old monarchy was powerful TV advertising to his poorer constituency. Such viewers were the virtual witnesses and participants in a continuing fairy tale.

In a private meeting before his departure for home, he used his remarkable interpersonal gifts to calm angry members of the family of Jean-Charles de Menezes, the Brazilian electrician wrongly identified as a suicide bomber and killed by London police. In Brazil, deaths of poor people at the hands of the police were unremarkable; in the United Kingdom, this one was the subject of an independent inquiry and public controversy. When a year later it was decided that no policeman should face trial, but the Metropolitan Police should be prosecuted for lack of care for the public's health and safety, it was reminiscent of trying Al Capone, the Chicago gangster, for tax evasion.

The polls began to favor Lula, implying that he would be reelected; by mid-2006, they indicated that he could win outright on 1 October in the first round. The turnaround became clear in March and April when the anticorruption campaign largely collapsed and the government rode out the departure of Antonio Palocci. In a scandalous effort to protect Palocci, the bank account of the commissionaire at a building in Brasília—who had witnessed nefarious goings-on by the finance minister and his friends from Ribeirão Preto—was illegally opened. Brazil's high interest rates came down slightly and there was no speculative attack on the real linked to the replacement of Palocci by Guido Mantega.

Between September 2005 and September 2006, the basic interest rate fell by more than five percentage points, from 19.75 percent to 14.25 percent. Though still high, this was the lowest level since 2001. It reflected international confidence in the economic management of Lula's team, and he made the strength of the economy a large part of his appeal to the wider, non-PT Brazilian electorate.

The seeming rundown in the salience of corruption as an issue was illustrated by the fact that five deputies who might have lost their political rights were absolved by the Chamber of Deputies in late March. A PT deputy, Angela Guadagnin, danced a little jig of celebration in the Chamber when one of her friends, the PT deputy João Magno—accused of receiving more than four hundred thousand reais in the scandal—was acquitted. Deputies were failing to turn up to vote on expulsions. Despite a fairly clear-cut case against a PT deputy from São Paulo— whose wife had withdrawn fifty thousand reais from a Brasília bank account belonging to the *mensalão* businessman Marcos Valério—the proposal that João Paulo Cunha should lose his political rights was voted down by 256 to 209.

Of parliamentarians accused of involvement in the *mensalão* scandal, only three had lost their political rights, four had resigned but were free to run again in elections, and eight had been absolved. In the early phase of Lula's presidency there had been attrition from the PT on policy issues, and this had accelerated with the exposure of systematic corruption in 2005. Deputies had left to join the PSOL; Fernando Gabeira had joined the Greens; Crístovam Buarque had joined the PDT, for which he was running as a presidential candidate in 2006. In 2005, one of the founders of the PT, Eduardo Suplicy, had voted in favor of parliamentary inquiries into the scandals.

But by April 2006, all politicians were beginning to position themselves for the upcoming election. The PT in particular, threatened with revenge by disillusioned voters, was pulling together in Brasília. Brazil's procurator-general, Antonio Fernando de Souza, named forty persons who had been bribed, and talked of "a criminal organization installed in the government." His naming and shaming had, initially, less impact than might have been expected. A parliamentary commission of inquiry, looking into the over-invoicing of ambulances, which had involved bribes to deputies from the small parties in the government majority, also failed to hit Lula, or even exclusively the PT.

How was it that, phoenix-like, Lula could rise again? It was a puzzle. But the best explanations related to the opposition, to the attitudes of the Brazilian public, and to Lula himself. Many within the PSDB and PFL pulled their punches over the corruption scandals. Although ex-President Cardoso spoke out against Lula, there were others in the conservative opposition who feared that a wholesale attack on corruption would uncover malpractices of their own. They could see that the disclosures of 2005 had seriously damaged the total political class. This left the most consistent and disinterested critiques to come from Heloísa Helena of PSOL, and Fernando Gabeira, now with the Greens, who were somewhat outside the mainstream.

The PSDB-PFL opposition was also at a disadvantage in that it did not have a popular, well-known presidential candidate for the 2006 elections. It chose Geraldo Alckmin, PSDB governor of the state of São Paulo, who had a PFL running mate. Alckmin had done a perfectly reasonable job as governor, backed by Serra as mayor of São Paulo city, but he was uncharismatic and not widely known outside his state. He was said to be prickly in personal relations.

For much of 2006, Lula had the unopposed promotional advantages of incumbency. He toured Brazil, inaugurating public works, inspecting public works that were already in operation, or talking of plans for the future. And he drew on his genuine and continuing popularity. Nearly twelve million families were now receiving the Bolsa-Família, the welfare payments for the poorest that followed up the Fome Zero campaign of his first year. For many Brazilian voters who had a low opinion of politicians anyway, cash in hand and a steady currency counted for more than corruption in Brasília.

Furthermore, his above-party stance, distancing himself from the PT when it suited him, was also attractive. Yet he had responded to nationalist feeling. He had made much of the early repayment of IMF loans in 2005, and of self-sufficiency in oil products a year later, which was accompanied by an aggressive advertising campaign by Petrobrás; he had put a stop to the Cardoso strategy of privatizations, which had strengthened the reach of international companies in Brazil. Yet he was not a scary leftist like Chávez, who would have worried the middle class. If Brazil was now a country for everyone, this too was the aspiration of its president.

Family life for Lula had always been hectic and snatched, ever since his days as a strike leader in the 1970s. As president he was constantly hosting, traveling, and conferring. His own life was perhaps less changed than was his wife's. Marisa entered the role of first lady with grace and aplomb, accompanying Lula on many of his international travels and handing out medicaments to the entourage of journalists that accompanied them. Traditionally in Brazil the first lady's role had involved charitable works, and Ruth Cardoso had run a nongovernmental organization (NGO). But, instead, Marisa continued to focus her time and attention on providing her husband with the emotional and political support that had been a feature of their lives together.

They spent very little of their time in the Palácio Alvorada, one of Oscar Niemeyer's beautiful but somewhat impractical state buildings in the center of Brasília. It was more than forty years old and, for most of Lula's first term, it was being renovated to make it both more family-friendly and more fit for presidential purposes in the twenty-first century.

Instead, Lula and Marisa lived in the Granja do Torto (literally the "twisted farm"), just over twelve miles north of Brasília. This was one of several farms outside Brasília which, in the original city plan devised by Lucio Costa in the late 1950s, would have provided fresh food for government offices in the new capital. But the *granjas* had been taken over by bureaucrats for use as weekend retreats.

The Granja do Torto was first used by the military presidents, and President Figueiredo bred horses there. It is simple, cozy, and comfortable, a place where a president can relax, swim, hold barbecues, and play soccer. It is away from the prying eyes of journalists and safe from terrorists. For Lula and Marisa, who came and went by helicopter, it was a place of relaxation and business. Foreign dignitaries and Brazilian politicians met them there. Every year the couple held a big party to celebrate their wedding anniversary.

Lula reveled in his job most of the time. He spoke to a Brazilian astronaut in space. He had a video conference with the Brazilian soccer team in the run-up to their unsuccessful World Cup in Germany, complaining that Ronaldo appeared to have a weight problem—an issue that Ronaldo cleverly turned against his president. An accusation by the *New York Times* correspondent Larry Rohter that Lula drank too much led to a temporary row, which also had the effect of killing a PT plan for a national journalism council, which media proprietors thought smelled of state censorship.

Although there was no doubt that Lula enjoyed a drink—now more likely to be whisky than beer or the national sugarcane liquor, *cachaça*—there was little evidence of alcoholic excess. Cynics said that Marisa tried to keep him under control. But after nearly four years as president, he was in good shape. After a health diet in early 2006, which had him drinking Diet Coke, he lost a lot of weight and found that suits he had worn in the 2002 campaign were too big for him.

More troubling than the effect of the presidency on the couple at its center was the impact on Lula's family. There were some dangerous traditions in Brazil, most notably that politics is a business, and that a politician is entitled to use his connections to assist his family. The PT, trying to promote the interests of poor Brazilians, had been highly critical of these old habits when it was in opposition. It explained why the party had been so vehement in calling for the resignation of Collor.

Such practices were deeply engrained in the northeast, where the da Silvas originated, and were exemplified by Severino Cavalcanti.

Would the first family be touched by this kind of scandal? There is little doubt that efforts were made to cash in on Lula's good fortune. Gijó, the São Bernardo restaurateur who had been a comrade in the Metalworkers' Union executive, told me in September 2005 that there was a small but steady stream of people who asked him to put in a good word for them with the president.

But Lula himself was careful to provide general rather than particular assistance. Hence he would be photographed with fifty cousins in Garanhuns, and would open a branch of the University of Pernambuco in the town, and would sponsor a long-debated scheme to divert the water of the São Francisco River, which could benefit much of the arid northeast. But he was not providing a direct pay-off for his blood relations.

Some continued to work in humble circumstances. His sister Tiana, for example, was a cleaner in a school in a dangerous *favela*. Indeed, according to his Brazilian biographer, Denise Paraná, he was criticized by some for not doing more for his family. He did, however, make an effort to provide medical assistance to his immediate relations if they were ill.[26] Lurian, his first child by Miriam Cordeiro, worked modestly for the PT.

Attacks for exploiting his position focused chiefly on his eldest son, known as Lulinha, and his brother Vavá. Fábio Luís da Silva, Lula's eldest son, had been born nine months and twenty days after his parents married. He was twenty-seven the year his father was elected president. He had a university degree in biology but had hardly built a career and was described in a critical article in *Veja* as "underemployed."[27] He was giving classes in English and information technology. All this changed in December 2003, when he entered the PR business in conjunction with two sons of an old union and PT colleague of Lula's, Jacó Bittar.

The story was a complex one, but it involved the building of a succession of companies—G4, then BR4 (set up in October 2004 with capital of R2.7 million), and then, a few months later, a firm called Gamecorp. Gamecorp, designed to provide games for mobile phones, was substantially funded by Telemar, a major Brazilian telecommunications firm. A quarter of the shares in Telemar are held by BNDES, the state development bank, and another 19 percent belong to pension funds, some of them related to the Banco do Brasil and to Petrobrás.

The key player in this process, which had not been publicized before *Veja* got on to it, was Kalil Bittar; he and his brother Fernando had been childhood friends of Lulinha. Telemar paid for Kalil and Lulinha to visit the United States, South Korea, and Japan in 2005, at a time when President Lula was on an official visit; their task was to talk to firms making games for cell phones and involved in third-generation telephony.

Veja, which broke the story of Lulinha's path to riches, claimed that in reality he had not invested a centavo of his own in the creation of these businesses. It argued that for state companies to fund the president's eldest son was an abuse, involving conflict of interest. Nonetheless, coming hard on the heels of the exposure of the politically damaging *mensalão*, these disclosures did not lead to retribution for the first family; they just added to the public's sense of rot at the top.[28]

The allegation against Vavá—Lula's older brother, Genival Inácio da Silva—was that he had set up a consultancy to peddle influence. He had been a worker and, like Lula, a metalworker, before retiring from a modest job as a civil servant. In 2005, he set up an office in São Bernardo to offer a service to firms that wished to deal with federal ministries, state enterprises, and towns controlled by PT mayors. The assumption was that, with his name, he could make contacts with government that other consultants could not.

Again the story was launched by *Veja*, no friend to the Lula administration, and it was not clear how successful Vavá's operation was. He told journalists that he had been able to arrange a meeting for the Brazilian Federation of Hospitals with an aide to the presidency. The federation was involved in a financial dispute with the government. But the results had not been satisfactory. Vavá was also being approached by NGOs, anxious to access funds from different government agencies.

Although the Vavá story ran for a few days and Lula said he knew nothing about his brother's activities, it seemed less serious and harder to pin down than the specifics of Lulinha's enterprise. Apart from the fact that Vavá seemed rather ineffective, what he was doing was not so different from the work of public affairs consultants in many democracies. In some of these it was considered proper for relations of ministers to work as lobbyists.[29]

In June 2006, shortly after the PSDB launched Geraldo Alckmin as its candidate for the presidency, the PT did the same for Lula. The free TV advertising for all candidates was due to start in August and the PT was already planning huge demonstrations in major cities that the president could address. As a modest reaction to the scandals of illegal election financing in 2002, the Election Commission was banning the *showmícios*, or big entertainment rallies, as well as the selling of buttons and shirts.

The continuing capacity of the PT and its friends to get people out on the streets had been demonstrated on 1 May, when the CUT had assembled around a million supporters in Avenida Paulista to hear pro-Lula speeches. The rival union movement, Força Sindical, however, got out 1.5 million north of the city, where its president, Paulo Pereira da Silva, asked, "Which of us doesn't have a friend or relation who is unemployed?" Lula himself attended a special mass with Marisa and close supporters such as Marta Suplicy, Aloizio Mercadante, and Luiz Marinho, his labor minister, in the São Bernardo church that had offered refuge during the strikes—Nossa Senhora da Boa Viagem.

There was a sense in which Lula, after all the difficulties, was trying to reconnect with his roots. He went to the northeast. On 13 July he began his formal campaign for reelection at a meeting with three thousand PT members and supporters in São Bernardo. There had been a renewal of the serious crime upsurge in São Paulo, where a criminal mafia controlled from jail had again been setting buses on fire and wreaking mayhem. A PFL ally of Alckmin, Cláudio Lembo, was substituting for him as governor, and both government and opposition had been blaming each other for the outbreak. The Paulista authorities rejected offers of help from Brasília. Lula attacked them for their "frivolity" in suggesting that the criminals were acting to support his election.

The scale of the violence, launched by a mafia that called itself the Primeiro Comando da Capital (PCC) was frightening and took everyone by surprise. The transfer of its leaders between prisons triggered armed PCC attacks on police stations, buses, and even schools in São Paulo in May. There were 299 violent incidents, 82 prison rebellions, and at least 36 police were killed; this was followed by revenge attacks by the police in which 126 people died, 75 of them showing signs of physical abuse. A second wave of PCC violence, between 11 and 16 July, was less serious but reminded the nation of the power of armed criminals.

What were the issues, and what was the electoral terrain, in Lula's fifth presidential campaign? For Lula, reenergized with mass meetings and opportunities to meet the people, the issues were clear. His government was constructing a welfare state. It had broken with at least some aspects of the neoliberal program of Cardoso, especially its privatizations. It was helping to build a South American community of nations on the basis of Mercosur, the southern regional grouping known as Mercosul in Portuguese, which had just admitted Venezuela and made a commercial agreement with Cuba in defiance of the United States. It was winning respect for Brazilian national sovereignty. It had done more in nearly four years than FHC had done in eight.

A propagandist book by Alizio Mercadante—*Brasil: Primeiro tempo*—put facts and figures behind the claim that Lula had significantly outperformed Cardoso.[30] This became a key part of Lula's appeal for reelection. For observers from across the Atlantic, it was a little like Tony Blair's UK campaign for reelection in 2005, when many Labour voters were disillusioned with the Iraq war but were told of the government's other successes. PT voters were being reminded that, whatever the scandal, the government had delivered on its social programs.

Lula also found ways of dealing with the corruption crisis of 2005. One was to charge that this was an attack by the Brazilian elite designed to destabilize the first popular government in forty years; he, and the PT in its election manifesto,[31] compared this experience to the crisis that had led to the suicide of Vargas, and military threats to Kubitschek and Goulart.

More positively but somewhat vaguely, Lula argued that there had to be political reform to deal with systemic problems; otherwise corruption scandals would recur at regular intervals for the next twenty years. Speaking at Olinda in the northeast, on 23 July 2006, he talked of the need to reform party structures, the mandates of congressional representatives, and the workings of Congress itself. He distinguished between bogus parties and genuine parties, and blamed Congress for being dilatory in voting on the federal budget. He hinted that reforms would come if he had a second term.[32]

Although some might be disillusioned with Lula personally, or with some of his government's actions, it was hard to imagine that he could be defeated. Indeed in mid-2006 it looked as though he could even win outright in the first round, on 1 October, though this prospect then faded. Pollsters had demonstrated a hardening of support among poorer Brazilians. The PT suggested in its manifesto that as many as thirty million had benefited from the Bolsa-Família, which was now going to twelve million families; but there were many other social programs, ranging from health to rural electrification (Luz para Todos) and agrarian reform, that had an extensive reach. Millions were seeing him as a father of the poor (*pai dos pobres*).

A strong factor in Lula's favor was the weakness of the opposition, though this applied only at the presidential level. Geraldo Alckmin was simply not a national figure to compare with Lula. He had been chosen by the PSDB/PFL alliance in preference to Serra, who had not only been beaten in 2002 but was more closely associated with the FHC government, which was Lula's continuing target of comparison. The criminal explosions in São Paulo, in May and July 2006, did not reflect well on Alckmin's state government's management of its overcrowded and anarchic prisons. Although he attacked the corruption under Lula, Alckmin was not offering a sufficiently attractive or different program. He argued that Brazil's growth rates were too low and its interest rates too high, but he would continue the Bolsa-Família. There seemed little to trouble Lula or his campaign strategists.

The other presidential candidates were peripheral to the main struggle but potentially damaging to Lula's image. Both Heloísa Helena of PSOL and Crístovam Buarque of the PDT were angry ex-members of the PT who could draw off some of its ideological supporters. Both criticized government corruption and, this from Senator Helena in particular, Lula's apparent betrayal of the left. Although Helena was unwilling to back campaigns for abortion and was therefore not seen as an advanced feminist, she was also benefiting from being the first serious woman candidate for the presidency. Poll evidence that Helena's support was getting into double figures in July, even before the free TV advertising for candidates, was enough to suggest that Lula just might be forced into a second round.

The battle was essentially between Lula and Alckmin, but altogether there were eight candidates. In addition to Helena and Buarque, there were four relative nonentities—Ana Maria Rangel, José Maria Eymael, Luciano Bivar, and Rui Pimenta.

Technical issues would affect the election, particularly for state governorships and Congress, where the PT was not expected to do well. After some debate, the Congress had maintained its rule for "verticalization," under which alliances for the presidency had to be copied at the state level as well. This meant, for example, that the PSDB and PFL had to work together right down the line, which caused conflict where local parties were hostile or thought they had an equal chance of winning a governorship or seat.

But the effect on the government side was more striking. For the first time since Lula ran in 1989, the PT was campaigning almost on its own, backed only by the PCdoB and Vice President Alencar's tiny Partido Republicano Brasileiro.[33] There is little doubt that this was because former allies such as the PDT saw the PT as a liability after the crisis of 2005. There was an important impact, therefore, on the free election advertising available to the presidential candidates. The Electoral Commission ruled that Alckmin, backed by PSDB and PFL, would get 10 minutes and 22 seconds of free TV advertising daily, whereas Lula would have only 7 minutes and 21 seconds. In the calculations of the campaign publicists, each second was vital.

In other ways, however, Lula's strength in the opinion polls was setting up its own waves. His first triumph was in preventing the PMDB from running its own presidential candidate. Had it done so, it would almost certainly have forced Lula into a second round and, conceivably, into defeat.

The PMDB was the unwieldy behemoth of Brazilian politics, a series of regional fiefdoms, powerful at the state level and likely to do well in the 2006 elections. But it was divided into pro-Lula and anti-Lula factions, and the only person seriously interested in being its presidential candidate was the party-hopping Anthony Garotinho, a former governor of Rio de Janeiro, who was widely suspect. Lula talked to the PMDB. The PMDB, looking ahead, decided that it was wiser to keep formally out of the presidential fray, so that it could make the most advantageous deals at the local level without being bound nationally either to the PSDB/PFL or PT.

Lula's abiding popularity was shown by cross-party alliances in the states: for example, there was a committee for Aécio Neves,[34] the PSDB governor of Minas Gerais seeking reelection, that was also working for Lula—a committee Aécio-Lula. Similar groups were active elsewhere where, irrespective of party labels, supporters wanted to link candidates to the Lula bandwagon. A group of businessmen, not quite as large as in

2002, also got together a pro-Lula campaign committee. At the other end of the spectrum, the MST, the landless movement, was also offering him its support.

The outlook, therefore, was that Lula looked certain to win a second term but the party he had founded in 1980 could be less important in his second government. He would probably need the backing in Congress of the PMDB. He might build a cabinet of "all the talents," without much attention to party labels. There could be more friction between the federal and state governments, although they need each other in the Brazilian system.

The PT, perhaps with tongue in cheek, gave Lula a list of "ten commandments" on how he should conduct himself during the campaign. It knew his weaknesses. It advised him to beware of direct debates with his adversaries or general press conferences. It suggested that he should avoid off-the-cuff improvisation, which was so much part of his style, but which had led to grief in the past. Instead he should stick to reading his speeches. He should try to cool down the campaign, and appear always as a president rather than a candidate.

Lula, who was quite used to ignoring the PT when he wanted to, joked that on this basis he might as well do nothing at all. Those who knew him well were confident that he would break more than one of these commandments.[35]

6 DOMESTIC POLICY

Lula's personal experience as a hungry child informed his government's most attractive campaign promise in the 2002 presidential campaign. It would establish a program called Fome Zero—Zero Hunger—that would abolish starvation. In a country with many millions of poor people, this had the same attraction as the "Mandela Sandwich" in South Africa—the guarantee from the postapartheid democracy that every child should have at least one square meal a day. No matter that critics, later in his term of office, argued that Brazil suffered greater health problems from obesity than malnutrition, this was a defining program for his government.

Fome Zero brought together several ideas. It would be a way of organizing poor people into neighborhood groups, to which individuals would have to belong in order to be eligible for assistance. Food would be provided from the agrarian reform settlements. There would be cheap "people's restaurants";[1] food banks to hold supplies, and food cards for the poorest families; direct support for family-based agriculture; access by all family workers to social security benefits, whether in the formal or large informal sector; and income guarantees for children from the poorest families, and incentives to get them into school.[2]

The program was linked to a minimum income guarantee and to promised increases in the minimum wage (*salário mínimo*). It made up an antipoverty policy designed to offset Brazil's huge wealth inequalities.

The total scheme had utopian overtones and demanded a lot of the country's not-always-efficient bureaucracy and Lula's new coalition government. It required federal, state, and local town officials to work together, and in 2003 and 2004 it ran into criticism from the media and disillusion from the PT grass roots. The complaints were that it was badly administered and was not reaching many needy people. After such a long time in opposition preparing alternative policies, more had been expected of a PT government.

Initially the Fome Zero idea was that poor families would be given coupons worth up to R250, which could be exchanged for food at certain named shops. But this did not work. In January 2004, Fome Zero was effectively overtaken as a strategy for income transfer to the poorest by the Bolsa-Família. Building on Fome Zero and the educational allowance of the Cardoso government (Bolsa Escola), this aimed to provide financial benefits for poor Brazilians in a simpler, coordinated fashion.

Bolsa-Família pulled together existing programs—including the requirement that children from families receiving welfare benefits should attend school. It was managed much more efficiently, and the number of families that benefited rose rapidly from 3.6 million in 2003 to between 11 million and 12 million in 2006. On that basis, between 50 million and 60 million Brazilians would have been lifted out of poverty, defined as living on less than a dollar a day.

Workers' incomes had been squeezed during the second Cardoso administration, and it took a while before the minimum wage raised the threshold. The neoliberal policies of FHC had resulted in a sharp reduction in manufacturing jobs, not least in the PT's original São Paulo heartland. The first two years of the Lula administration saw the president and Antonio Palocci keeping to tight fiscal and monetary policies. This was to satisfy the IMF and external investors, and also suspicious middle-class Brazilians. Partly because interest rates were high, the value of the real was maintained.

By the end of 2004, employment levels were rising and it was possible to hike the minimum wage in real terms. In 2005, it went up by 8 percent to R300 a month (around $115), and in April 2006, it went up again to R350, estimated by the Ministry of Labor to be a gain of 13 percent above inflation. Although Lula had originally called for a doubling of the *salário mínimo* in his election campaign of 2002, the 2006 increase was handsome, it came a month sooner than usual, and it directly benefited forty million of Lula's traditional supporters in an election year.

But did the social programs make any difference to the shocking inequality of wealth distribution?[3] Or were they just cosmetic, making Lula's working-class constituency feel better but doing little to change the profoundly conservative and economically unjust nature of Brazilian society? Statistics on wealth and poverty are never wholly reliable, but near the end of the four years of Lula's first term, his social policies seemed more ameliorative than dramatically redistributive.

Critics complained that the welfare approach was primarily one of assistance, promoting dependence, rather than one emphasizing jobs and training. But, as will be considered later, the Brazilian economy was not growing nearly as fast as developing countries such as China or India, and its manufacturing base was under attack.

In August 2006, after the election campaign had formally begun, Volkswagen announced that it would be cutting more than eleven thousand jobs from its factories in São Paulo's ABC belt. The Metalworkers' Union Lula used to lead went on strike, but Luíz Marinho, who had been called from the presidency of the CUT by Lula to take over as minister of labor in 2005, refused to intervene. In the end, only three thousand jobs were lost straightaway, and the government poured money in to compensate those who lost their jobs.

Beneath much of the social inequality in Brazil lay another dimension—race. Many of those who were poor were black, or darker in appearance. Most of those who were middle-class, and nearly all who were rich, apart from select groups of soccer players and entertainment stars, looked white. It was much to Lula's credit that his government tried to confront what for long had been a taboo subject in Brazil.

Back in the 1930s there had been a national commitment to "whitening" the population. For most of the twentieth century thereafter there had been a complacent view, which reflected the high degree of intermarriage and miscegenation over centuries, that race was not an issue. Nonetheless, snobbery, discrimination, and sharp objective differences based on skin color persisted. Movements for black rights and equality, partly inspired by the civil rights campaign in the United States in the 1960s, grew in the 1980s.

Lula created a Special Secretariat for Policies for the Promotion of Racial Equality (Secretaria Especial de Políticas de Promoção de Igualdade Racial) in Brasília. It was involved in research, the controversial program to promote racial quotas for university entrance, and support and recognition for two thousand *quilombos*, the settlements for escaped slaves in the seventeenth to nineteenth centuries that were symbols of the survival of African (often Yoruba) culture in Brazil. Some black urban settlements, far more recent than the historic rural villages of runaway slaves, were given *quilombo* status.

In fact, the government was building on enlightened movement in the private sector,[4] and some action by the Cardoso government to widen recruitment to the civil service. This had already resulted in the reduction of wage differences between those describing themselves as black, around 48–49 percent of the population, and those describing themselves as white, a narrow majority.

The differences were still big—on average whites had twice the income of blacks, and half of blacks were unemployed—but they were coming down slightly. A study published in September 2005 showed that in 1990, a white worker age 48–50 was earning on average 130 percent more than a black person of the same age. By 2002, this difference had fallen to 90 percent. Among younger workers, age 24–26, the difference in favor of whites had dropped only a little, from 62 percent to 55 percent.

Most of the difference in salary was explained by disparities in education, the region people lived in, and their occupations and actual jobs. But, according to age, discrimination still explained 25–29 percent of the variation. A report of the study in *Folha de São Paulo* highlighted a well-qualified black woman, age 33, from a poor family in Rio de Janeiro. She had an MBA in marketing from Rio's Catholic University and spoke five languages. She had been passed over for several jobs and at least one of her interviewers admitted that she was not being employed because she was black. She ended up as a salesperson in a Canadian-owned cosmetics shop in fashionable Ipanema.

The Lula government sought to confront discrimination as part of its antiracist and antipoverty stance. Matilde Ribeiro, the minister for racial equality, commented on this report, "Twenty years ago, this difference [in pay levels] would have been denied. Today it is evident. The improvements are the fruit of two decades of struggle by the black movement, but there is still much to do."[5] Other research, however, pointed to the weakness of the public education system in Brazil as a major handicap for black families and other poor Brazilians,[6] although the 2001 UN conference against racism had sparked some improvement for black and dark brown Brazilians. In his 2006 presidential campaign, Lula promised to give more priority to education.

The sheer inequality of Brazilian society would have been hard for the most radical government to overcome, given inherited disparities of wealth and education, continuing high interest rates, and distortions in tax and pensions. But a World Bank study, released in late 2005, showed Brazil as the most unequal country in Latin America, and outstripped only by four African states—Namibia, Botswana, the Central African Republic, and Swaziland.[7] The Bank argued that there was too little interaction between rich and poor in Brazil, that although the Bolsa-Família was helpful it did not go far enough, and that groups such as parliamentarians and judges were feathering their own nests.

The trouble was that the Lula government was not conducting an all-out campaign against inequity, in spite of what the president had said in earlier election battles. It was constrained not only by relatively orthodox economic policies, but also by an unwillingness to challenge the vested interests that benefited from the status quo. Some of those were traditional electoral allies, such as university professors and organized (as opposed to unorganized) labor. Subsidies to the public universities, which had maintained their prestige and tough competitive recruitment against the challenge of private universities, were actually a subsidy to the upper middle class, which could afford good private secondary schools.

Hence the government made the most of gestures, such as raids on employers who were hiring what amounted to slave labor. The evil tradition of debt peonage among farmhands for ranchers or the producers of charcoal for pig iron in eastern Amazonia had continued into the twenty-first century. It was a continuing exploitation of poverty in the northeast. Desperate men from the region were hired by labor managers called *gatos* (cats), put on trucks and driven hundreds of miles, and put to work for long hours in poor conditions with inadequate food and shelter. It was almost impossible to repay the loan they had had to take out to get there. Every year under Lula, several thousands of such men were released, with publicity, after federal inspectors or police raided their workplaces.[8]

This was also an aspect of the government's attempt to strengthen human rights in Brazil. In spite of a vigorous attempt to raise awareness by civil society organizations, and progressive aspects of the 1988 Constitution, human rights still had difficulty in winning public support. Legal procedures were slow. There was much corruption at the local and state levels. It was particularly hard for semiliterates to obtain justice. Many people denigrated the human rights movement as defending criminals rather than victims—an attitude that led to defeat of the attempted ban on gun sales in a 2005 referendum.

Lula's Special Secretariat for Human Rights (Secretaria Especial dos Direitos Humanos) launched a phone-in service to enable victims and witnesses to denounce abuses. Initially in Brasília, but to be rolled out across the country, it reserved the number 100 for a free confidential service that would reach a team of advisers and lawyers at Disque-Direitos Humanos (Dial Human Rights).

Minister Nilmário Miranda recognized that it would be getting calls from everywhere. He anticipated denunciations of racism, torture, death squads, and all sorts of violence, including assaults on women, children, and homosexuals. Miranda called this a key element in a national system for human rights, but recognized that the real challenge would be to make sure that complaints were followed by action, whether by the Ministério Público (the independent prosecuting authority), parliamentary committees of inquiry, or specialist agencies.

The image of the social programs—which also included efforts for women's equality, for microcredit, and against domestic violence[9]—was that they meant well, made for good publicity, but might not make a great deal of difference. They also suffered from a feeling that Lula, who himself had lived in shantytowns when he first arrived as a boy from the northeast, had not tackled the enormous problems of crime and squalor in the *favelas*.

Under Brazil's federal system, most responsibility for crime and the urban environment lay with the states and the municipalities. But crime, related to drug trafficking, police corruption, and the appalling state of the prisons, provided front-page news and a reason why tourists avoided certain parts of Brazil. Longtime supporters thought that one of Lula's worst decisions, in manipulating his coalition government in Brasília during the political crisis of 2005, was the sacking of his old friend Olívio Dutra as minister for cities. A placeman of Severino Cavalcanti was put in that position instead.

Periodically the crime in the *favelas* or the shoot-to-kill practices of police or off-duty policemen in death squads shocked the country. This was particularly the case when the violence took place in the media capitals of São Paulo and Rio. The underlying figures were serious, tragic, and little altered by the arrival of Lula in the presidency. In the first year of his presidency, 2003, Rio police killed one thousand people. The homicide rate a year later in the city's poorer northwest suburbs, the Baixada Fluminense, was running at 76 per 100,000, half as much again as in metropolitan Rio, which has one of the highest rates in the world.

Cidade de Deus, the novel by Paulo Lins based on anthropological research in a Rio *favela*, brought to international attention the lawlessness of a poor suburb when it became the prizewinning film, *City of God*.[10] This revealed the power of the drug lords, the youth of these armed and intimidating criminals, and the state of war that existed with the police. It is estimated that in Rio there are between 600 and 750 self-built *favelas*, inhabited by 20 percent of the population, and the response of the authorities oscillated among demolition, relocation, and assistance to *favelados* to build their shacks on a more permanent basis.

In March 2006, Lula announced a housing program with a direct investment of around one billion reais (about U.S. $360 million) and tax incentives worth eighteen times as much, payable through state banks. While it was estimated that the country needed eight million new homes, the Congress had been sitting on proposals for a grand housing plan for twelve years. But Lula's program was criticized as an election ploy, which could help the middle classes more than the poorest. For the *favelas*, the idea was that the inhabitants could get finance for materials to rebuild their homes. In his weekly radio chat show, *Coffee with the President*, Lula said that every Brazilian would have his own home.

Because of the nature of a federal system, there were often quarrels between the government in Brasília and the state and municipality when gun crime became front-page news. This was the case in São Paulo in the middle of 2006, when gangsters, from prison, orchestrated an extraordinary orgy of violence and destruction—murders of police and burnings of buses, shops, and public buildings. Nothing like it had been seen before. Riots inside prison, caused by overcrowding and the low quality of prison staff, had taken place at intervals throughout Brazil's brief democratic era. But the mayhem in São Paulo, taking place in three waves and moving beyond the state capital, seemed to conjure up something more alarming. It was the vision of a state in which gangsters took control after a civil war—precisely what so many *favelados* lived in on a day-to-day basis.

The sequence of events was as follows. On 22 May, the rebellion broke out after a bank robber nicknamed Marcola, otherwise Marcos Camacho, was threatened with being taken to a high-security prison, Artur Bernardes. He controlled the PCC (Primeiro Comando da Capital), the biggest criminal faction in São Paulo state.[11] At the same time, 765 detainees linked to the PCC were due to be transferred to the Presidente Venceslau jail, where they also faced more rigid discipline. Marcola, who had moved the gang into the drugs business, used a mobile phone inside the prison to order a mass uprising of his members inside and outside. Hundreds of prison guards were held hostage. Outside, in a period of a hundred hours that brought terror to the citizens of the São Paulo metropolis, the PCC organized 299 attacks that led to 152 deaths among police, criminals, and ordinary citizens. An additional 126 people died in subsequent days, supposedly in confrontations with the police, leading to accusations that the police were operating as death squads.

A second wave of attacks began on 11 July and involved 106 attacks spread over five days, with considerable damage to property, but only eight deaths. The targets were public and private buildings, banks, shops, buses, and police attacked either with gunshots or with firebombs.

The third wave took place on 10 and 11 August, when the PCC launched one hundred attacks in eighteen towns and small cities of São Paulo state, though not in São Paulo metropolis itself. Lula himself traveled to the city to urge the deployment of federal troops—something that had happened in earlier crime crises in Rio.

On 13 August, Globo TV broadcast a 3-minute, 36-second DVD on behalf of one of its journalists, Gulherme de Azevedo Portanova, who had been captured by the PCC and threatened with death. This complained about the jail system and the special regime for the most serious criminals.

Inevitably, such a dramatic and well-publicized upsurge in crime fed into the election campaign. São Paulo was controlled by the opposition. Alckmin had been the governor. He had been replaced after joining the presidential fray by his PFL vice governor, Cláudio Lembo, whose political ancestry went back to the promilitary ARENA party of the 1970s. The man leading the polls for the governorship now was José Serra, the PSDB mayor and Lula's defeated opponent of 2002. Lembo talked tough and said that São Paulo's security forces could deal with the crisis. The PT's candidate for governor, Mercadante, called for federal troops and pointed to the financial losses the state was suffering.

One thing the crisis had illustrated was that gangsters had no problem in arming themselves with guns. Yet the previous year, when a referendum on the sale of guns took place, there had been a remarkable change in public opinion, led by the media. It was a story that illustrated an underlying social conservatism in Brazil, the fickleness of the popular mood, and the power of money to change the way people vote.

The background was that Brazil had an appalling record of gun crime, one of the worst in the world. In 2004, some thirty-four thousand people had been murdered with guns, and in other years the death rate had been even higher. This amounted to a hundred killings a day, or nearly

twenty-two deaths per hundred thousand people annually; it was reckoned that more than 9 percent of citizens had guns.

Local NGOs and others, supported by the worldwide IANSA coalition (the International Action Network on Small Arms) had been challenging this situation. In a two-year amnesty, coinciding with the start of
the Lula term, around 440,000 weapons were handed in. The government also negotiated an agreement with its neighbor Paraguay, the
source of many smuggled items, in an attempt to prevent the import of
illicit weapons. Most of the guns used in Rio murders, however, had
been licensed, or stolen from or sold by soldiers or policemen.

In 2003, the gun laws were reformed to restrict legitimate sales.
They fell by 92 percent between 2003 and 2005, and the number of
shops licensed to sell was drastically reduced, from 1,730 to 120. With
the amnesty and greater public awareness, the death rate fell in 2004
by 8.2 percent.

As part of this drive against gun crime, parliamentarians in Congress
succeeded in getting it to vote in favor of a referendum on a total ban on
gun sales. The referendum, as a tool of democracy, was allowed by the
1988 Constitution but had never been activated before. This was not an
exclusively PT campaign in Congress, nor in the country, where the referendum was set for October 2005. Indeed, NGOs felt that the government could have been more helpful.

While Lula himself voted for the ban, so too did his old PSDB opponent José Serra, then mayor of São Paulo. Serra wrote an article in the
Folha de São Paulo under the headline "I Say Yes to Yes."[12] Marisa, Lula's
wife, made her only direct political gesture in the whole period he was
president when she indicated that she too would vote yes.[13]

The referendum was conducted under the rules of the Electoral
Commission, with compulsory voting for those aged eighteen to seventy, and each side was given free airtime on television and radio. Those
wishing to say yes to a total ban showed tear-jerking images of bereaved
widows and mothers. Those against a ban likened the proposal to a Nazi
threat to the right to self-defense of honest citizens.

But what was extraordinary was the turnabout in public opinion.
Early in 2005, some 70 percent of voters were in favor of the ban. But the

No camp won with 64 percent of the poll in October. Much of this switch took place late in the campaign when the gun lobby spent heavily, and the most powerful organs in the media came out on its side.

Veja, the best-selling newsweekly with a middle-class audience, produced a front-page story on 5 October titled "Seven Reasons to Vote No." It argued that countries that banned gun sales saw an increase in criminality and the cruelty of gangsters; that a yes victory would not take arms out of circulation; that disarmament of citizens is one of the pillars of totalitarianism; that Brazilian police cannot guarantee security; that prohibition will stimulate the illegal trade; that criminals will not obey a prohibition; and that the referendum deflects attention from the need to clean up the police, the justice system, and the prisons.[14]

Not all these arguments were well founded, and in reality only 10 percent of gun deaths in São Paulo, for instance, were the result of shooting by criminals; the great majority had miscellaneous causes including bar brawls, road rage in traffic, and domestic or family disputes where the presence of weapons escalated a conflict to a murder.

For Brazilian activists and the international arms control campaign, this, the outcome of the first national referendum on guns anywhere in the world, was a great setback. They explained it in terms of the insecurity of the public and distrust of the police. It was also thought that less-educated voters may have got their vote the wrong way around—thinking that they were voting No to guns, rather than No to a ban on gun sales. Activists were also suspicious of the heavy outlays by the gun interest, believing that it may have had assistance from the powerful gun lobby in the United States.

The outcome was not only an implied criticism of Lula's law and order policy, it also reflected the fact that Brazil's still-new democracy had failed to provided efficient, uncorrupt policing that served all communities equally, not just the rich. The vote may also have resulted from irritation with the government at a time when the *mensalão* crisis had been dominating the media: there was a widespread fear that the corruption would be covered up—"it will all end in pizza," to use the popular expression.[15] The electorate was having a crack at some in the political establishment.

What would the Lula government do about the festering land issues in Brazil? The injustice of Brazilian land ownership had been a theme for reformers for a half-century but the relationship between the PT and the MST, the landless movement, had had its ups and downs. Although both the party and the landless movement had received encouragement from progressives in the Catholic Church in the exciting era of transition in the 1980s, the two bodies were quite separate and sometimes in conflict. Members of the MST might dislike electoral politics; elected PT politicians were worried that MST radicalism would put off voters. The Cardoso government, with its links to landowners among its PFL allies, had been particularly tough on the MST, although there had been some land reform. Leaders of the MST had reacted by supporting Lula in 2002.[16]

But from the viewpoint of a government, even one led by the PT, the issue of landlessness and the big unproductive estates, the *latifúndios*, was only one of many involving the use of land. Others involved family agriculture on one side, and Brazil's need for export revenues, the clarion call of the powerful agribusiness industry, which was exporting soy, citrus, and beef, on the other; contentious environmental questions, which had created international concern about deforestation in Amazonia, but which also arose when Lula brought down from the shelf a long-discussed scheme for the diversion of the Rio São Francisco in the northeast; and the continuing controversy over the land rights of between 460,000 and 734,000 Indians, Brazil's indigenous peoples.[17]

Government apologists, such as Lula's close associate Aloizio Mercadante, who wrote a book in 2005 comparing Lula's federal government favorably with its FHC predecessor, stated that an average of nearly eighty-two thousand families were being settled on the land annually. This, he said, was 21 percent more than the average under Cardoso.[18] He argued that an agrarian reform of this kind, which brought more money into the countryside and linked small producers to major projects such as Brazil's biofuel program, was a contribution to rural regeneration and a brake on fast urbanization. The government was seeking to get its services to MST settlements and to provide more support to the federal settlements set up in the past by INCRA, the federal colonization agency.

But the MST did not see things the government's way. It was impatient with the slow rate of reform in Lula's first year, 2003, when only fourteen thousand families were settled. João Pedro Stedile, the MST leader, threatened to raise hell—which produced a government promise that four hundred thousand families would be settled by 2006. Occupations continued. In September 2005, Stedile said that the government was "finished"—and criticized its conservative economic policy and its reliance on figures such as Severino Cavalcanti, Renan Calheiros (then the president of the Senate), and José Sarney.[19]

Followers of the MST were developing a culture of their own in their encampments—radical, democratic, exploring feminism and green agriculture, and often hostile to state institutions. Its ethic remained confrontational. In April 2004, it invaded properties belonging to Klabin, a big paper manufacturer. In September 2005, it occupied a ranch in Paranapanema belonging to the national president of the conservative landowners' body, the União Democrática Ruralista; in the same month, its members occupied the offices of INCRA in several states.

A fringe breakaway from the MST, the MLST (Movimento pela Libertação dos Sem Terra), had been founded in 1997. It was even more impatient than the MST. In April 2005, around twelve hundred of its members invaded the Ministry of Finance in Brasília to complain about cuts in the agrarian reform budget. In June 2006, its supporters invaded the Chamber of Deputies and got involved in fights with deputies and the police. The police were called by Aldo Rebelo, who was presiding over the Chamber; 497 MLST people were sent to prison, considerable damage was done, and forty-one people were injured.

Critics of the government recalled that in 2004 the leaders of the MLST had visited Lula in his office at the Planalto Palace. He had been photographed wearing one of their caps, and had authorized a government grant of nine million reais to the organization. But the government's response to the invasion of the Chamber two years later was uncompromising.

The government's difficulty in policing Brazil's huge extent, with its many specific land conflicts, was illustrated by the murder in February 2005 of an American nun, Dorothy Stang, who had been working with the Catholic Pastoral Land Commission (CPT) to stop violence against peasants in Amazonia. She was murdered close to the Trans-Amazonica highway in Pará state, which had seen more than one-third of the 1,349 deaths in land conflicts in Brazil between 1985 and 2003. Because she was well loved locally and an American, there was national and international publicity. In recompense, Brasília protected four million biodiversity-rich hectares (approximately ten million acres) in two conservation areas in Pará. Yet preventing potentially fatal land conflicts was as hard for the Lula government as for its predecessors.

In addition to the settlement of the landless, the government gave support to what was called family agriculture—small farmers, not growing much more than they needed for subsistence, who in the south of the country had been almost wiped out with the growth of the big ranches. It was exactly from this culture that Lula's own family, in the northeast, had come.

In 2003, his government renegotiated the debts of some 825,000 farm families, set up a national program for the strengthening of family agriculture, which lent as much as nine billion reais (some four billion dollars) for the 2005–6 crops and was active in more than five thousand districts, mostly in the north and northeast. Rural extension programs were revived, and Petrobrás bought biofuel (labeled "social fuel") from small producers.[20] Also of importance in the countryside was a rural electrification program, Luz Para Todos (light for all), which was an extension of a Cardoso project.

But in a sense this activity, like the settlement of the landless, was peripheral to the big agricultural story. Lula's Brazil was becoming more dependent on large-scale export agriculture, with its ruthless impact on fragile environments in the cerrado scrublands and Amazonia's forest. At the end of 2004, the then minister of agriculture, Roberto Rodrigues, put it bluntly: "Don't let's get mixed up about this. Agribusiness is the most important business in this country. It represents 34 percent of GNP, it generates 37 percent of employment, and it is responsible for 42 percent of Brazilian exports. It is the biggest surplus heading in the balance of payments, which guarantees the national surplus as a whole."[21]

Agribusiness was a Brazilian tradition. Sugar and coffee were intertwined with the country's history over more than two hundred years.

What was different now was the power of big money and sophisticated machines to attack the environment, and the range of products and export markets involved. Soy was going to China, orange juice to the United States, beef to Europe—with a few variations according to the state of concern over mad cow disease. Coffee was still important. Sugar cane had become an ethanol fuel source.

The power was displayed in huge mechanized ranches, most dramatically in the state of Mato Grosso in the central west. It became the epicenter of the newest revolution in agribusiness—Brazil's biggest state in the production of soy, cotton, and beef, and the second state for rice, a staple in the national diet. Much of this was driven by agricultural entrepreneurs from southern Brazil and, when Lula was elected president, the richest of them, Blairo Maggi, was elected as governor of Mato Grosso, appointing his wife as secretary for labor.[22]

The Maggi group was founded by Blairo's father, André, who moved from Rio Grande do Sul to Paraná in the 1950s, and decided to invest in the cerrado scrublands of Mato Grosso in the 1970s. The group then moved into the state's forested lands, on the edge of Amazonia, turning them over to soy. By the start of the twenty-first century, the firm was the biggest single soy producer in the world. Brazil itself was producing almost a quarter of the global soy output by 2005, earning more than $10 billion, and six million hectares (nearly fifteen million acres) of Mato Grosso were being used for the purpose.

According to Greenpeace, Maggi had had World Bank loans of thirty million dollars to open up a third of this land.[23] Maggi used his position as governor to improve roads and infrastructure in the state, and ruthlessly promoted deforestation and agricultural expansion.[24]

Inevitably, Maggi ran into heavy fire from environmentalists, who protested that Mato Grosso alone was responsible for 48 percent of Amazonia's destruction in 2004 and 2005. The level of deforestation in 2004—ten thousand square miles—led to a withdrawal of support for Lula by the Green Party's seven federal deputies in May 2005, just before the *mensalão* corruption scandal broke. The minister of culture, Gilberto Gil, nominally a Green, did not leave the government, however.

Lula on this, as on other issues, was trying to straddle opposites. On the one hand, he knew the significance of exports to Brazil's economy and the need to run a balance of payments surplus in order to service the nation's debt. On the other hand, he was trying to show some commitment to sustainability in the development process. After all, Brazil had hosted the Earth Summit in Rio de Janeiro in 1992; its growing environmental movement had touched the PT itself, which was no longer an urban party but linked with social movements in the countryside and the rubber tappers in the forest, for whom Chico Mendes was a martyr.[25] The idea that Brazil's land was an inexhaustible free good, which had dominated policy and practice for most of the twentieth century, was no longer viable.

Lula tended to let the different parties contend—creating conservation and indigenous reserves at one moment, while boasting of the contribution of agricultural and raw material exports at another. The conflict went to the heart of the government. Roberto Rodrigues, as an agricultural minister, was actually a major soy grower in the northeastern state of Maranhão. Marina Silva, Lula's respected environment minister, was on at least one occasion driven to tears by her president's attitude, when he authorized experiments in genetically modified crops.[26]

International opinion, and consumer opinion in particular, could sometimes do more than Lula or his ministers. Ironically, one reason why Maggi soy had become so dominant, especially in Europe, was that it was not genetically modified. In July 2006, Maggi and U.S. multinationals responded to consumer concerns about deforestation, after investigators had shown European supermarkets that Amazon-grown soy was feeding the chickens they sold. The big commodity groups promised not to use soy grown on illegally cleared land. Monitoring such undertakings, however, remained as tricky as it was with existing conservation laws.[27]

Lula was not averse to big developmental gestures, indeed, he was actively attracted by them. One of these was the government's expensive project to divert the São Francisco river, in the drought-stricken northeast, to provide water and irrigation for farmland. When the author was talking to da Silva cousins around Garanhuns in 2005, it was clear that this was a popular decision and it was one of many reasons why Lula looked impregnable in polls of the northeastern states in the run-up to the 2006 election. Nonetheless, it was opposed by some on ecological grounds; one bishop went on a hunger strike.

Lula was also willing to make propaganda about Brazil's biofuel program, developed over several decades in the twentieth century by different governments. An important part of this involved the production of alcohol from sugar cane to drive motor vehicles. It had proved a salvation for the northeastern sugar industry, which, in the second half of the twentieth century, had been looking old-fashioned and uncompetitive.

Controversy over tree felling in Amazonia continued unabated throughout the government's term, inside and outside Brazil. The actual reduction of forest cover—particularly due to burning in northern Mato Grosso, but with logging and burning all around the forest's perimeter—went on in spite of satellite detection and an action plan involving thirteen ministries and several state governments. The destruction of more than 25,000 square kilometers (nearly 10,000 square miles) in Lula's first full year, 2003–4, was the second worst since 1977; some 18,000 square kilometers (roughly 7,000 square miles) of woodland disappeared in 2004–5.

By late 2006, an environmental group, the Instituto Socioambiental, was claiming that there had been more deforestation in the Lula era than in any four-year period since 1988.[28] But the last year of Lula's first term saw a sharp decline in the rate, particularly in the state of Amazonas, where the state government was switching its support from deforestation to conservation. Problems of corruption in the forestry agency, IBAMA, added to the difficulty of law enforcement over huge, thinly populated areas, and even PT officials in one state were exposed as benefiting from illegal logging.

Ever since the Medici military regime in the early 1970s had launched its Trans-Amazonica roads program, ecologists internationally had been on red alert about the danger to one of the world's largest forests. Many other tropical rainforests, such as those in west Africa and Indonesia, had been decimated. Increased understanding of the extraordinary biodiversity of the rainforest and of the role of its disappearance in climate change had, sadly, not been accompanied by any letup in predatory assault, or a capacity to halt the destruction entirely.

The realization that the loss of tree cover was having dramatic results was brought home to Brazilians by serious droughts in Amazonia in both 2005 and 2006. Starting in Acre, in western Amazonia on the border with Peru, these droughts affected the river capital of Manaus in the central region, killing fish, disrupting river transportation, and isolating river towns. They also gave Marina Silva, the environment minister, a handle with which to strengthen her regulatory powers, and in the year there were three hundred arrests, fifteen hundred firms were shut down, and six hundred thousand cubic meters (nearly eight hundred thousand cubic yards) of illegal logs, often mahogany, were seized.[29] Middle-class opinion, especially, was waking up to the reality of global warming.[30]

Mixed up with the future of Amazonia, of course, was the future of Brazil's indigenous Indians, although Indians are in fact spread throughout the country. By the year 2000, 11 percent of the land mass of Brazil was reserved for Indians, regarded as the best curators of the country's ecology.[31] Indeed, a respected environmental institute demonstrated that only 1.14 percent of forest on Indian lands had been cut down, compared with 18.96 percent elsewhere.[32]

Traditionally, the PT had been sympathetic to the Indians, seeing them as part of the excluded poor. There were frictions on the ground, however, among Indian groups and poor peasants and rubber collectors, who were also part of the PT coalition.

Indians were threatened by the advance of loggers, ranchers, and soy growers, who often had state governments on their side. Lula gained some credit in 2005 by signing into law the ratification of land occupied by fifteen thousand Indians, many of them Makuxi, in Roraima, on Brazil's northern border.[33] Those celebrating this act in the area were cut off, however, when rice growers opposed to the decision isolated them by destroying two bridges; the growers on Indian land would have to be relocated. The delimitation and protection of this area, known as Raposa-Serra do Sol, had been a holdover from the 1990s and the subject of a major international campaign of support led by Survival, the

U.K.-based NGO. Indians were still dissatisfied after the problem had theoretically been solved.

Indians had acquired increasing visibility in recent years, and from 1991, more and more people were describing themselves as "indigenous" in the national census. But even under Lula, the sums allocated for their health care were not getting through to them, and it was reckoned that around half of the tribes and ethnic groups had fewer than five hundred people. At least twelve, with between five and forty individuals, were likely to disappear.[34]

Of all the social areas with which any government is concerned, the one causing most irritation and anxiety to ordinary Brazilians was probably education. The public education system in the country was, and is, thoroughly inadequate for a country seeking first-world status. Comparisons with Asian countries that were developing faster than Brazil, such as South Korea, China, Malaysia, or Singapore, often came back to the higher priority they had given to the education of their citizens. Recognizing this, Lula promised in the 2006 election that he would put much more effort and resources into this field.

But many felt that, in his long years on the campaign trail, Lula should have set a better personal example; while other prominent trade unionists had found the time to get degrees or legal qualifications, Lula had never bothered. Whereas Nelson Mandela, for example, had studied for external degrees while he was in jail, and had encouraged poor black South Africans to go back to school when he was president, Lula appeared to glory in teasing better-educated Brazilians with what he had achieved after only a vocational course at SENAI.

There was not much doubt about Brazil's backwardness. A study of fifteen-year-olds by the Organization for Economic Cooperation and Development (OECD) showed that, out of forty-one countries that were compared, Brazil came in fortieth in mathematics and science, and thirty-seventh in reading standards. Mexico and Indonesia were ahead in mathematics and science, and the South Koreans were in the top four nations in all three subjects.[35]

Other analyses were also worrying. Parents who could afford to were avoiding public education and, in 2005, the Fundação Getúlio Vargas found that more than ten million students were in private schools and their families were spending 13.6 percent of their income to send them. In the state schools, more than half of the heads and principals were being appointed by political patronage.

The 1990s should have seen real progress; it was one of the "finger promises" of Cardoso's five-finger election program in 1994. By the time Lula was finally elected president in 2002, many of the jibes at his own modest educational experience had been dropped and a PT-led government, helped to power by so many teachers and academics, was expected to achieve a lot.

The Lula government launched a blizzard of initiatives. Among these were the requirement that children start school at age six, and that basic education be extended from eight to nine years. The free school meals system was extended to reach thirty-seven million pupils, and better reporting was required to ensure that families receiving the Bolsa-Família sent their children to school. Research showed that the Bolsa-Família was proving particularly effective up to the age of thirteen.[36] New programs were started for young children, for the improvement of teacher quality, and for the thirty-three million adults who were defined as functionally illiterate.

Universities were not ignored, as the government started a program called "University for All"—ProUni (Programma Universidade para Todos), which aimed to provide whole or partial remission of student fees for low-income students. Full costs were paid for students from families whose income was less than 1.5 times the minimum salary, and in the first semester of 2006 there were eight hundred thousand students enrolled under this program; two hundred thousand students at private universities benefited. Lula founded ten federal universities, some of which were based on previous faculties.[37] Expansion of the university sector was accompanied by advice to institutions that they provide a minimum quota for black, the poorest, and American Indian students.

Some academics complained of dumbing down and pointed to the unhappy experience of racial quotas in the United States and the real difficulty of defining race in Brazil. The overall thrust of the educational policy—which was complemented by a strategy of the Ministry of

Culture to bring computers and information technology to the *favelas*—was to ally a drive for social justice with a drive for higher educational standards. Crístovam Buarque, a former education minister and PT member dismissed by Lula, made education the key plank of his presidential campaign for the PDT in 2006.[38] He argued that Lula's government was simply not doing enough. Lula had had three education ministers in four years.

Brazil's education system was socially skewed,[39] and teachers in the public system were not well paid. In a federation, a great deal of power lay with the states and municipalities. Other democratic countries, as different as the United States, the United Kingdom, and the east European states that had emerged from communism after 1989, were also facing difficulties in modernizing their education. The best that could be said for Lula was that he had made a start; education systems cannot be changed overnight, and it would be easier to see how much his governments had achieved at the end of his second term.

What about the health sector? At its most expensive, private medicine and the best-equipped hospitals were among the finest anywhere. In a country where a woman's appearance was a matter of permanent private angst and cosmetic surgery was a leading topic of debate, it was not surprising that surgery to improve the body's looks was at the forefront of global medicine. Both Marisa and Lula were thought to have had Botox injections to remove unwanted wrinkles. But Brazil was also in the front rank for immunology.

Yet this was a world away from the health services available in the slums or the forgotten towns of the interior, or Lula's own experience with intestinal diseases or a chopped finger as a child and young man. Health care for poor Brazilians was still underfunded, or of poor quality, at the start of the twenty-first century.

The 1988 Constitution had marked a real advance. With PT support, it had created a single health service designed to reach all Brazilians. Up to 1988, it was estimated that 30 percent of Brazilians were excluded from any health service. The new one created after 1988—Sistema Único de Saúde—was designed to be inclusive, not unlike Britain's National Health Service, which had started forty years earlier. There had been several financial crises already for the new service, however, and paying for good doctors to work in it was expensive.

The Lula government sought to coordinate the federation, states, and municipalities more effectively, to invest in preventative medicine, and to focus on priorities such as infant and maternal mortality, ambulance services, cheaper medicines—where the government joined forces with South Africa in successful struggles against the drug companies to make generic medicines available—and dentistry. Dentistry could not be overlooked in a country where ten million people had neither teeth nor dentures.

The government had some successes, notably in infant and maternal mortality. Nearly half the population was covered by a family health service (PSF), and in the first two years, from 2002 to 2004, infant mortality in districts with PSF dropped from 31.3 deaths per 1,000 live births to 26.7. Investment in dental health rose more than six times between 2003 and 2006. The struggle against AIDS, TB, and malaria was intensified. Brazil's now aging population received more attention, and a campaign for the vaccination of those over sixty, in April 2005, reached nearly 84 percent of this age group.

Brazil's strategies for the control and reduction of HIV/AIDS had been admired for some years. When in 2005–6 there was international concern about a possible avian flu pandemic, the government increased its vigilance; flu was always a problem causing lost days at work. The government installed investigative units in the states to monitor the types of flu virus and the spread of illness.

But as with education, it was impossible to claim that enormous advances had been made in four years, although clearly the health of poor Brazilians, and of the traditional PT electorate, was getting attention. Aloizio Mercadante, Lula's close associate, was frank: "The challenges for public health in Brazil are still enormous, as a result of the persistence of social inequality, of the tendency of medical costs to rise, of demographic change with the aging of the population, and of the lack of cooperation between elements in the federal system."[40]

Culture was an area where the government wanted to be seen to be doing something different. Lula had had personal support for many years from artists and intellectuals such as Chico Buarque, the singer, songwriter, and novelist. Although Lula recognized the limitations of what some years before had been nicknamed the "festive left" (*esquerda festiva*), he was grateful for the appearance of popular artists at the big rallies, a mixture of entertainment and politics, that were a feature of all his campaigns prior to 2006.

He appointed Gilberto Gil as minister of culture. Gil was a black singer originally from Bahia, who was part of the *tropicalismo* movement in the 1960s and 1970s, which had made samba known throughout the world. Although technically a Green, Gil wore his political allegiance lightly and was committed to Lula personally. He stayed in the government when the Greens withdrew support, and organized a meeting for the president with artists in Rio in August 2006, at the start of the election campaign. But he could not bring all artists with him: the singer Caetano Veloso, for example, refused to vote for Lula, on the ground that he was opposed to presidents having second terms.

Inside Brazil, Gil launched various programs to bring art, film, and information technology to the people. He supported efforts to crack down on the illicit export of cultural goods, and rehabilitation of museums, for which he trebled spending over three years. Using investments released by the government and company fiscal incentives, he steered extra money into regions that had been poorly served in the past—the north (Amazonia), the northeast, and the central west.

He also promoted a vigorous cultural policy internationally, building partnerships with China and running a "Brazilian Year" in France in 2005 and a "cultural cup" in Germany to coincide with the soccer World Cup. In July 2006, the governments of Brazil and Chile cooperated to back a regional conference for the Americas on discrimination, intolerance, and xenophobia, five years after the UN world conference on the same issues in Durban. The Ministry of Culture was one of the Brazilian ministries involved.

But Gil ran into criticism because he sometimes mixed his private interests as a performer with his ministerial visits abroad. In a hostile article, the newsmagazine *Veja* suggested that his performing career as a singer had stagnated prior to his ministerial post, but that he was now able to raise his concert fee from R70,000 to R200,000 (or U.S. $80,000).[41] Undoubtedly his hosts and partners outside Brazil often wanted to hear him play, and he did not always charge them. His own prestige as an artist was actually of benefit to his country, and his concerts may have been on days off from his official duties. Nonetheless, there was a grey area here, exploited by the government's enemies.

What about religion? There was no doubt that Lula was a loyal Catholic, and progressive clergy and laity had helped to build the PT from the beginning. But in government the president was careful. The evangelical Protestants had become more powerful, not least among poor Brazilians, in the late twentieth century. Vice President Alencar was an evangelical. Spiritist and traditional beliefs were still important among Afro-Brazilians. There were currents of secularism and charismatic Catholicism coursing through society.

The Catholic Church had long been divided into factions, and Don Eusébio Scheid, the cardinal archbishop of Rio de Janeiro, who was one of the president's critics, punned that he was "not Catholic, but chaotic." At the same time, Lula was suspected of helping his friend Cardinal Cláudio Hummes behind the scenes in the race to become pope following the death of John Paul II. He traveled to Rome for the pope's funeral with three former presidents—José Sarney, Itamar Franco, and Fernando Henrique Cardoso.

Abortion was the one area where Lula's Catholicism seemed to influence his policy most obviously. In August 2005, Lula wrote to Dom Geraldo Majella during the general assembly of the Brazilian bishops to reaffirm his position to "defend life in all its aspects and extent." This effectively ended a proposal to legalize abortion, which had been pushed forward by feminist groups and a number of deputies in the PT and PCdoB. A year later there was a possibility that the progressive wing of Catholicism would hit some of Lula's former allies, when bishops called on electors to avoid voting for deputies who had been mixed up in corruption.

The biggest political factor in Brazilian culture, and arguably in society, was the dominance of private media. The PT had always been suspicious of the concentration of power, particularly in television ownership. Lula himself at times had been wounded by attacks, notably in his 1989 election campaign. Whereas he had readily made himself available to the press in opposition, in government he avoided collective press conferences.

But the media were operating in a competitive environment, subject to change. A paper that had been of the highest quality in the 1960s and 1970s, the *Jornal do Brasil* of Rio, was a pale reflection of its past by the beginning of the twenty-first century. The Globo group, combining television and press, had built a strong position all over the country by the late twentieth century. Web sites, blogs, and the Internet had all become significant, especially to the educated and professional groups, by the time of Lula's presidency.

The PT in opposition had wanted to establish a national council of journalism to license journalists. It argued that it wanted to professionalize and raise standards in the media. But there had been a long history of friction between the PT and the big media groups, which saw this as an attempt at censorship by unreconstructed authoritarians in the party.

The scheme was thrown overboard after the failed attempt to expel a *New York Times* journalist. Instead, in May 2006, Lula signed the Declaration of Chapultepec, a document drawn up by the Inter American Press Association that affirms the freedom of the press. Nonetheless, in the run-up to the 2006 elections, the PT was still seeking to break up concentrations of media power. Compared with other democratic countries, it was hard to conclude that the media treated the Brazilian government particularly unfairly.

Finally, it is worth saying something about the wider universe of social movements and civil society. They had provided the milieu in which Lula had built an authentic union movement and they had helped to construct the PT. They had grown together, in the struggle to democratize Brazil. At the same time, they all cherished their independence, just as Lula and his friends kept the PT separate from the unions. In government, Lula and his ministers claimed to consult the social movements, including them in discussion and advisory groups. But it was inevitable that there would be frictions, for civil society had its own missions.

Disappointment that Lula could not change the world ranged from big issues, such as the tight control of economic policy in his first two years, to specific grievances that he had not done enough to open the files and pursue the guilty involved in human rights abuse under the military. At the end of the third year of his government, a thorough survey of nongovernmental opinion revealed deep disillusionment and the sense that the government was not really listening to what the social movements were saying.

This study rested on the experience of thirteen NGOs and was coordinated by Ibase (Instituto Brasileiro de Análises Sociais e Econômicas). It examined how far the government had been listening to public opinion in elaborating its policy, and specifically regarding eleven social conflicts, from deforestation in Amazonia to security in Rio de Janeiro. It complained about the government's support of genetically modified crops even though the national environmental conference was against it, and concluded that much of the government's "consultation" was bogus.

This critique resonated with other evidence that the PT had lost touch with its roots and its earlier ideals. One of the party's founders, Plínio de Arruda Sampaio, said that the findings echoed the motives that had caused him to leave. "There is no intention to promote a transformation of society. The government has stopped having a dialogue with the popular sector. It is seductive, it offers crumbs, but it doesn't have a dialogue. It is having a good dialogue with the dominant class, and in a fraternal way."[42]

It is a worldwide experience that no NGO is ever satisfied with what any government does. One of the difficulties for Lula was that, after his long struggle to the presidency, so much had been expected.

7 INTERNATIONAL AND ECONOMIC POLICY

Many regarded the foreign policy of Lula's government as the aspect that most truly reflected the original ideals of the party he founded, the PT, while its economic policy was the biggest betrayal. Although neither the foreign nor the economic policies were entirely consistent, each represented attempts by the president and his associates to find fresh paths for Brazil through the maze of globalization, pursuing the national interest as they saw it.

In opposition, the PT had, over many years, formulated an international policy that focused on defense of national sovereignty, the solidarity of developing nations, the values of the Non-Aligned Movement, and growing unity within Latin America. This approach placed emphasis on the United Nations, challenged the hegemony of the United States in the post–Cold War system, and looked for new ties with Africa, the Middle East, and Asia to balance traditional connections with Europe.

There were also economic aspects to this international thrust. It was obvious that at least some developing countries—notably China and India—were growing at a rate much faster than the United States and Europe, and they had a hunger for Brazilian commodities. An upturn in oil prices after the beginning of the Iraq war in 2003 meant that oil-rich Arab countries, as well as Venezuela in South America, again had money to invest. A foreign policy that asserted the solidarity of poorer countries could actually be good business as well as good politics. Lula's numerous trips to Africa did not go amiss with Afro-Brazilians; his hosting of a summit for Arab and Latin American states in 2005 was also a positive signal to the *turcos*—a large Brazilian population of Middle Eastern descent, particularly strong in São Paulo state.[1]

The African dimension was perhaps the most idealistic, for it offered little short-term economic gain. Visiting the Slave House on Gorée Island in Senegal, Lula apologized in April 2005 for his country's role in the transatlantic slave trade. Slavery was not abolished in Brazil until 1888, more than sixty years after independence from Portugal, and Brazil had been the biggest importer of slaves to the New World. "I want to tell you . . . that I had no responsibility for what happened in the sixteenth, seventeenth, and eighteenth centuries, but I ask your forgiveness for what we did to black people," Lula said, in the presence of President Wade of Senegal.

Lula's firsthand experience of Africa had another consequence. He was shocked to see that nearly all Brazil's diplomats on the continent had white skin. Coming home, he insisted that the Rio Branco Institute, the prestigious school for diplomacy, should recruit more black students.

But there were problems in trying to practice what the PT had preached. Brazil did not have interests identical to those of the Spanish-speaking countries of Latin America, some of which actively feared Brazilian aggrandizement. Although very many Brazilians were poor, the country itself, and its GNP per capita, were much better off than countries such as China and India and nearly all the African states. Furthermore, it was locked in a complex political and economic web with the United States and Europe; political ties went back to the Brazilian Expeditionary Force in Italy in World War II and to Brazil's being on the anticommunist side in the Cold War; and even into the twenty-first century, the "Brazil risk" and the value of the real depended on financial opinion on Wall Street and in London and Zurich.

Lula himself was well traveled by the time he became president, with a range of contacts, particularly on the center-left. He was an international celebrity in his own right even before he moved into the presidential palace. In office he was backed up by a longtime associate and one-time Marxist, Marco Aurélio Garcia, who had been a policy coordinator in earlier elections and was campaign coordinator and then acting PT president in the 2006 campaign.[2] Garcia acted as Lula's personal adviser on international relations. He also had the support of the professionals in the Itamaraty, the Brazilian foreign ministry, which for years had had the pick of the public service. Lula's foreign minister, Celso Amorim, had been ambassador in London and New York.

By the start of the twenty-first century, the nature of diplomacy had changed radically compared with its slow-moving canons a century earlier. News was a twenty-four-hour business. Frequent summits, where presidents and prime ministers met hurriedly, had personalized the exchange between nations. There were fewer distinctions between "home" and "abroad," so journalists questioned leaders at overseas press conferences on domestic crises. Leaders themselves used foreign trips to promote their status among voters.

Lula enjoyed this hugely, using his demotic and larger-than-life personality to boost Brazil. The sheer quantity of his foreign travel, and the amount of time he spent on foreign dignitaries coming to Brasília, was remarkable. In 2003, he was out of the country for at least 58 days on official visits, taking in 32 states. In 2004, he was out for 44 days, visiting 22 countries. In 2005, he was away for an exceptional 70 days, visiting 28 countries. He traveled more in three years than Cardoso had in four. Often returning hospitality, or hosting state visits to Brazil, he gave time to 41 heads of state or government in 2003, 21 in 2004, and 30 in 2005.[3] He traveled extensively even in an election year, 2006.

But what did this activity achieve? Brazilian businessmen, who often traveled in his party, appreciated the effort he put in on their behalf. But it is arguable that, diplomatically, he had more success in the wider global sphere, winning recognition for Brazil at G8 meetings, support for the country's claim for a permanent seat on the UN Security Council, and significant South-South alliances, than in Latin or South America.

In his inaugural speech in early 2003 Lula had stated, "The great priority of foreign policy in my government will be the construction of a South America that is politically stable, prosperous, and united, based on ideals of democracy and social justice." He went on to say that, to realize this aim, it was essential to revitalize Mercosul,[4] the economic alliance of countries of southern South America, which had been damaged by crises in each of them and by narrow and egotistical visions. Mercosul was essentially a political project.[5]

There is no doubt that the Lula government sought to strengthen the processes of integration, but different political agendas had a habit of getting in the way. On the positive side, Brazil backed an agreement between Mercosul and the Andean Pact countries that, in December 2004, brought into existence a South American Community of Nations with some 350 million inhabitants and a GNP of around U.S. $2.6 trillion. Colombia, Ecuador, and Hugo Chávez's Venezuela were brought into association with Mercosul.

At the same time, Brazil stimulated the setting up of a parliament for Mercosul. It put seventy million dollars into a development fund for Mercosul's poorer countries and regions, around 70 percent of the total. Talk of a common currency was knocked on the head by the central bankers. But the Brazilian state development bank, BNDES, invested heavily in infrastructure works aimed at physical integration, such as two more bridges over the Orinoco to link Brazil and Venezuela, and doubling the width of the Mercosul motorway joining Brazil and Argentina.

The politics, however, remained obstinate. Part of the problem lay in the propaganda of Lula and his government that they wanted to "lead" Latin America, and be seen by the outside world as representing the region in international discourse. Yet leadership cannot just be asserted; it has to be conferred by those who wish to be led. Prior to Lula's presidency, the Brazilian Foreign Ministry had tended to pursue a softly, softly policy. It was aware of the widespread suspicion of Brazil's economic and demographic strength among Spanish-speaking neighbors, and a history of geographical penetration by Portuguese speakers going back more than four hundred years.

Inevitably there were continued frictions with Argentina. A joint commission was set up to monitor bilateral commerce between the two countries, but Argentina imposed duties on Brazilian exports and Brazilian businessmen complained that Lula was not doing enough to defend "national sovereignty." In a private dinner with Brazilians at the ambassador's residence in Tokyo, in May 2005, Lula was vitriolic about

President Kirchner, because Argentina was blocking Brazil's Security Council ambitions.[6]

The official line in Brasília was that all was friendship with Hugo Chávez, whose country was buoyed up with oil revenues and an anti-American leader who had headed off several undemocratic attempts to overthrow him. But there were signs of friction. Chávez liked to throw his weight around on the world stage, offering fuel to the poor of the United States and to the transportation fleet of the mayor of London, making friends with the Iranian regime, and launching Tele-SUR, a TV service for Latin America. He sponsored a samba school in the 2006 Rio carnival. His anti-Americanism played well with the traditional left in the PT and in Brazil, and it must have grieved Lula when Chávez was cheered and he was booed at the World Social Forum in Porto Alegre in 2006.

A more serious problem arose when President Evo Morales of Bolivia, the indigenous leader strongly backed by Chávez, announced the nationalization of oil and gas in a May Day speech in 2006. Petrobrás, in which the Brazilian government has a controlling share, was the biggest outside investor in Bolivian energy; Brazilian industry depended heavily on Bolivian gas supplies. The Lula government seemed unprepared for a measure that had appeared in Morales's campaign manifesto the previous year.

Morales talked of Lula as "my oldest friend," but his energy ministry proposed to take a half share of foreign companies within 180 days, and in the transition period proposed to grab 82 percent of the production revenues, leaving only 18 percent for the companies. This was a challenge Lula could not shirk, and Marco Aurélio Garcia complained bitterly that the seizure would damage Lula's chances during the election campaign. Lula referred to it openly as "a dirty trick."

Lula commented, "Obviously, if Bolivia insists on taking these unilateral actions, Brazil has to think of doing something tougher to Bolivia." In fact, Brazil exerted diplomatic pressure and got results. Andrés Soliz Rada, a radical nationalist who was the Bolivian energy minister, resigned on 15 September 2006. Although Morales was not going to back down on nationalization, and Petrobrás was still talking of pulling out of Bolivia, space was opened for negotiation.

There were important differences between Brazil, on the one hand, and Venezuela and Bolivia, on the other, which made shorthand efforts to bracket Lula in a lurch to the left in South America in 2005 somewhat misleading. Both Venezuela and Bolivia depended heavily on oil and gas, whose rewards had made little dent in the poverty of the majority of their people. Redistribution was overdue. This was especially the case in Bolivia, where an indigenous majority had for centuries been dominated by a Hispanic elite descended from the conquistadors.

Lula's sentiment in favor of the poor was undoubted, but the social, economic, ethnic, and political situation in his own country was so different that he had ruled out a massive extension of public ownership on the Chávez-Morales model. Ideological friendship could go only so far; it was an influence on, but not a determinant of, his foreign policy with neighboring states.

Brazil's desire to be seen as a Latin American rather than a South American power was demonstrated by its leadership of the UN force in Haiti. It provided the largest contingent. Haiti was arguably the poorest country in the Western hemisphere, and its original revolution by black Jacobins against slavery had been betrayed by corruption, incompetence, and frequent political upheavals. The UN soldiers had gone in as a stabilization force, committed to development—rather as the NATO troops advertised their original mission in Afghanistan. In Haiti, too, this became a difficult peacekeeping exercise, however.

The Brazilian commander died unexpectedly in January 2006, but another Brazilian general was appointed. Although Haitian politics seemed a morass and the Brazilian contribution was not inexpensive, Lula was determined to stay the course. While some of his conservative critics at home saw this as a waste of money, Lula saw it as a tangible down payment on a permanent Security Council seat. It was also another signal of respect to Brazil's African tradition, and a hint to the Brazilian military that it could still make an honorable contribution under the civilian dispensation.

Lula had made it clear in his election campaign that he was not keen on the Free Trade Area of the Americas (FTAA) being pushed by the Bush administration, seeing it as an attempt to extend U.S. economic ascendancy in the region.[7] Instead he preferred a growth in regional cooperation, and a worldwide trade deal in the so-called development round—the Doha round—of the World Trade Organization (WTO) negotiations. While the pro-American Mexican leader, Vicente Fox, led the states that wanted to press forward with the FTAA, a summit of the Americas in Mar del Plata in November 2005 effectively baulked the proposal. Lula's Brazil, Nestor Kirchner's Argentina, the rest of the Mercosul states, and Hugo Chávez's Venezuela were a strong caucus blocking its adoption.

Somehow Lula managed to ride with both the hare and the hounds in the relationship between Latin America and the Bush administration. George W. Bush stopped in Brasília on his way home from Mar del Plata. Lula showed him, on a big map in the Granja do Torto, where he had been born in Pernambuco, and the state and city of São Paulo, where his trade unionism and politics took off. They signed a communiqué that was civil but anodyne. It talked favorably of UN reform, the need for a Doha deal, and support for TRIPS, the WTO's treaty on intellectual property rights.

Many Brazilians combined feelings of both attraction and repulsion toward the United States. After the attacks on the World Trade Center in New York in September 2001, tough new passport checks were introduced that made life difficult for Brazilian visitors to the United States. They seemed to go beyond any reasonable security precaution, and the Brazilian authorities responded in kind. After a few days, when U.S. tourists and businessmen got stuck in slow and lengthy lines at Brazilian airports, the U.S. authorities relented.

Brazil also stood up to the Bush administration over HIV/AIDS. The U.S. government, influenced by its evangelical Christian supporters, was pushing an antiabortion, pro-abstinence, and antiprostitution agenda in financing overseas work. Brazil rejected an offer of forty million dollars in U.S. assistance for its AIDS programs, because it refused to agree to a declaration condemning prostitution. The country had a subtle and effective anti-AIDS strategy and had no wish to exclude sex workers and their clients from its benefits.

Lula had criticized the U.S. invasion of Iraq in 2003, and before becoming president he had shared much of the anti-American rhetoric of the PT. But in office his relationship with Washington was good, if not precisely warm. The United States needed Brazil's support, for economic as well as political reasons, just as Brazil had to retain a comparable relationship with the United States. President Bush might be vague about the geography of this large country and traditional ally, but Lula could play a useful role as an interlocutor with the mercurial Chávez and Brazil's economy could not be ignored.

Professional diplomats could be cynical about the more utopian aspects of Lula's foreign policy. In his inaugural speech he had said, "In my government, Brazil's diplomatic action will be oriented by a humanist perspective, and will be, above all, an instrument of national development." Yet there is no doubt that this was meaningful to Lula. It reflected his own Catholicism, his experience as a poor boy, his long political struggle, and his commitment to the needs of the core PT constituency.

At international occasions he would speak about the need to conquer hunger and extreme poverty, and the importance of the world reaching the UN's Millennium Development Goals by 2015.[8] It was why he devoted effort to trying to broker a deal in the stymied world trade talks. It was all of a piece with the Bolsa-Família inside Brazil, which, by late 2006, was being cited by an IMF expert as a successful strategy for reducing poverty.[9]

The South-South stance of the Lula government was pursued with persistence, and dovetailed with both the effort to obtain a permanent Security Council seat and the president's regular attendance at the annual G8 meetings of the strongest economic powers. But it was impossible to avoid controversy. Conservative Brazilians with links to North America and Europe sniped at seeing the PT ideology in action; they noted that Brazilian economic growth was much slower than growth in China or India, and that Brazilian tariff barriers were still high.

On the more idealistic side, human rights supporters of the government were worried when they saw Lula glad-handing African dictators such as President Bongo of Gabon, who had been president since 1967. They were uncomfortable with what was not said about democracy and human rights at the summit meeting of Arab and Latin American states in Brasília in May 2005, when the focus was on trade and investment and the Arab countries sought support for the Palestinian cause.[10]

More difficult still was the fact that Brazil was following a two-pronged strategy to promote the national interest. It was preaching, and to some degree practicing, a policy of solidarity with developing countries in Latin America and the rest of the world. But at the same time, its policy of picking "strategic partners" for different purposes—for its campaign for a seat on the Security Council, for trade growth and trade negotiations—had the effect of separating other states into two tiers, with a capacity for jealousy between them. This was particularly the case with the Security Council.

One of the great successes of Lula's foreign policy was that he became a regular attendee at G8 meetings. But it was the G8 members that decided whom they should invite as additions, and by the Gleneagles meeting in 2005 and the St. Petersburg one in 2006, Brazil, India, and China were seen as essential guests. Indeed, there was talk of their becoming full members.[11] In a notional way they were representatives of the developing world; in a real way—especially because China was an engine for the whole global economy and a key trading partner for the United States—they came because of their presumed economic clout.

But to expand the membership of the Security Council, every state's vote would count. UN reform had been talked of for years, and the permanent Security Council status exclusive to the victors of World War II—the United States, Britain, France, China, and Russia—was increasingly outdated sixty years later.[12] President Cardoso had never made a permanent seat for Brazil a major priority, though it was certainly an aim being quietly pursued by the Foreign Ministry. There did seem a chance, early in the new century, and with the UN's reputation battered by various scandals, that inertia could be overcome by an institutional reform.[13]

Under Lula, a permanent seat for Brazil became a key, publicized goal. He was persuaded to adopt it by his foreign minister, Celso Amorim.[14] Brazil allied with Germany, India, and Japan in a well-organized campaign. Support was sought all over the world, and Brazil did well, for example, in the European Union. It ran into trouble, however, in Latin America and Africa. As mentioned earlier, other Latin American states were suspicious of a Portuguese-speaking country "representing" them. Argentina and Mexico in particular were jealous of

Brazil's pretensions.[15] Each believed it had a better claim. Furthermore, each of Brazil's allies had its opponents—Japan had China, India had Pakistan, Germany had Spain and Italy.

The biggest obstacle for Brazil lay in Africa, where Lula had visited so many states and the Foreign Ministry had opened several new embassies. The problem lay in a numbers game. The Africans wanted two permanent Security Council seats for themselves; the leading contenders were Nigeria and South Africa, though this did not please the Francophone countries. But if they succeeded, it would mean there would be eleven permanent members, which UN reformers thought were too many when they had to be added to by temporary members from each region.

There were other issues too. Why could there not be a Middle Eastern power with a permanent seat? Might not Brazil have done better on its own than with allies who brought opponents as well as assistance? By the end of Lula's first term, therefore, it was obvious that Brazil wanted to get onto the Security Council very badly, but much less certain as to when or whether it would succeed. Somehow Brazil had to combine the goodwill of the existing permanent five with sufficient votes from everyone else.

In 2005, Brazil also suffered two setbacks in elections to international posts, at the WTO and the Inter-American Development Bank (IADB). Lula's government backed Luiz Felipe Seixas Corrêa to run the WTO, but he was knocked out in the first round; developing countries were backing Mauritian and Uruguayan candidates instead. By the time Brazil switched to support the candidate of its Mercosul partner, Uruguay, it was too late, and Pascal Lamy of the European Union won. In the IADB race, Brazil put up its own candidate, João Sayyad, but he was defeated by a Colombian. Only one Mercosul government voted for Sayyad and, ironically, that was Argentina.

The world of the twenty-first century was moving away from reliance on large institutional collectives such as the Non-Aligned Movement or the Organization of American States, and giving more space to "coalitions of the willing" such as the G4 states that hoped to get onto the Security Council together. Brazil was involved in several of these pragmatic pressure groups.

1. Approximate birthplace of Lula, Caetés, 2005. The two boys are Luciano Godoy and Vali Vicente. Photo by author.

2. Lula (third from left) with Dona Lindu (far left) and family on the beach at Santos. Presidential Palace, Brasília.

3. Lula (third from right, back row) as a teenager on a soccer team. Presidential Palace, Brasília.

4. Lula at his wedding to Marisa, 1974. Presidential Palace, Brasília.

5. Lula at a metalworkers' strike meeting in São Bernardo, 1979. Folha de São Paulo.

6. Lula at the negotiating table, 1979. Abril/Gamma/Camera Press, London.

7. Killing time playing cards during the 1980 strike. Abril/Gamma/Camera Press, London.

8. Lula with José Dirceu, 2001. Reuters.

9. Lula after voting in the 2002 presidential election. Reuters.

10. Lula with President George W. Bush, 2002. Folha Imagem.

11. Lula with President Fidel Castro at the Havana airport, 2003. Folha Imagem.

12. Lula with Marisa and Oscar Niemeyer outside the Palácio Alvorada, Brasília, 2005. Reuters.

13. Lula with Marisa at the Taj Mahal, 2005. Reuters.

14. Lula with President Hugo Chávez, 2006. Reuters.

In the first year of the Lula government, at Cancun in September 2003, Brazil joined nineteen other developing states in a Group of 20 that argued for an end to agricultural and export subsidies by the United States and the European Union. The position was unified but, when a crisis arose over the Doha trade round at Hong Kong in late 2005, it was clear that the G20 and its member countries were disunited in what they could offer the developed countries in return. The developed states wanted to open up industrial and retail sectors, service industries, and public purchasing in the developing states.

The issues were complex, and there were more than two sides involved. Although neither the richer nor the poorer states wanted to give away too much, some analysts believed that the true benefit from a trade deal, for the poorest nations of all, was likely to be small. Big agricultural exporters, such as Brazil and Australia, stood to do well. But a deal that wiped out European Union preferences for countries such as Guyana would leave them worse off than before.

Lula himself did not lose faith in the need to succeed with the Doha round, even though its timetable kept slipping and commentators wrote that it had collapsed. After the G8 meeting in St. Petersburg in July 2006, Lula was part of a group—which also included China, India, Mexico, the EU, and Australia—that, along with the G8 themselves, tried to rescue the "suspended" talks.

Two other significant pressure groups to which Brazil belonged were BRICS (Brazil, Russia, India, China, and South Africa) and IBSA (India, Brazil, and South Africa). These were as much about promoting trade among themselves as about adopting a common line in world trade negotiations. The presence or absence of China was an important difference in these two sets of initials.

For Brazil, China was both a blessing and a bane. It took Brazilian raw materials and commodities, but the low price of its manufactured goods was a constant threat to Brazilian industry in products ranging from textiles to electronics. And, from a PT viewpoint, it was a dictatorship relying on cheap nonunionized labor, anathema to all those who had struggled for free unions and better wages against the military regime.

Lula visited China in May 2004, signing deals for food and steel exports; that year Brazil had a surplus of U.S. $9.1 billion in its trade with China. Commercial cooperation was wide-ranging, with China launching Brazilian space satellites, and Brazil building passenger jets in northeastern China. But the anxiety on the Brazilian side was shown a year later when the minister for development, industry, and external trade, Luiz Furlan, visited Beijing in an effort to get a gentleman's agreement to moderate the surge in Chinese exports to Brazil.

IBSA was strongly promoted by Lula himself, who visited New Delhi in 2004 and hosted a summit in Brasília with President Thabo Mbeki of South Africa and Prime Minister Manmohan Singh of India in September 2006. He ran this in the midst of his campaign for reelection. The three countries had agreed to set up a free trade area among themselves, and Brazil-Indian trade rose by 170 percent in two years. "We are the largest democracies respectively on each of our continents, and these values bind us in a unique way," said Manmohan Singh. The three aimed to raise trilateral trade by 25 percent in one year, to ten billion dollars in 2006.

Behind IBSA lay not only the topical interest in trade, the IMF, and UN reform, but also energy cooperation, in which Brazil was strong in ethanol, South Africa in synthetic coal-based fuel, and India in wind and solar power. Lula took advantage of the meeting in a characteristic way, by offering Brazilian soccer coaches to India's extremely underdeveloped soccer league.

Lula was keenly aware that, in the twenty-first century, diplomacy was not only conducted between states. The world held many forces that were more powerful than nation-states—multinationals, campaigning nongovernmental organizations, the media, and armed groups such as al-Qaeda and Hezbollah, which could take on the strongest armies. His own background, in the ferment of social movements at the end of the military dictatorship, had given him insight.

He therefore took advantage of several opportunities to talk with and meet people at unofficial gatherings. In particular he was a regular at the World Social Forum, which had begun in Porto Alegre as an antiglobalization rally against the World Economic Forum in Davos, Switzerland.

And he also turned up in Davos. The theory was that he was carrying a message from the radicals at Porto Alegre to the representatives of the world's rich in Switzerland. As his presidency went on, this became a harder act for him. In Porto Alegre he was no longer seen as a militant. In Davos, Brazil's economy was regarded as sluggish and its president damaged by the corruption scandals.

In international opinion, Lula remained categorized as a "center-left" politician. In July 2003, he visited London for a meeting of progressive leaders, mostly European, promoted by Tony Blair, the "New Labour" prime minister, and his friend Peter Mandelson. The "New Labour" project was designed to bring together traditional socialist concerns for the relief of poverty and greater equality, with the reality of the apparent success for capitalism after the fall of the Berlin Wall, and middle-class desire for choice in public services. This strategic compromise had proved effective in winning elections and was touted in theories of a "third way" or, in Bill Clinton's version, "triangulation"; but critics on the left saw an abandonment of ideals of equality, with the state as its engine, and a creeping conservatism.

Lula was not unfamiliar with these debates, but he was no theorist. At the progressive summit in London, and on similar occasions, he tended to play his personal card as a celebrity who—unlike people such as Blair, who had had a comfortable upbringing—had worked his way up from poverty and had helped create a union movement and the PT.

At the same time, he came away comforted that the kind of compromises he was making in Brazil were paralleled elsewhere. Specifically, the tough economic policy that he had foreshadowed in his Letter to the Brazilian People, and which was designed to reassure investors and the middle class, was similar to the Blair strategy. Blair's Labour government had preserved its Conservative predecessor's spending priorities for two years, and had also given autonomy to the Bank of England to set interest rates. Lula's intention too was to calm fears and make it easier to promote policies of social inclusion.

But the downside for Lula, as it had been for Britain's Labour government, was that the orthodox economic policy tended to continue. Brazil did not default on its foreign debt when Lula took power in

Brasília. It did not introduce exchange controls, as the prime minister of Malaysia had controversially but successfully done in the late 1990s currency crisis in Southeast Asia. It kept faith with international financiers, and very high interest rates at home.

For the traditional militants of the PT, this was a betrayal. For ordinary Brazilians, the high interest rates, which had been as high as 25 percent a year in January 2003, were particularly burdensome.[16] The country was still paying high interest on its overseas debt and was committed to a large current account surplus in order to do so. Economic growth, averaging some 2.6 percent a year during Lula's term, was too low for a developing country trying to catch up with the richer states and only half the South American average.

The one clear success that had a redistributive impact was the decrease in inflation, which was estimated to be around 29 percent cumulatively over the four years 2003–6.[17] The real became a reliable currency, traded at airport currency shops around the world.

For the first three years of the Lula government there was a fairly tight control of expenditure, although more civil servants were hired. In 2006, for obvious political reasons, the purse strings were loosened.

The government did stop the privatization program begun by Cardoso, which had seen the privatization of telecommunications and some state banks. It made slow progress with public-private partnerships, a device much used by the Blair Labour government in the United Kingdom to pay for public sector infrastructure with private money, at the risk of burdening future generations with debt. It used remaining state-controlled entities, such as Petrobrás, for developmental purposes. It tried to make up for the regional disparities that meant that the north and the northeast of the country were so much poorer than the south and southeast.

Essentially, Lula and his team had decided that they wanted Brazil to be one of the big players in the world economic system, albeit with nationalist flourishes. The Brazilian development bank, BNDES, had funded privatizations under Cardoso. Under Lula, it not only paid for Mercosul infrastructure, it also funded the purchase of Argentine businesses by Brazilian ones—such as the Swift meat business by Brazil's

Friboi group. The government adhered to Cardoso's IMF agreement, the response to the speculative attack of 2002, and in December 2005 it repaid the whole of an IMF loan of $15.5 billion two years early. A weak U.S. dollar and high commodity prices enabled Brazil to amass dollar reserves quickly. Lula and Palocci made much of this IMF repayment.

The trouble was that Brazil, in spite of its size and export capacity, was still lumped together with other so-called emerging markets. Events elsewhere, over which it could have no control, affected investment flows, the value of the real, and the trend of the São Paulo stock exchange, the Bovespa.[18]

Although the Lula government had proved resilient to international volatility, Brazil's open economy was still exposed to shocks. In September 2006, only ten days before the first round of the presidential election, a batch of bad news—including a coup in Thailand, a possible default in Ecuador, and political crises in eastern Europe—drove the real and Bovespa trading down. The latest scandal to hit the Lula government was only one of the items foreign investors had in mind. In May, when American investors saw higher interest rates at home, money had been pulled out of Brazil and the real had dropped by 20 percent.

The concept of "emerging markets" had been devised to lure money into developing countries from traditional financial centers in the United States and Europe. Greed for high returns was linked to the undoubted fact that developing countries had plenty of catching up to do. But the bigger returns were often linked to higher political and economic risks. Every so often the North American and European investors took fright. This factor—the "Brazil risk"—helped to explain Brazil's persistently high interest rates and its relatively poor economic performance.

Brazil's own firms, and its own rich, added to the merry-go-round. Brazil was the fifth largest exporter of capital among developing countries. Yet much of this was not going into investment overseas: 70 percent was spent in or via tax havens.

Lula seemed baffled by the complexities of the Brazilian economy, and was inclined to telephone the head of the Central Bank and demand reductions in interest rates, irrespective of the underlying competitive requirements for the real. The traditional economic advisers for the PT were not always helpful, especially now that Lula's coalition had the responsibility of governing, rather than the luxury of opposition. Back when Cardoso had introduced the real, Aloizio Mercadante was only one of the PT economists who said the new currency would not last more than three months.[19]

Lula had won the election with two different economic programs. The first was the PT's, running to forty pages, which provided a leftist critique of Cardoso's government that was the result of much internal discussion. The second was the much briefer four-page Letter to the Brazilian People, in which the PT leadership promised to continue the key lines of the Cardoso program and maintain international commitments, but would seek to reduce interest rates, end privatization, and create more jobs. Some joked that this was a letter to the international markets.

The circumstances in which Lula won in 2002 were not propitious. Argentina had defaulted on its debts. There had been a run on the real, virtually halving its value, and a Brazilian needed four reais to buy one U.S. dollar. Inflation was back up at 30 percent a year. Intuitively, Lula approved a rigorous economic policy to calm the fever. Palocci and Henrique Meirelles at the Central Bank were austere in carrying out commitments to the IMF and in achieving the "primary fiscal surplus" that was needed to service the public and international debt. Many traditional PT supporters, who had taken the Letter to the Brazilian People with a grain of salt, were disappointed.

The surplus agreed to was of 4.25 percent of GNP. By 2004, Brazil was getting a surplus of 4.59 percent. Even though the agreement with the IMF ended when the IMF loans were repaid, the government maintained its target, and continued to overshoot. It reached 4.84 percent in 2005 (R93.5 billion), and 5.77 percent in the first six months of 2006. Brazil's public debt, which had been climbing since 1994, came down under the new government to 50 percent of GNP.[20] At the same time, the government maintained one of Cardoso's key instruments in cleaning up the public accounts: the law of fiscal responsibility. It was an anti-inflationary device that limited public spending to what could be raised in taxes.

This tight approach, only slightly loosened after Palocci was forced to resign by a scandal in early 2006, irritated many PT militants. They pointed out that the excess over the government's target in 2005 was worth R11.4 billion, or 27 percent more than all the money invested in the Bolsa-Família. The government seemed to be doing exactly what the PT had criticized previous governments for: it was curtailing social programs to please international bankers. When the presidential election came around in 2006, both Heloísa Helena and Crístovam Buarque attacked Lula on this ground.

Lula's reply was that he was creating space for social programs—hikes in the *salário mínimo*, the Bolsa-Família, and jobs. Probably his weakest point was employment. In a populist flourish, in the 2002 campaign he had claimed that he could create ten million new jobs. The Brazilian economy, as in other developing countries, included both registered and informal jobs. Registered jobs provided more security, yet covered only a minority of the workforce.[21] Independent analysis suggested that, with most of his term gone, his government had seen only 4.8 million new registered jobs.[22]

Inevitably, job creation was erratic, following ups and downs in the economic cycle. In 2005, there were 1.83 million new registered jobs, slightly fewer than the 1.86 million of 2004. Growth was greatest in services, commerce, and construction, but disappointing in agriculture. Significantly, 24 percent of the jobs created in 2005 were in the public sector, principally at the municipal level. The PSDB-PFL opposition fastened on the public sector growth, attacking it as a brake on the economy and a source of patronage for the PT and its allies. But social programs needed staff to deliver them, and much of the anger over the slow start to the Bolsa-Família derived from local incompetence.

For Lula's poorer supporters, one of the government's most valuable achievements was a drop in the price of food and other necessities, at exactly the same time that rises in the minimum salary and the Bolsa-Família were kicking in. It was an argument he used in interviews, and at his last public rally prior to the first round of the presidential election, in São Bernardo on 28 September. Where a housewife had had to pay R13 for a standard bag of supermarket rice in 2003, she was now paying R5.90. He claimed credit and asked housewives to vote for him.

Others argued that the fall in prices had little to do with the government as such, but reflected the inability of the agricultural sector to raise prices, and the impact of imports when the real was strong. In fact there were various features of the Brazilian economy that perturbed analysts and different constituencies. There was the slow growth of the economy. There was the size of the public sector and the tax burden—a burden that was unequally shared, as companies and rich individuals found many ways of avoiding it. There was a growing export dependence on primary products, and deindustrialization, especially in the ABC suburbs around São Paulo that had been the cradle for the PT.

The slow pace of the economy—running at half the South American average in the last year of Lula's first term—was extremely disconcerting. The PT had been founded in reaction to the compression of wages during the "economic miracle" of the dictatorship. But that did not mean that the party and its leaders did not want to see growth; they were aware that it was a necessity, given the degree of poverty and the rate of growth of the population, which was heading toward the two hundred million mark. Talking to ordinary Brazilians, one is constantly asked, "If the country is so rich in resources, why are so many of us poor?" And, "Why doesn't this country get a move on?"

In August 2006, the newsmagazine *Veja* asked seven Nobel prizewinners in economics to say why they thought that Brazil was not doing as well as China or India. It pointed out that in the decade from 1996 to 2005, those two countries had had annual growth rates of 9 percent and 6 percent, respectively, while Brazil had had only 2 percent.[23] Other statistics suggested that while the other two had greatly increased their participation in world trade, Brazil had actually seen a decline.[24]

All the Nobel economists were North American, in general subscribing to neoclassical economics, and not specialists in Latin America. But what they said had resonance, even though they pointed out that China and India were starting from a much lower base than Brazil and therefore could expect to expand faster.

Among their criticisms were that Brazil was too bureaucratic for those starting or doing business, and still too protectionist; that it showed signs of the "crony capitalism" that had been criticized in southeast Asia, where the state and certain commercial sectors were too close to each other; that savings were too low and basic education too poor; and that the sociopolitical culture of Brazil, inherited from Portugal, was insufficiently dynamic. From where they stood, these economists disliked the populism they saw in Brazil and the "assistencialism" of the government. They did not recognize persisting inequity and continuing poverty as part of the problem.

Two economists who had specialized in Brazil, Werner Baer of the University of Illinois at Urbana-Champaign and Edmund Amann of the University of Manchester, argued that the Lula government's attempt to move on from economic orthodoxy to measures of equity and social inclusion was always going to be difficult. The tight monetary policy had impeded growth, the government's scope for discretionary spending was restricted, and it had not made the structural reforms in taxation and social security that would enable the country to escape the trap of low growth.[25]

By 2005, the corruption crises in Brasília were also beginning to cast a shadow on the country's ability to attract inward investment, although it was still the fifth most attractive country.[26] A World Bank study of the ability to do business in 155 nations, published that year, had Brazil near the bottom at 119. Pakistan, Russia, and many Latin American countries came in ahead, and it was reckoned that it took an average of 152 days to open a business in Brazil, 460 days to obtain necessary licenses, and the equivalent of more than 300 working days to pay taxes due to the complexity of the corporate tax system.[27]

The government was not doing a lot to reduce this bureaucracy, and although it had tried a modest social security reform, it made no attempt to simplify the tax system or make it fairer. It was prepared for quite drastic tariff cuts in the Doha round of the world trade talks, however, with the Finance Ministry proposing a reduction from 35 percent to 10.5 percent in the tariff protecting industrial goods made in Brazil. The Finance Ministry was supported by the Foreign Ministry, which realized that something had to be offered in exchange if the United States and European Union were to drop their agricultural subsidies and Brazil was to increase its agricultural exports. The proposal inevitably ran into opposition from the Development Ministry and industrial interests in São Paulo.

From the arrival of President Cardoso to the end of Lula's first term, the Brazilian economy went through substantial change. Its exports became more dependent on agricultural products, natural resources, and steel and iron ore. The role of services inside the economy increased. There had been deindustrialization in the greater São Paulo area, with firms moving to other parts of Brazil, or production leaving the country altogether.

The cutbacks at Volkswagen—which had started making cars in Brazil during the Kubitschek years, and whose profits at one stage had been crucial to the viability of the Wolfsburg company in Germany— were symptomatic. The firm said that it might close its São Bernardo do Campo factory entirely in 2010, and claimed that it was paying workers twice the rate of its competitors.[28]

The long, slow agony of the VARIG airline in 2005–2006 showed that not even the greatest names in Brazilian business were safe. This had been the national flagship for decades, and the romantic story of its founder, Rubem Berta, was known to schoolboys. Berta had developed a local airline for Rio Grande do Sul into an international service; at one stage, he had kept it from bankruptcy by using his stamp collection as collateral. But VARIG became uncompetitive, effectively went bust, and survived only in diminished form as VARIG-log.

The Brazilian economy could be caught in a pincer movement between low-cost imports from China and high value-added competition from Europe and North America. Lula visited China in 2004 with businessmen in his party, and his minister of agriculture, Roberto Rodrigues, spoke optimistically of the sales of soy and other foodstuffs that Brazil could make; but a year later, Luiz Furlan, the minister of development, was sent to China to try to persuade the Chinese to make voluntary restrictions on their exports. Brazil was concerned at the arrival of huge quantities of cheap textiles, shoes, tires, and machines. The fear of Chinese competition was not dissimilar to that shown by the European Union and the United States.[29]

Higher-end competition was also contributing to deindustrialization in Brazil. A good example lay in a decision by BMW, the German firm making the Mini small car in Britain, to transfer production of the engines from Brazil to Birmingham. The director of the British plant, Harald Kruger, said that although labor costs in Brazil were a third lower than in Britain, they made up only 15–20 percent of production costs. By making the engines closer to the Mini plant near Oxford, the firm would save money on transportation and storage, and improve efficiency.[30]

Nonetheless there were bright spots for Brazil. These included the export surplus in the Lula years, the success of Petrobrás in achieving self-sufficiency in petroleum and the exploitation of natural gas, and worldwide recognition for the country's biofuel program. Lula himself propagandized for the success of biofuel, which had some seventy years of research and development behind it. It became a serious gasoline substitute in the 1970s, as the "Proalcool" program, part of the military regime's response to the oil price shock. By 1985 this fuel, based on sugar alcohol, was powering 90 percent of the new cars in Brazil.

But with the coming of democracy, a reduction in subsidies, and stability in oil prices, biofuel lost its charm in the 1980s. In the new century, with worry about greenhouse gas emissions and a new spurt in oil prices, biofuel suddenly became attractive again. A Fiat subsidiary in Brazil, called Magneti Marelli, devised a computer control unit that allowed cars to switch use among biofuel, compressed natural gas, or gasoline, in combinations that reflected availability and price. This flexi-fuel solution offered advantages. Brazil was in a position to export not only biofuel, but also an advanced technology.

The Agriculture Ministry was optimistic that, with improvements in technology, the country could greatly increase its position in international markets. While Brazil remained the world's biggest producer of coffee beans, it had only 2 percent of the market in instant coffee. It had similar opportunities for condensed milk. But the instant coffee issue had been an irritation for decades: multinationals based in the developed countries juggled their preferences and commercial strategies to retain for themselves the added value from converting beans to instant coffee.

Brazil's faith in world trade rules, as compared to bilateral arrangements or the U.S.-driven Free Trade Area of the Americas, was based on its successes with the WTO. The Lula government continued the steady campaign against agricultural subsidies by the United States and European Union that had been begun by trade diplomats in the Cardoso presidency.

Brazil picked product areas, such as sugar and cotton, of economic significance and it chose appropriate allies for its appeals to the WTO. In 2005, in conjunction with Australia and Thailand, it scored a big victory over the EU on sugar. The EU was paying its sugar beet farmers three times the world price for every metric ton exported, and was also subsidizing the reexport of cané sugar. After the Uruguay trade round ended in 1994, the EU was permitted to export 1.27 million metric tons of subsidized sugar, but the Europeans cheated. The exports crept up to 4 million metric tons, and Brazil and its sugar producers estimated that they could reach 7 million by 2007.

The WTO, in two successive rulings, told the EU to cut back. Brazil, as a large-scale and relatively cheap grower, with 40 percent of the world market already, could expect to benefit in the international arena. It was a blow against the distortions of agricultural subsidies, also debated in the Doha trade round. But it was not good news for some higher-cost developing countries that had been selling cane sugar to the Europeans. Producers such as Mauritius and Jamaica, which had preferential access to the European market under the special postcolonial arrangements for African, Caribbean, and Pacific states, could expect to suffer. By 2006, small traditional producers such as Barbados had pulled out of sugar almost entirely.

Brazil also took on the United States successfully at the WTO over cotton. In spite of the WTO's ruling against it, the United States continued to subsidize its cotton farmers illegally. Luiz Furlan, the minister for development, decided that it might be more in Brazil's interest to use the ruling as a bargaining chip, to obtain entry into the U.S. market for more Brazilian products, rather than to insist on immediate compliance, however.

The successes at the WTO, and the country's actual significance in certain world markets, explained why Lula in power could not go along with the simplistic anti-WTO and antiglobalization cries of his former allies in the World Social Forum. His government saw trade rules as an advantage, not a conspiracy. They allowed all countries, and especially the stronger developing countries, to limit the economic power of the North Atlantic blocs.

8 CORRUPTION AND SCANDAL

Brazilian history is replete with stories of corruption, both large and small. The country is geographically immense, and for a long time communications were poor. Policing, even when honest in intention, has proved difficult. Family and local obligations have often been valued more highly than obedience to the law or scrupulous probity. Brazil is a federation in which spending powers are distributed among central government, states, and municipalities, and alliances are essential in politics. A pork barrel approach among politicians can degenerate rather easily into the frank abuse of public money.

The PT, in the gradual return to democracy in the 1980s, was the chief proponent of a more ethical approach. Representing workers, it criticized unjustified rewards for managers and shareholders. Standing up for the poor, it attacked the misuse of public funds by politicians and the rich. Above all, in a new democracy, it wanted to see higher standards in public life. The various ideological currents in the party, whether derived from Marxism, Catholicism, or the new social movements, were united here. It was why the PT harried Fernando Collor to impeachment via a parliamentary commission of inquiry (CPI in Portuguese). The party also attacked Cardoso for buying the votes that changed the Constitution so that he could run for reelection, and smelled a whiff of payoff in some of his privatizations.

So why was it that, at the end of Lula's first term in 2006, his government was seen as exceptionally corrupt, and voters took their revenge by denying him reelection on the first round? It is worth running through a number of the key scandals and then looking at some of the issues that lay behind them.

The first serious scandal was exposed early in Lula's first term, when the magazine *Época* ran a front-page story, backed up with tape recordings, that showed that Waldomiro Diniz, secretary for parliamentary affairs in the Casa Civil of the presidency, had attempted to extort money from the boss of a popular illegal gambling game, the *jogo de bicho*. He had attempted to get money from one Carlos Cachoeira in the 2002 electoral campaign.

The story ran at a bad moment for the government, when Fome Zero was starting poorly, and before the new Ministry for Social Development and the Combat of Hunger had been created to get Bolsa-Família running in its place. Diniz was responsible to José Dirceu, who was the minister for the Casa Civil. Dirceu offered to resign, but Lula, who wished to show loyalty to those who had helped build the PT, rejected the offer instantly.[1]

Only a few days later, Lula told Ricardo Kotscho, his press secretary, that he had just committed the worst political error in his life; later still, Dirceu also told Kotscho that he should have insisted on resigning then. Worse was to come for Dirceu and Lula, but in retrospect this probably was one of Lula's biggest mistakes, in that it failed to distance him, his party, and the government from the crime and political accountability for malpractice. It also raised questions, which became more pressing later, as to how the PT had financed the expensive election campaign of 2002.

The defining scandal of the middle period of Lula's first term exploded in an edition of *Veja* on 18 May 2005, which showed Mauricio Marinho, a manager of the Correios—the state postal service—taking a bribe. He had been appointed by Roberto Jefferson, president of the PTB, one of the venal allies of the government whose votes were essential to Lula's majority in Congress. The report, backed up by secret video footage, stated that the PTB was milking these appointments to raise money for the party.[2] This was a party that had emerged from the 2002 elections with twenty-six federal deputies, but which by the time of the scandal, using time-honored inducements to others to change their party colors, had as many as forty-seven.

Around a fortnight later, Jefferson, criticized on all sides for corruption, detonated what the press described as a "human bomb." Essentially, he said that the government led by the PT had a system for paying a monthly salary—the *mensalão*—to deputies in other parties to vote with the government. He put the blame on José Dirceu, who was coordinating the government majority; Delúbio Soares, the PT's treasurer; and Silvio Pereira, the PT's secretary-general. Two days after Jefferson spoke to the *Folha de São Paulo*,[3] the Council of Ethics in Congress opened hearings on his possible expulsion; the day after that, in spite of strong efforts by the government to prevent it, a parliamentary CPI was set up to investigate corruption in the post office. Only fourteen PT deputies and one PT senator, Eduardo Suplicy—who was in tears as he did so—were among the 236 deputies and fifty-two senators who signed the request for a commission.

After that the scandal rapidly escalated. TV and press provided a stupefied nation with daily briefings on the crisis in Brasília. Jefferson explained that an advertising man named Marcos Valério was funneling monies to the deputies, a channel that was nicknamed the *valerioduto*. He said that Silvio Pereira was in overall command of a system for taking money from state entities, which was used to reward the small parties that supported the PT in Congress. This funding was being transferred via what was described as a "second account" (*caixa dois*), an illegal, unreported account.

Very shortly there were three parliamentary commissions sitting simultaneously—on the postal service, on gambling (Bingo), and on the *mensalão*. Their hearings were televised. Heads were rolling. By 13 June, Dirceu had left his ministerial post in the Casa Civil, and was soon having to defend himself in the Council of Ethics because he was also a federal deputy.

Three banks were incriminated in the illegal transfer of funds—the Banco do Brasil, Banco Rural, and Banco de Minas Gerais. José Genoino, the president of the PT, resigned after an aide to his brother was arrested with R200,000 in a bag and $100,000 in his underpants.

Silvio Pereira resigned as PT secretary-general after it was revealed that the Banco do Brasil had lent the party R20 million in the first two years of the government.

Increasing attention was given to Marcos Valério and his testimony, from which it appeared that he had been overcharging the government for publicity and advertising work, and had been sending money abroad via accounts used for money laundering. The CPI investigating corruption in the post office asked that eighteen deputies be expelled, while Severino Cavalcanti, now presiding over the Chamber of Deputies, tried to protect Dirceu from expulsion.

Fingers also started to be pointed at Duda Mendonça, the marketing genius behind Lula's "peace and love" campaign in 2002. By August he was telling a CPI that the PT had paid him for his services through an offshore account in the Bahamas, and that R10.5 million had been hidden from the Electoral Commission in an illegal second account. The federal police asked for Supreme Court permission to block the accounts of his company in the Bahamas.

Later in August, the hue and cry moved against Antonio Palocci, whose conservative management of the Ministry of Finance had calmed the fears raised in advance of a Lula victory. A former aide of his, when he was mayor of Ribeirão Preto, said that he had been receiving monthly payments of R50,000 in 2001–2 from businessmen in the city. Palocci had been passing this money on to the PT. Lula stated that he would keep Palocci in his ministry.

The scandal-hunting was largely focused on the PT and the government, but was not exclusive to them. By September, Severino Cavalcanti, the president of the Chamber of Deputies, was being attacked for taking bribes from the owner of a restaurant in the Congress building. Sebastião Buani, the restaurateur, said that he had paid Severino R110,000 in 2002 and 2003 to extend his concession. Severino gave three different accounts of his actions, denied that he had signed the contract for the restaurant, and when it became clear that he had, denounced the document as false.

Severino Cavalcanti was the self-styled "king of the low clergy"—the backbenchers in Congress who seemed more concerned with their spoils and privileges than with their role as legislators for the good of the country. After a pilgrimage through a succession of conservative parties, he was now in the PP, the small party that included Paulo Maluf and was also supporting the government. He had denied that the *mensalão* existed, and told the *Folha de São Paulo* on 29 August that the fact that deputies had benefited from an unreported second account did not justify their expulsion from Congress.

Lula had given the impression of working with him, to try and tamp down the crisis, but opposition deputies threatened to boycott the Chamber if Cavalcanti continued in office. By the end of September, he had been forced out and, in an important victory for the government, Aldo Rebelo of the PCdoB was elected in his place.

The Greens and the PSOL, the newly established leftist party, were violent in their criticism of corruption in the PT and its allies. But there was a certain hesitancy in the attitude of the PSDB and PFL. One reason why many Brazilians remarked that "it will all end in pizza"—that politicians would get together to make sure no one was really punished—was a suspicion that the opposition parties also might not look good in the spotlight. In fact, Senator Eduardo Azeredo, the president of the PSDB, resigned his position in October, after information emerged that showed that his election campaign in 1998 had benefited from Marcos Valério and his *valerioduto* of illicit money.

The crisis in Brasília in 2005 had damaged Lula and the PT. It had spawned other stories, such as an allegation by *Veja* that the party's campaign in 2002 had been subsidized with millions of Cuban dollars.[4] There was common gossip among conservative opponents that the PT had a plan for twenty years in power, and that Dirceu was masterminding this by tapping the incomes of parastatals, using his skills as a Havana-trained apparatchik learned thirty years previously. Along the way there was an exposure of the rapid rise to wealth of Lula's eldest son, known much to his annoyance as Lulinha, which Lula dismissed as an invasion of his son's privacy.

But the crisis had also shown that the institutions of Brazil's young democracy were actually working. Even if there were systemic weaknesses in Congress and the parties, the parliamentary inquiry commissions were effective. Their processes might not always be fair to witnesses and they allowed for grandstanding by deputies, but they were putting information into the public domain.

Furthermore, although it was also political, the ethics council had sought to do its job: by the end of 2005, both Jefferson and Dirceu had been expelled from Congress. The media and the federal police, operating in tandem with the CPIs, emerged with their standing enhanced. In March 2006, when the *mensalão* scandal was running out of steam in Brasília, the procurator-general listed forty persons he described as crooks, and fearlessly denounced "a criminal organization installed in the government." The public prosecution machinery, the Ministério Público, also seemed to work apolitically.

What was serious for the PT was that so many of its leaders, people hitherto respected who had worked hard to build the party, were casualties. The departure of Dirceu, Genoino, Pereira, and Delúbio Soares knocked out key personalities at the top. Those on the left of the party saw them as controllers in the dominant Campo Majoritario faction; they had made crucial compromises with Brazilian and international business in the year before Lula's presidential win. No one really knew what reassurances had been offered by this group, or how much money had been paid into party coffers in consequence.

The fact that some of them, like Genoino, had plainly not enriched themselves personally was no justification. In general the corruption coming to light was for the benefit of the party or, in the case of the *mensalão* payments, to maintain a governing majority in Congress. But it was not what the PT was supposed to be about. The PT was founded to be different. The critique of occult money was linked to a critique of shameless alliances and secret, undemocratic processes by the party leadership.

The problems were not only at the federal level. In the course of 2005, the police and campaigners made more effort to resolve the mystery of the murder of Celso Daniel, the PT mayor of Santo André, in the ABCD industrial belt around São Paulo. Daniel had been popular, a rising star in the PT, and was coordinating Lula's presidential campaign when he was kidnapped, tortured, and killed in January 2002. Two of Daniel's brothers made statements to the CPI on gambling (Bingo) two years later, and public interest was renewed because several of those involved in the case, including a lawyer who was trying to get to the bottom of it, were also murdered.

What became clear was that the PT in the city was requiring bus firms to make regular payments to the party. At a certain point this had blown up in the party's face and Daniel was killed. How far Daniel himself was responsible for this, or even knew of it, was still a matter of conjecture. But this picture of municipal corruption correlated with what was being said about Ribeirão Preto when Palocci was mayor.

The Daniel mystery was not resolved, but a non-PT case of corruption was. Paulo Maluf, the one time "bionic" governor of São Paulo in the military era, subsequently elected city mayor with Duda Mendonça's help, was sent to prison for forty-one days. He was by then seventy-four, and had been fending off accusations of corruption for years. A huge effort by the Ministério Público, lasting three years and probing his family's accounts in the Cayman Islands and Liechtenstein, produced evidence to the judiciary that he had made off with U.S. $500 million during his term as mayor. At a tough time for the PT, this win gave some satisfaction to Lula's supporters. But it was another sign of reduced tolerance for corruption by institutions required to combat it, and added to the public feeling that most politicians are rogues.

The corruption scandals of 2006 were perhaps less devastating to Lula's government than those of the previous year, though the so-called dossiegate helped prevent him from winning a first-round victory in the presidential election in October. It was not until after that failure that he and the PT acted to expel members under suspicion. There were four main cases: the scandal that forced Lula to get rid of Palocci; the case of the overpriced ambulances (nicknamed the *sanguessugas*, or bloodsuckers); the case of the "vampires"; and the attempt by an unintelligent intelligence unit of the PT to buy a dossier that was supposed to incriminate José Serra in the overpriced ambulances scandal.

Palocci was finally fired by Lula on 27 March 2006, after a steady buildup of reports and rumors of financial misbehavior during his administration in Ribeirão Preto that had started the previous August. Two of his aides were involved in the *Veja* allegation in October that the Cubans had smuggled three million dollars to the PT in 2002, to help pay for the election campaign. Hearings in the parliamentary commission on gambling produced evidence in early 2006 that Palocci was directly involved in taking illegal gaming money for the party. The final straw came when it emerged that one of the state banks, the Caixa Econômica Federal, had illegally broken into the bank account of a commissionaire in Brasília who had witnessed dubious comings and goings by Palocci. On the side there were also allegations that he and a group of friends from Ribeirão Preto were involved in louche parties in the capital.

Palocci, who had undoubtedly been hoping that the orthodox management of the economy and his international stature would help him survive, said that the economy was in heaven but he was in hell. His replacement by Guido Mantega, who had gone from the Planning Ministry to run the development bank BNDES, caused hardly a ripple. But any credit Lula might have won by getting rid of Palocci was offset by his speech at Palocci's farewell party, where he called him a dear companion and "more than a brother."

The ambulance scam operated by a firm called Planam was, to begin with, more damaging to the Lula government than to the PT. It had begun during the Cardoso government and illustrated the way in which congressmen could abuse their positions to enrich themselves. The scam involved deputies in Brasília passing amendments to the federal budget that permitted municipalities to purchase ambulances at inflated prices, with the deputies then getting some 10 percent of the money.[5] Members of small parties supporting the government—the PTB, PL, and PP— were key beneficiaries.[6]

It was a complicated scam, because it involved some sixty mayors as well the congressmen, and it came to light in 2006 as the key players in Planam—Luiz Vedoin and his father, Darci Vedoin—began to explain what had happened. A CPI was set up, and it discovered that a scandal that had started during the Cardoso years had carried on into the Lula government. This implicated Humberto Costa, the first of Lula's health ministers.

Lula had decreed a stop on debts contracted by the previous government, which created a problem costing R8 million for Planam. After a meeting with Humberto Costa, however, and payment of a "commission" to his office of R400,000, Costa released R30 million for the purchase of hospital equipment in the interior. With a tendering process that was not transparent, Planam was able to get its money.

This bloodsuckers scandal, as it became known, overlapped with a wider issue of nontransparent tendering that was nicknamed the "vampires" scandal. It turned out that the Ministry of Health was a disaster zone, with corrupt and manipulated purchasing of supplies and equipment. Lobbyists, corrupt officials, and businessmen were all involved. The federal police made high-profile arrests of sixteen people in three cities in May 2004 in "Operation Vampire," and the scandal got new attention two years later in the context of the bloodsuckers.[7]

It was suggested that the "vampire" racket had started way back in Collor's time, and police thought that it might have skimmed off the enormous sum of two billion reais over the years. What was most serious from the viewpoint of the Lula government was that resources for the health service, a social service that needed investment rather than robbery, were being wrongly diverted.

These two scandals involving the Ministry of Health took on a completely different political complexion during the 2006 election campaign. In the middle of September, when Lula seemed to be comfortably ahead in the polls and looking forward to reelection in the first presidential round, Luiz Vedoin was arrested, and the PT treasurer in Mato Grosso and a former police agent working with the PT were picked up in an Ibis hotel in São Paulo. These two were arrested with R1.7 million and $248,000 in cash.

The police who arrested them indicated that this large sum was to buy a bloodsucker dossier from Vedoin. The dossier would implicate José Serra, Cardoso's former minister of health and now the favorite to be elected governor of São Paulo for the PSDB opposition. A video would show him at the handing over of some of the overpriced ambulances in Mato Grosso and suggest that he was personally involved in the fraud.

Attention shifted from the possibility that Serra had in any way been involved—there were also rumors of a second dossier that would implicate the PT—to the undoubted fact that the PT was involved in dirty tricks. The dossier was linked to an attack by Vedoin on Serra in an issue of the newsmagazine *IstoÉ*. But where had all the money come from? Was it true that the PT had been using underworld funds to buy the dossier? Lula, talking to journalists on his way to New York for the UN General Assembly meeting, had said it was time for the election campaign to get a bit dirty. Was this what he meant?

What had seemed like a plot to knock out Serra in the São Paulo race rapidly took on national consequences and created a serious reverse for Lula himself, because those involved in planning what the journalists labeled "dossiegate"[8] were not just in São Paulo, but were close to the president in Brasília. In São Paulo there was really only one person directly blamed, Hamilton Lacerda, who had been press secretary for Aloizio Mercadante's governorship campaign. He was sacked and Mercadante's campaign, which was already struggling, took a lethal blow.[9] Inevitably people asked how much Mercadante, who professed absolute innocence and total disgust, had known; he was accused at the least of poor judgment in selecting subordinates.

The real impact was felt in Brasília. Ricardo Berzoini, president of the PT and coordinator of Lula's reelection team, was accused of authorizing purchase of the dossier. Lula dismissed him, saying that he would not be able to do his job if he spent the next fortnight having to answer questions from the police and a CPI. He replaced him with Marco Aurélio Garcia.

Three people close to Lula had helped to buy the dossier and negotiate with *IstoÉ*. They formed part of an "intelligence unit" for the PT that had spectacularly misfired. They were: Freud Godoy, involved in the president's security, who resigned; Osvaldo Bargas, an old friend of Lula's from the days of the Metalworkers' Union, who had had a post in the Ministry of Labor and whose wife was Lula's private secretary; and Jorge Lorenzetti, a favorite of Lula's because of the quality of the barbecues he grilled for the president's private parties, who was supposed to be in charge of the intelligence unit.

Once more Lula's own judgment was called into question—his leniency to old friends, his lack of grip on his coalition government or even the party that owed him so much. Once more the involvement of the PT in dirty tricks seemed to undermine the stands it had taken in the past and the better aspects of Lula's government. Once more the media could ask how Lula's campaign was being paid for and whether all leftists were crooks, who would hang on to power at all costs.

Lula described the conspirators as "nuts" and "imbeciles." But the questions would not go away. On the eve of the poll an agent of the federal police released photos of all the cash, piled up in notes, to the press.[10] The public saw the money that would have bought the dossier. To an average voter it looked like a great deal of money. It would not make electors more likely to vote for Lula or candidates of the PT.

Behind much of the corruption that came to light in the Lula years was the tradition that politics was a business. It cost considerable sums to win an election; the type of proportional representation system that elected federal deputies, combining a party list with the percentage of votes needed to return a deputy, emphasized the need for individual popularity; rewards for a winner were considerable, in terms of income, the power to legislate, and even the right to award R2.5 million from the budget for a public facility such as a school or health clinic in his or her district. The biggest reward, if a deputy or party was part of the government majority, was the ability to nominate people for jobs. José Dirceu, at the height of his prime ministerial powers early in the government, when Lula described him as "the captain of our team," was responsible for twenty thousand positions of trust.

When in early 2005 there was an election for the president of the Chamber of Deputies, won by Severino Cavalcanti, it was reckoned that one million reais were being spent by the five candidates. A calculation at the time suggested that seventeen thousand people worked for the Chamber and its 513 deputies, and that each deputy was costing the country R70,130 a month. While each deputy was being paid R12,850 a month, he or she was getting a further R35,000 to hire staff, and R15,000 to keep an office in the district.[11]

A significant proportion of the deputies were already wealthy by Brazilian standards. After the 2002 election, more than one-fifth, 116 deputies, declared assets of more than one million reais to the election commission; after the 2006 election, this proportion was close to one-third, 165.[12]

But the relative luxury of the deputies themselves was nothing compared to the power of appointment. There were reckoned to be around fifty posts within the gift of the government that brought with them enormous power and budgets. They included presidencies of state banks, such as the Bank of Brazil, Banco do Nordeste, and Banco da Amazônia; Petrobrás and Eletrobrás; Brazil's airports corporation, Infraero; and IBAMA, which licenses timber extraction. Many of these posts were handed to PT loyalists or shared among members of the governing coalition.

The *mensalão* scandal exposed by Roberto Jefferson showed, for instance, that the president of the government reinsurance corporation, IRB, was expected to pay R400,000 a month to Jefferson's party, the PTB. But there was far more to this than such payments. People and firms would provide financial support to parties or candidates in return for the promise of lucrative appointments. Contracts given by parastatals could be overpriced, or handed to companies that were backing the relevant party.

Much of the coming and going in Brasília could be explained by this spoils system. Deputies would be paid to switch parties—which was why the PTB raised its total substantially in the course of 2003–6. Valdemar Costa Neto, then president of the small Partido Liberal (PL), said that the PT had obtained his party's support in Congress for a price of ten million reais. When the PMDB talked to Lula about providing more backing for the government in return for getting two ministries, it was the patronage the party would acquire that was as important as the ministerial posts themselves.

At the same time, while Congress was making waves in 2005 with its parliamentary commissions, its own standing suffered. There was little accountability to electors between elections, so deputies could switch parties with impunity. The actual output of Congress in terms of new laws was modest, and much legislation was coming from the presidency in the form of "provisional measures" (*medidas provisorias*). The initiative that led to a referendum on gun sales, although properly within the competence of Congress, had been the result of an unusual burst of energy.

Lula himself, and the PT he had helped to found, knew all about the weaknesses of Congress and how the political system worked. At one point during the *mensalão* crisis Lula claimed that his government was doing more to combat corruption than its predecessors, and although this did not get much of a hearing then, and did not deal with the kind of big political corruption exposed in 2005, he had a point.

Among the measures the government had taken was to issue a presidential decree in June 2005 that required all federal government tenders to be advertised on the Internet. Following a commitment he had made to Transparency International Brazil when he was a candidate in 2002, Lula also established a Secretariat for the Prevention of Corruption in Brazil's federal audit mechanism, the Controladoria-Geral da União (CGU). In a partnership agreement with the CGU, Transparency Brazil prepared a "risk map" for public institutions in Brazil, showing where secret or poorly controlled decision making can lead to corruption.[13]

The government also launched a national strategy to combat money laundering, with the involvement of more than forty public entities, and encouraged an increasingly efficient and professional federal police force. As was seen in arrests of PT members who had tried to purchase the anti-Serra dossier, police action could be embarrassing to the government. But before he himself was hurt by those arrests, Aloizio Mercadante had written with pride that the police had conducted sixty-seven anticorruption operations, arresting 1,300 people (515 of them federal civil servants), and in twelve big swoops had put an end to frauds costing R67.8 billion.[14]

As for Congress itself, there was continued discussion of the need to strengthen party loyalty; talk of a switch in the electoral system, so that deputies would be chosen by defined geographical districts and not as part of a statewide list; and limits on party spending. Lula himself in 2006 spoke for a while about the need for a new constitutional assembly to carry through political reform. He backed off the idea, however, when opponents pointed out that the 1988 Constitution had not been in operation for very long, and that Hugo Chávez in Venezuela had given constitutional reform a bad name.[15]

Some changes had taken place. The 2006 election took place under new rules designed to reduce party spending, and hence the party's dependence on questionable campaign financing. Parties were not allowed to hand out shirts or gifts, and the expensive *showmicios*—rallies with top-class singers and entertainers—were banned. The Electoral Commission remained small, however, and not well geared to police the problem of the *caixa dois*, the hidden party funds.

Two alterations to the rules were also aimed at increasing party loyalty—the verticalization rule, discussed earlier, and the barrier clause, which was expected to take effect in 2006. Lula himself had wanted to change the verticalization rule, which required parties to stick to the same alliances through presidential, federal, and state level elections. Presumably he thought that he, and perhaps the PT, would have more room to maneuver if party consistency were not required and he could give preference to deals with personalities.

But the barrier clause was aimed directly at the small parties, usually the most venal and "physiological" in the post-1988 democracy. A law passed in 1997, but due to take effect only in 2006, stated that a party would have to obtain at least 5 percent of the national vote for federal deputies, and 2 percent in at least nine of the twenty-seven states. Those that failed, and it was anticipated that around a half-dozen would, would lose the right to state funding, have only minimal rights to free TV time, and would lose privileges not only in the Chamber of Deputies but in state assemblies and town councils.[16]

The impact of the barrier clause was likely to see a rush, after the 2006 elections, by small parties wishing to join together to get enough deputies, or by individual deputies wanting to join one of the bigger parties. In December of that year, however, the Supreme Court ruled that the law creating the barrier was unconstitutional, in that it rode roughshod over the rights of minorities.[17] But politicians had worked on the assumption that the law would stand.

The general tendency in Brazilian politics since 1994 had been to see an increasing grip, particularly at the federal level, by four large parties—the

PT, the PMDB, the PSDB, and the PFL. Of these, the PT had made the most of its anticorruption stance before Lula won the 2002 election. The PMDB had emerged from the parliamentary opposition to the military dictatorship, but its hands had become soiled by the "physiological" traditions of horse-trading. The PSDB, although more middle-class than the PT and willing to make ideological alliances to its right, had also included victims and exiles from the dictatorship.

The PSDB had started and remained powerful in São Paulo, and it claimed to stand for a modern approach in administration and public tendering. One of the advantages quoted for Cardoso's privatizations was that, if the scope of state firms was reduced, the opportunity for political corruption would likewise be reduced. But the PT and other critics thought that some privatizations had put money into the hands of friends of the PSDB, and its anticorruption claims were suspect.

The fourth big party was the PFL, whose ancestry lay in a liberal breakaway from the promilitary ARENA and PDS parties; its prominent members, such as Marco Maciel, had helped to end the dictatorship by congressional action in the mid-1980s. Their subtle operations in Brasília had converged with the street protests of the PT and its allies in the *Diretas Já* campaign. Nonetheless, it was the most conservative of the big parties, with powerful bastions in the northeast, the most economically backward and politically corrupt region. The military had introduced electoral rules that favored the northeast, giving it more federal deputies than it was entitled to on a population basis. Although the PFL was vigorous in attacking Lula's administration for corruption, few thought its own record was unblemished.

Although there was a strong consensus that increased party loyalty would diminish systemic corruption, the parties themselves were coming to seem more alike in policy. Hence the focus on personality, family, and local loyalties and the exchange of favors was likely to continue to play a large part in voters' choices. Ideology, outside the small Marxist parties, had rarely been a determining factor in Brazil; its hold was weakening in Europe and North America also.

The growing similarity in party policies by 2006 was analyzed by *Veja* on the eve of the elections.[18] On a wide range of issues the four big parties were taking the same line: each was in favor of inflation targets, continuing political reforms to strengthen party fidelity, targets for surplus in the government accounts, and the Bolsa-Família. Each was cautious about racial quotas and divided over suggestions—which Lula himself had made—that the country should return to the 1988 Constitution and limit presidents to a single term of five years.

The PT parted company with the others in that it was against independence for the Central Bank and against exchange controls to protect the agricultural sector from bankruptcies. It was with the PFL but against the other two in seeking to deal with the deficits in pensions and welfare (Previdência Social) by combating fraud rather than more drastic action, such as increasing taxation on the retired. One area not looked at by *Veja*, which featured in the election campaign, concerned privatization. Lula and the PT had made a commitment not to continue Cardoso's privatization policy, and they had stuck to it during Lula's first term. It was fairly clear that if the PSDB-PFL coalition won the 2006 election, it would look to sell other state assets.

But how had the PT reacted to the reports of corruption that were dominating the media by the middle of 2005? The party was not being given strong leadership by Lula. Lula himself was depressed, doubting whether he should run for reelection the following year, and saying that he had been betrayed and had had no idea what was going on as senior party colleagues came under attack and resigned.

The truth was that the PT had changed from its early idealistic days at the start of the 1980s. There was a *nomenklatura* of apparatchiks. There were jobs to be had in the party, and members of the party could get certain jobs outside it, in local government and elsewhere. As one observer told me, "In the 1980s, the PT was against the establishment. In the 1990s, it engaged with the establishment. By the 2000s, it was part of the establishment."[19] It had become dangerously like the other parties, even if those of its leaders who were tainted were apparently using corruption to support a cause, rather than for personal enrichment.

To begin with, the PT seemed punch-drunk with the rapid explosion of disclosures. Some members left to join other parties, especially the PSOL, but also the Greens and the PDT. An act of "refoundation" took place in São Paulo, in September 2005, at which PT members took stock and decided that the party needed to get back on track. It was anticipated that the party would be punished at the polls in 2006. A few prominent sympathizers expressed their disgust openly.

One of the most pained and pertinent was the progressive Catholic Frei Betto,[20] a former Dominican and journalist. Back in the 1970s, he had gone underground, been imprisoned by the military, and sheltered people on the run. He had stayed with the da Silva family at the height of the strikes, when Lula's life was in danger, as a comfort and protection for Marisa and the children. He said, "Not even in the years of the dictatorship could the right manage to demoralize the left as this PT nucleus has done in such a short time. Under the dictatorship, in spite of all the suffering, persecutions, jailings, and assassinations, we went forth with our heads held high, sure that we were contributing to the redemocratization of the country. Now, no. These leaders will demoralize the party and splash mud over the whole of the Brazilian left."[21]

But the bulk of the party stayed loyal. It was not clear whether this was out of appreciation for what the government was doing, a sense that the PT was entitled to do what the rest were up to, or weary cynicism at one more blast of hostility from the media. The basic solidarity with the leadership was demonstrated in the election for a new president of the PT, caused by Genoino's departure, in September and October 2005.

Out of a total party membership of more than 800,000, nearly 315,000 voted in the first round, with seven candidates representing different factions. Ricardo Berzoini, from the progovernment Campo Majoritario, was comfortably ahead of the divided groups further to the left. Berzoini, a former minister of education, had been parachuted in to become secretary-general of the PT after Silvio Pereira departed during the *mensalão* crisis. Although the Campo Majoritario lost ground in the national executive, it maintained control in most of the states.

In a runoff against Raul Pont, former PT mayor of Porto Alegre in Rio Grande do Sul, Berzoini was safely reelected. Attempts to review the PT membership of some of those involved in the corruption crisis were postponed until after the 2006 election and, as will be seen in the next chapter, a number, including José Genoino and Antonio Palocci, ran as PT candidates for the Chamber of Deputies and were successfully elected.

Furthermore, the PT's membership was not hurt numerically by the crisis. There was a clear disconnect between the outrage felt by much of the media and expressed by Brazilians on the street and the attitudes taken by those who belonged to or were joining the party. In January 2006, the party had 864,273 members, an increase of 2.1 percent compared with the previous January. Altogether it had lost 5,418 members and recruited 29,583 in the crisis year.

It is instructive to compare this reaction with the sharp reduction in membership of the British Labour Party, especially after a Labour government embarked on the unpopular Iraq war in 2003. As in Brazil, many Labour Party people disliked the conservative economic policy of their government, and the war triggered further disillusionment. But in Brazil, in spite of a few high-profile defections, the party held together.

In Brazil, of course, it had taken a quarter of a century to elect the first PT-led government, and militants did not turn their back on it lightly. Also, there was the Lula factor. Opinion polls at the height of the crisis suggested that a majority of Brazilians thought that their president was at least aware of the corruption, even though he might not have connived at it. Roberto Jefferson claimed that he had mentioned the *mensalão* strategy to Lula some months before it became public knowledge. But, for many in the PT, Lula remained a messianic figure. Jefferson, by contrast, was remembered as an attack dog for the unquestionably corrupt President Collor; to PT loyalists, his testimony would always be suspect.

And where was Lula on the long-drawn-out corruption crisis that dominated headlines in the second half of his government? Why did he not act more firmly to maintain the PT's ethical tradition, which, as Frei Betto implied, had been a product of the hard struggle against the dictatorship? Why was he so reluctant to exercise leadership in attacking corruption and the corrupt—so that the Brazilian law society (Ordem dos Advogados Brasileiros, OAB) seriously considered mounting a case for impeachment?[22]

Lula's public reactions seemed inconsequential and feeble, suggesting that he did not know what was going on, that he had been betrayed, that it was all a diversion from his important task of governing Brazil. By 2006, he was claiming credit for sacking Dirceu and Palocci. It was only after his failure to win reelection in the first round of the 2006 presidential election that he got the PT to sack those accused of buying the anti-Serra dossier.

But there was far more to it. Lula was seriously implicated in the secretive business of party funding, in the manipulation of alliances in Congress, and in the unpleasant political culture of postdictatorship Brazil. Party funding has been an issue in other democracies where demand for funds outstrips the members' subscriptions; in the United Kingdom, for example, there was a police investigation into the alleged sale of honors to finance the Labour Party. The costs of the Lula campaign in 2002 seem to have been met by business donations, set against the prospect of overpriced government contracts and jobs with the ability to spend large federal budgets. Whether it was true that Dirceu planned to use the government's patronage to entrench a PT hegemony remains unclear. But Lula himself, at the time of his Letter to the Brazilian People during the 2002 campaign, must have been aware that there were financial aspects to the statement. Later he implied that every party has its *caixa dois*, and always did have.

It was Lula's own decision, overriding the views of Dirceu, to make alliances with the PTB and the smaller, least-principled parties in Congress. Knowing what he did about the reasons why such parties would back a government, he could not have been entirely surprised to learn of the *mensalão*. He may have felt that this way he had more freedom of political action. But these alliances were bound to have a price.

Finally, the corruption scandals symbolized the extent to which Lula himself had come to terms with the prevailing political culture. He was not going to go on tilting at windmills. He needed the votes of the two-thirds of the electorate that had refused to back him on three previous occasions. He did not want to retire as a gallant loser; he would do anything Duda Mendonça suggested and make whatever compromises were required in order to win the presidency.

The story left open the question of what a reelected Lula and a renewed Congress might do about these issues after 2007. Thanks to good if not always unbiased journalism, the nature of corruption in the Brazilian system was much better understood at the end of his first term than at the start. Lula was making favorable noises about reform, but it was not clear whether this would be a serious commitment by the PT or a second coalition government. Much would depend on pressure exerted by bodies outside politics, such as Transparency Brazil, the Catholic Church, the OAB, and the media. There was still a slight possibility that if the president was found to be directly linked to egregious corruption, an impeachment campaign might be mounted.

9 THE ELECTIONS OF 2006

Lula's last big rally, on the eve of the first round of the presidential election on 1 October 2006, was a vintage occasion. He spoke to a crowd of more than three thousand people, the majority waving PT flags, at a big open space called the Area Verde in São Bernardo, his hometown where he himself voted. For an observer, buying a can of beer and watching with the excited crowd, it was a reminder that Lula and the PT were still a force to be reckoned with. Both had been seriously battered over the previous four years; both would survive.

Lula's voice was hoarse after speaking all over the country. Yet he marched up and down the stage, talking for thirty-five minutes, acting like a much younger man. He joked that the mayor was trying to sabotage the meeting, because the lights in the square had been switched off. He hugged José Alencar, his vice presidential colleague.

He brought Marisa before the audience, and praised and thanked her. Women used to be prisoners; now they had equality. Marisa herself had never complained when he had gone to prison; she was part of the struggle. He had half the cabinet on stage with him and, at a certain point, asked Luiz Marinho, his minister of labor, to give the latest figures on job creation. He had even been patient when Eduardo Suplicy, running again to be PT senator in São Paulo, sang his traditional rendering of Bob Dylan's "Blowin' in the Wind."

Lula's speech was populist and nostalgic. He recalled the police and military helicopters flying over the Vila Euclides in the days of the dictatorship, his drinks with union colleagues at home, his vow that "Nothing can hold back the Brazilian worker," even before he helped to start the PT. He attacked the elite; the press, which had run so many hostile articles against him;[1] former president Cardoso, who he said would have preferred that only those who would vote for him should have the vote. The elite was so prejudiced it "would like to change the people."[2] He did not directly mention the crisis over the anti-Serra dossier, or why he had chosen not to take part in the final TV debate with Alckmin, Buarque, and Helena.

Lula was not pronouncing policy, he was rallying the faithful. Other speakers from the platform said that he had done more in three and a half years than his predecessors had in five hundred. The slogan was "Lula de novo, com a força do povo" (Lula once more, with the support of the people), and the call was for Lula to win on the first round, and Mercadante, the PT candidate to govern São Paulo, on the second. The crowd let off firecrackers and sang, "Olé, olé ola, Lula, Lula!" Journalists noticed that on the platform were two federal deputies questionably absolved by the Chamber of Deputies as the mensalão scandal wound down, José Mentor and Luiz Carlos da Silva, always known as Professor Luizinho, and a businessman named Paulo Okamotto, who had paid off a debt for the president.

Lula's team seemed fairly confident at this point, three days before the election, that he would gain the 50 percent of votes plus one that would mean victory in the first round. It was already clear that Mercadante and the other candidates for the São Paulo governorship had little hope of stopping a runaway victory for José Serra. What would happen elsewhere was less predictable, although the PSDB was also coasting to victory in the big state of Minas Gerais, where Aécio Neves, the popular grandson of Tancredo Neves, was seeking reelection as governor. As usual, voting was compulsory, and in some states including São Paulo, there was a ban on alcohol sales during the hours the electronic election machines were running.

The election campaign had been less hectic and participative than in previous years. In the city of São Paulo, for example, there were few posters displayed in flats and houses. The limitations on free gifts and on the appearance of singers at rallies dampened enthusiasm. Even so, Lula's campaign spent R41.96 million in the first month, and Alckmin's R18.89 million.[3] Lula himself seemed more populist, more focused on getting out his poorer supporters, than in 2002.[4]

But what actually occurred, when the Electoral Commission tallied the results a day or so later, surprised many. Lula, who had seemed comfortably ahead, got only 48.6 percent of the vote. The underrated Alckmin, who had been below 40 percent in recent opinion polls, and below 30 percent three months earlier, came in with 41.6 percent. The two candidates to the left of Lula, Heloísa Helena of PSOL and Crístovam Buarque of the PDT, got only 6.8 percent and 2.6 percent, respectively—less than expected. When at the last moment many Brazilians made up their minds whom to vote for, apparently around 6 percent of voters backed away from Lula after his final rally. He said that the infamous anti-Serra dossier, and the pictures of the money to pay for it, had shot him in the foot.

So what had gone wrong for Lula? This was the first time in Brazil's young democracy that a ruling president had been forced to fight again. He had in excess of six million fewer votes than he had received four years before, when he beat Serra in the second round.

In reality, Lula had been competing for reelection since early in 2006, using the various government tools at his disposal, from the release of "pothole money" to mend federal roads, to the steering of government and parastatal support to the states and municipalities governed by the PT and its friends.[5] A package to help homebuyers with low interest loans and to provide incentives for firms to build houses for their staff was launched a fortnight before the election.[6] Overseas visits, such as the one in March where Lula was the guest of the Queen of England, or his appearance again at a G8 meeting, were managed for their impact at home.

He was arguing that he had started a transformation of Brazil from an unjust society and a slow-moving economy. He kept comparing his government favorably with that of Cardoso. His speeches in the 2006 election were noticeably more populist than they had been four years before.

This reflected some poll findings that working-class Brazilians were unimpressed by the endless reporting of corruption in Brasília, seeing this as a conspiracy by the elite against a government that was trying to do something for ordinary people. He warned that the PSDB-PFL coalition would resume privatizations and might cut back on the Bolsa-Família.

Sometimes Lula seemed hubristic, suggesting that he was a martyr like Tiradentes, the pioneer of independence, or even Jesus Christ. In free TV propaganda he said, "Lula has the face of Brazil and Brazil has the face of Lula"—rather as General de Gaulle in his heyday had seen himself as the embodiment of France. He quoted Fidel Castro in the dock, before his successful revolution in Cuba—"History will absolve me."

Still criticized by his opponents for his bad Portuguese and his use of slang and swearwords, Lula retained his instinctive ability to communicate with ordinary people, his extraordinary common touch. Members of the PSDB are known as toucans, because of their party colors. Lula said that they were always predatory birds: "I'm not an expert on toucans but in the Granja do Torto there is a little flock. From time to time a little group of toucans flies in from the National Park to the Granja do Torto. Do you know why? It is to eat the eggs and the fledglings of the birds in their nests. They are predators, in spite of their beauty. And what they did to Brazil was exactly the same. Look at the results—that was the treatment the poor got."[7]

Significantly, in the first-round campaign Lula dismissed the corruption allegations as essentially unimportant, though the authorities would investigate and if necessary prosecute. But candidates caught up in the *mensalão* or other scandals were allowed to stand again for the PT or with PT support—this included both Genoino and Palocci, who were looking to become PT federal deputies from the state of São Paulo—and some of them appeared on platforms with Lula.

But Lula's opponent, Geraldo Alckmin, was a more serious threat than he appeared. He was seven years younger than Lula and came from a small town in São Paulo state, Pindamonhangaba. His father had been a veterinarian and he had qualified as a doctor and anesthesiologist. Just as Lula had entered union politics by a fluke, so Alckmin at the age of nineteen had become a town councilor rather by chance. The then MDB, the tolerated opposition to the military, was looking for candidates and approached Alckmin after another had refused. In 1976, he became mayor.

Alckmin appeared to be a cold fish, introverted and uncharismatic. But he got elected as a state deputy in 1982, and a federal deputy in 1986. He was therefore a participant in the constituent assembly that Lula found so frustrating. For Alckmin it was a breakthrough. He was spotted by Mário Covas, then leading the PMDB in the Chamber of Deputies, who made him his deputy. His gifts as a practical politician, going through the Constitution line by line and negotiating with others, impressed Covas, who made him his vice governor when he was elected governor of São Paulo in 1994.

Although he failed in an attempt to get elected as mayor of the city of São Paulo in 2000, when Marta Suplicy for the PT defeated Maluf in a runoff, he became governor unexpectedly when Covas died in office, and he was reelected for the PSDB in 2002. He established a reputation as a quiet, competent administrator. But he too, like Lula, had to fight off attacks during the 2006 campaign. He was calling for a "decent Brazil" (one of Lula's slogans in 2002) and an end to corruption. Yet his own administration was blamed for the PCC mafia uprising in May to July; his wife, Maria Lúcia, known as Lu, was criticized for her willingness to accept gifts of dresses. Lula's supporters pointed out that Alckmin's state administration had succeeded in preventing a large number of CPIs that would have investigated alleged scandals in São Paulo state.

In temperament, therefore, Alckmin was a complete opposite to Lula. He was so uncharismatic that he was nicknamed "chuchu," after a bland green vegetable. But he had shown toughness in getting the PSDB/PFL nomination, elbowing aside the claims of Serra and Aécio Neves for the presidency. Some who had been close to Cardoso did not exert themselves too hard for Alckmin in the first round, and admitted surprise when he forced a second presidential vote. But a certain distance between the candidate and Cardoso's government protected him from a key line of Lula's campaign.

The presidential campaign was of course only one of the many election battles going on all over Brazil, because a limited number of senators, all the federal deputies, and state deputies were also being chosen. Lula, touring the country, had an eye not only for PT candidates but also for those who had supported him in the past and who might support him in future. Some of these alliances would raise eyebrows for those with long memories. For example, Lula worked hard to help ex-president José Sarney get reelected as PMDB senator for the small state of Amapá in the north. Sarney was now a key player in Lula's congressional coalition.

For much of the presidential campaign it was not clear how far the corruption issue, as against the policy changes introduced by the Lula government, would sway electors. Both Lula and Alckmin were devout Catholics, and the National Conference of Brazilian Bishops, although keen to see issues debated properly, warned against use of the corruption issue to mount a "coup" against democratic institutions.[8] Many media organizations, and Transparency Brazil, ran Web sites in which it was possible for computer-literate citizens to see which candidates had been involved in scandal.

The final swing to Alckmin in the last few days before the election, however, reflected the renewed potency of the corruption issue, thanks to photos of the money to buy the anti-Serra dossier, and criticism of Lula for failing to participate in the final TV debate promoted by TV Globo. In fact, Lula had boycotted all the previous TV debates—as had President Cardoso when he was running for reelection—and it looked as though he decided against the final one only late on 28 September, the day it took place, as he wound up his campaign in São Bernardo.

Lula's hostility to a TV debate in which he would be outnumbered and where Heloísa Helena in particular was likely to be extremely confrontational was understandable, but it looked bad. People wanted to know more about the dossier and how the PT group had obtained the money to buy it. TV Globo placed an empty chair where Lula would have sat, and the other candidates addressed it ironically.

What happened on 1 October showed a divided Brazil, and a Brazil that was still ambivalent about corruption. Lula won all the northern and northeastern states, with the exception of Roraima on the Guyanese border. Alckmin won in the south and west, including the state of Acre adjoining Bolivia, but failed to win the wealthier states of Minas Gerais and Rio de Janeiro.[9] Broadly speaking, the poorer, blacker parts of Brazil chose Lula; the richer, better educated, and whiter ones chose Alckmin.[10] The people who felt that Lula was on their side, with his Bolsa-Família, rural electrification, ProUni, and other social programs, had voted for him. There was a correlation between federal investment on one side and the strength of the private sector on the other.

From a PT angle, the other elections, so important in a federal state where Brasília must rely on partners at other levels of government, were far from disastrous. The party won four governorships in the first round—Bahia, Piauí, Sergipe, and Acre—and had a chance in second rounds in Pará and Rio Grande do Sul. Pro-Lula governors won an additional seven governorships. The PT elected eighty-three federal deputies, only eight fewer than in 2002, to be the second largest group after the PMDB with eighty-nine. Although the outgoing PT-led coalition had lost nineteen deputies, it still substantially outgunned the opposition by 322 to 182, which would cause problems for Alckmin if he were to win on the second ballot.[11] The pro-Lula wing of the PMDB had done well.[12]

The most satisfying victory for the PT was in Bahia, where Jaques Wagner won. He had been minister of institutional relations for Lula until he resigned in May to take on a nominee of the seventy-nine-year-old PFL boss, Antonio Carlos Magalhães. On the other hand, in Rio Grande do Sul, so long important for the PT, Olívio Dutra only just managed to get into a second round to challenge the PSDB's Yeda Crusius, a former minister of planning in the Itamar Franco government. Dutra, one of the PT's founders and an old friend of Lula, had once shared an apartment with the president in Brasília, when they were both federal deputies. For the former leader of the bank workers' union, it was perhaps unfortunate that the election coincided with a bank workers' strike.

The PT's weakest performance was in the Senate, where each of the twenty-seven states, including the Federal District, chose one of its three senators. The only PT senator to get reelected was the veteran Eduardo Suplicy from São Paulo, and he only narrowly beat off a challenge from the PFL. This weakness would make it relatively easy for the opposition to create any CPIs it wanted in the new Congress.[13]

Public disaffection with the Chamber of Deputies was shown in a change of personnel. There was the biggest turnover since the election that followed Collor's departure, and 46 percent of the deputies were new or recycled. But it was not a clear-cut rejection of the allegedly corrupt. Paulo Maluf for the PP, who had the magic number for voting machines of 1,111, was elected a federal deputy in São Paulo with the highest individual vote in the country—739,827. Fernando Collor emerged from the disgrace of impeachment and his loss of electoral rights to be elected as senator for Alagoas for a tiny party, the PRTB. He said he would support a second Lula government. For the PT, both Genoino and Palocci were elected as deputies.

The *mensalão* and "bloodsucker" deputies fared badly. Of nineteen deputies caught up in the *mensalão* scandal, eleven sought reelection but only four succeeded. The cull among those involved in the ambulances affair was even more striking: only six were elected and forty-one were rejected. Severino Cavalcanti, who had renounced his seat in Pernambuco to avoid loss of his political rights, was not reelected. More positively, Fernando Gabeira of the Greens came out on top among federal deputies in Rio de Janeiro. His reputation had been enhanced by his interrogation of corruption in the CPIs, and it helped increase the number of Green deputies from five to thirteen.

Lula's failure to win on the first round was unexpected and a wake-up call. It called for a radical reappraisal both for himself and for his campaign team. After 1 October he presented himself differently, more rationally, more like the candidate of "peace and love" of 2002. He took part in TV debates with Alckmin and was more open with the media. He was more specific on policy positions. He insisted that the PT expel all those involved with the dossier, ensured that Berzoini could not return as party president, and said that the guilty should be punished. He worked hard on regional alliances with governors and others who could bring him votes in the second round. He also made use of the patronage and powers of government.

Both government and opposition indulged in what Brazilians describe as "electoral terrorism"—scaremongering that plays on fears of the other side. The Alckmin forces revived the propaganda that if Lula was reelected the PT would manipulate public funds and institutions so that it stayed in power for twenty years—even though Lula himself had made clear that he would like to revert to one-term presidents serving only five years. Government propaganda had it that a President Alckmin would cut back on the Bolsa-Família and other social programs, even though the candidate denied it and one of the clearest achievements of the Lula term was to show that income redistribution was not only essential but practical. It was alleged that Alckmin would privatize all state assets.

On both sides, and in the middle, there was a feeling that something akin to class warfare might come to Brazil. The recent presidential election in Mexico, in which the leftist candidate Lopez Obrador charged that the election had been stolen, had resulted in street demonstrations and the creation by Obrador of a rival government to the one that had been recognized. Some feared that, looking at the division between the north of the country for Lula and the south for Alckmin, a narrow result either way in Brazil could have similar consequences.

Both candidates tried to head off this risk. In a free TV ad, Lula appealed to the middle class, which had been an important part of his coalition in 2002. "Social justice also widens and strengthens the middle class," he said. "Brazil is seeing the emergence of a new middle class. If I'm reelected I'm going to give special attention to this group."[14] He would try to reduce the tax burden on small business. He denied that he was trying to divide the country between rich and poor. "I don't want to divide anything. I grew up poor before. If it was left to me I wouldn't have any rich or poor, only the rich."

Alckmin argued that Lula was less on the side of the poor than he claimed, since he was making friends with representatives of the oligarchy such as ex-President Sarney, and Delfim Netto, a former economic minister in the military government of President Figueiredo. Ex-President Cardoso, who earlier had been aggressive in criticizing PT-related corruption, also tried to tamp down class conflict. When it looked as though Lula was comfortably ahead in the run-up to the second round, Cardoso said that the voice of the people should be respected and he was not calling for Lula's impeachment, even though irregularities should be prosecuted.

In the four weeks between the two rounds, Lula strengthened his position and Alckmin was unable to make further headway. At a strategic level, as seen in debates and the free TV advertising, Lula did well with his claim that he had made progress in his first term and would do even better in a second. He asked for votes to enable him to work harder on the task he had begun. There did not appear to be enormous policy differences between the two sides.

Significantly, the corruption issue went quieter, although the federal police were still trying to find out how the PT conspirators had got hold of their money, and the owners of a currency exchange in the state of Rio de Janeiro were arrested three days before the second-round voting.[15] On the government side, Lula for the first time cracked down on the PT's dirty tricksters: Oswaldo Bargas, Jorge Lorenzetti, Hamilton Lacerda, and Expedito Veloso were all expelled from the party and Berzoini had to resign as PT president.[16]

Alckmin, by contrast, lost his moral standing on the issue by accepting support from Anthony Garotinho, the former governor of Rio de Janeiro state, and his wife, who succeeded him in the post.[17] Garotinho had been widely attacked as one of the most corrupt politicians in Brazil, and although Alckmin said he was prepared to accept help from any quarter, it was a severe embarrassment to his campaign. The mayor of Rio, César Maia, who was from the PFL, which was backing Alckmin, roundly denounced the presidential candidate.

Lula was still effective on the stump, and more relaxed with voters than the rather stiff Alckmin. In Manaus, in Amazonia, he complained that Alckmin was still "a Paulista in his head." While recognizing that some privatizations, for instance of telecommunications, had brought benefits, he said that he would not sell national assets. "Never in my life, when I needed more money, would I sell my fridge. Rather I would work an extra hour, and do overtime," he said.

But buoying him up were the strength of the economy, the power of the presidency, and shrewdness in alliance-building. The unemployment rate in the six largest cities was falling—from 10.6 percent in August to 10 percent in September 2006.[18] Interest rates came down again, from 14.25 percent to 13.75 percent. Business confidence was demonstrated in October when the Companhia Vale do Rio Doce (CVRD), the iron and steel company founded by Vargas and privatized by Cardoso, bought more than three-quarters of the shares of a Canadian company, Inco; it became the second-largest minerals firm in the world.[19] Such economic news slightly dented Alckmin's refrain that Brazil should be growing faster.

Lula's use of government financial muscle also helped his campaign and his alliances. He allocated three billion reais for the renegotiation of agricultural debt, a valuable contribution to the farming industry and farming states. One-third of this went to Mato Grosso, where the soy business had been suffering for climatic reasons. Blairo Maggi, the "soy king" who was governor for the PPS—the renamed PCB, the one-time orthodox Communist Party, now backing Alckmin—said that he would break ranks to support Lula.

In Maranhão, a northern state where Roseana Sarney was in a runoff on behalf of the opposition PFL, Lula appeared on a platform to support her. She was the daughter of José Sarney and a formidable politician in her own right. The local PT hated this, the national PFL planned to expel her, and she started making overtures to join the PMDB. But Lula had calculated that, if she got elected and supported him as her father did, it would strengthen his governing majority.

In Rio de Janeiro state, where the PMDB's Sergio Cabral was in a runoff against Denise Frossard of the PPS, Lula backed Cabral, and Alckmin's blunder over Garotinho was a handicap to Frossard, his ally. Such local battles intertwined with the presidential one, so that Aécio Neves, who won the governorship so comfortably in Minas, was exerting himself to help Alckmin, who had come in second there to Lula in the first round. In Rio Grande do Sul, the strengthening appeal of Lula in the course of October might be enough to help Dutra to victory, and the PT to another governorship.

In the complex game of Brazilian politics it was necessary to do two things: to put together a coalition that was powerful enough to win an election; and to put together a coalition that was capable of governing. These were not the same coalitions. In a multiparty system, where both PT and PSDB on their own had less than one-quarter of the votes and elected politicians, this was a major challenge to leaders. As his own confidence returned in the course of October, Lula was increasingly looking to the coalition he would need for a second term in government. It was obvious that the PMDB this time would be a key ally, in Congress and the states. Lula also talked of trying to reach consensus with the opposition on key issues.

Even the *nanicos*, the tiny parties, had to be taken seriously. The law, which everyone expected to become operational, had required them to achieve a minimum national vote to obtain funding and other privileges; it meant that fourteen parties with elected representatives had failed the hurdle. Two on the left—the PCdoB, which was pro-Lula, and PSOL, which was opposed—decided to carry on as they were. But two of the parties that had been punished by voters for their role in the scandals, yet had been part of the government majority—the PTB and PL—made judicious mergers with even smaller parties to rise above the threshold. The PL plus PSC alliance would have thirty-eight federal deputies; the PTB plus PAN would have twenty-three.

The affections of a new grouping, the Democrats of the Left (Democráticos de Esquerda), remained to be seen. It comprised the PPS (with 21 deputies), the Greens (with 13), and the PHS (with 2). The PPS had been part of the opposition, possibly because the PCdoB was with Lula. The Greens had earlier been part of Lula's government coalition, but Gabeira, as a PT man turned Green, had made a name for himself by attacking government corruption. It seemed likely that the Democrats of the Left would support a new Lula government only if they were confident of greater transparency.[20]

In the course of the four weeks between the two presidential elections, it became obvious that Lula was pulling ahead. Possibly because he had never expected to get into a second round, Alckmin had wasted ten days before his campaign restarted. His TV appearances mixed aggression and good humor in a confusing way. The Lula team, shocked and energized, were going all out to win.

The results, when they were announced on 30 October, were a vindication for the president. He had won a record number of votes—58.3 million—and had nearly 61 percent of the valid total, compared with 39 percent for Alckmin. His percentage of the vote was only 0.5 percent less than it had been when he beat Serra in the second round in 2002.

The drop of 2.4 million in support for his challenger meant that Alckmin came in first in only seven of the twenty-seven states.

Importantly, Lula emerged from the 2006 election with more support among state governors than he had had four years earlier. The PT won a fifth state in a runoff, the Amazon state of Pará, where Ana Júlia Carepa defeated the PSDB candidate. It had won only three states in 2002. The PSB, Lula's close allies, picked up two more northeastern states, Rio Grande do Norte and his home state of Pernambuco—where a grandson of Miguel Arraes was the winner.[21] There were a few setbacks for Lula in the second round. Olívio Dutra could not overtake the PSDB's Yeda Crusius in Rio Grande do Sul, and Roseana Sarney was beaten in Maranhão, putting an end to forty years' domination of the state by her family.

The party strengths in the state governorships were therefore: PMDB 7, PSDB 6, PT 5, PSB 3, PPS 2, PDT 2, PFL 1, and PP 1. Allowing for the actual relationship with Lula, it was reckoned that at least seventeen of these governors supported him, and he in turn would rely on them to lean on the deputies and senators from their states to provide backing for him in Congress. The key potential role of the PMDB in enabling Lula to achieve what was called "governability" was emphasized in these results. Although the PSDB had made gains, the PFL, its more conservative ally, had lost three states.

Lula and Marisa looked suitably triumphant. He told the crowds in Avenida Paulista, São Paulo, that he would continue to work for the poor, that it was a victory for those underneath against those on top, that it completed his achievement as a politician. He talked of a resumption of economic growth, of the need for political reform and for political unity in the country. And he said that the PT "has no right to commit ethical and political errors from now on."[22] Good wishes came in from leaders around the world.

So, after all the explosive revelations only a year earlier, Lula would remain in his post as the thirty-ninth president of Brazil until the end of December 2010. He was still the first president from a leftist party elected by universal suffrage,[23] the first who had been an industrial worker, the first who lacked a university degree. He took four days off to relax at a naval base in the northeast before meeting with politicians to start constructing a government for his second term.

10 **LULA SO FAR**

AN INTERIM ASSESSMENT

When Lula was reelected for a second term, on 29 October 2006, around four thousand of his supporters partied that evening on the Avenida Paulista in São Paulo. But the turnout was tiny compared with the celebration four years earlier, when one hundred thousand people came out into the street, filling the long commercial thoroughfare. Looking at it through British eyes, one could not help but compare this diminished enthusiasm with the gradual loss of excitement at the successive election victories won by Tony Blair and his "new" Labour Party. Is this the inevitable fate of a government of the left, which aspires to improve the lot of the mass of the population, when faced with the compromises, complexities, and disappointments of the modern world? Could Lula have done differently, or better?

Any assessment of this Brazilian president, who is arguably the most significant since Getúlio Vargas, can only be interim. Second terms, for both Latin American and North American presidents, can be very different from their first. In Latin America, reformist leaders often become more conservative. By definition, there is a time limit to their authority, and would-be successors start jostling to inherit. In the Brazilian case, it was not clear that the PT would be able to field a strong candidate in 2010, and the government forces might support someone like Ciro Gomes, of the PSB, a former minister for Lula, who was elected with proportionately the largest majority in the country as federal deputy for the northeastern state of Ceará.[1] On the opposition side there could be a struggle between two PSDB governors, José Serra and Aécio Neves.

But 2006 marked the renaissance of Lula, after the depth of his unpopularity during the *mensalão* crisis of 2005. In reality, had he dropped dead at any point in the previous decade,[2] his obituarists would rightly have pointed to his prominent roles in ending the dictatorship, building freer trade unions, establishing a large-scale party for workers and the left, and consolidating democracy. None of these things had he done on his own, but his career was a thread running through modern Brazilian history and, most would say, for the better.

He had two driving motivations. One was to end the worst poverty in Brazil. The second was to respect and reward the contribution of Brazilian workers. In a way, everything he did could be related to these simple but powerful concerns. At his inauguration in January 2003, he said that he did not want any Brazilian to go to bed hungry. The Bolsa-Família, hikes in the *salário mínimo*, and the other social programs were designed to transfer income and opportunities to the poorest Brazilians. Their votes in 2006 showed that they recognized that he was doing this; statisticians could prove it.[3]

His repeated phrase that nothing could hold back a Brazilian worker, and his personal identification with the "peasantry" of the industrial areas around São Paulo, had driven his participation in the strikes of the 1970s and his work to create the PT. The compression of wages in the "miracle" years was a source of anger and resolve. The day after his last rally before the first-round vote in 2006, he stood outside auto factories in São Bernardo, leafleting and talking with workers; it was as though he needed to reconnect with his own roots.

Ricardo Kotscho, the journalist who became his press secretary, understood this identification well. Writing of him at an earlier stage in his political career, he described how he always went home to São Bernardo between campaign journeys:

> Lula was his own hero; he had no idols or models. The saga of the Silva brothers, who left as little ones from the miserable depths of Pernambuco in a truck with benches (*pau-de-arara*) and suffered a lot until finding work in the factories of São Bernardo, he had told me in

verse and prose a thousand or more times. But what impressed me more was his relationship to those he called the "peasantry" (*peãozada*), the multitude of metalworkers who created a species of independent republic in the ABC.[4]

Lula was an instinctive rather than an intellectual leader, and he was happier at a mass meeting or in one-on-one talks than in interminable committee sessions. His frustration and ineffectiveness as a federal deputy, when the 1988 Constitution was being debated, was a pointer to one of his weaknesses.

There was a sense in which, in campaigning for democracy or setting up the PT, he was leading forces out on the street, rather than thinking through what was needed to institutionalize democracy or his own party. Building democracy was never going to be easy in Brazil. Party labels were often lightly worn.

There was a tradition of elite domination and control; there was the real power of rich civilian elites, both in industrial areas and in the agricultural northeast, where so-called colonels (*coroneis*) had managed politics in their own interest. Ever since the Army had overthrown the Empire in 1889, the military had lurked in the background, and it had taken power in 1964. Positivist attitudes,[5] and some elements in the Catholic Church, sought to dictate to the Brazilian people what was good for them.

Lula's first campaign was to free up the corporatist union structure by making unions more responsive to workers and more effective in fighting for better terms and conditions. As seen earlier, he came into union work almost by accident. The developing strikes were reactive, and took on more significance as the military government realized that the unions were a threat to its power. After the Metalworkers' Union had been reorganized, Lula went on with friends to create the CUT. But some outsiders felt that the democratization of Brazil's union movement was still incomplete; the small compulsory levy on unionists continued, as did other relics of the Vargista labor system; unions in Brazil could still be seen as a kind of business, rather than as entirely autonomous civil society organizations.

The creation of the PT, in which intellectuals as well as workers were involved from the start, was a home-grown Brazilian affair. The party was and remains a coalition. One of its strangest aspects is the role it recognizes for factions, with different slates running for election both at the state and at the federal levels. It maintains various tensions between the different groupings that compose it. Yet it also has a strong centralist direction—borrowed from the Marxist parties—which was represented by its successive dominant factions, Articulação and Campo Majoritario.

Lula worked enormously hard to get the PT running. Yet at times he seemed to have lost interest in it and, when the PT by the late 1980s saw that he was its best asset, he began to treat the party in an offhand way. In the 1990s, he was making clear that he would not be bound by its policies or its views on alliances with other parties. By 2002, with his Letter to the Brazilian People, which followed a radical party conference, he had publicly distanced himself from its positions.

He was lighthearted about, even occasionally dismissive of, the PT. Leftist or socialist governments in Europe have also parted company with the parties they supposedly represent. Lula had reason in 2005 to be really angry with those in the PT leadership whose corruption led to his unpopularity. The same happened in September 2006, when the anti-Serra dossier was all over the media. But he stayed loyal to his creation, remarking of former comrades that "to err is human." He did not immerse himself in party management and, until he fired him, Lula relied heavily on José Dirceu and others to organize the party.

The PT was an important invention, allowing for debate and internal democracy, and a participative approach to policymaking. These were all new to politics in Brazil. But Lula seems to have concluded in the 1990s that the PT was insufficient to achieve his election as president, or the introduction of the kind of social reforms he wanted. After his third presidential defeat, in 1998, he was more than ever convinced that he had to reach out to the middle ground and calm the fears of the more conservative. This would involve a cautious economic policy, behind which he could promote pro-poor social programs. It was a strategy that the Clinton administration in the United States, the Schroeder government in Germany, and the Blair team in the United Kingdom were also following.

As in these other countries, it meant that Lula was accused of betrayal of bigger social change. But he was knowingly working within the global free market, where money could be withdrawn at short notice, and no currency—particularly in an emerging market—was secure. Shortly after his reelection in October 2006, one of his PT ministers, Tarso Genro, incautiously cheered that the era of Palocci and financial conservatism was over. The real dropped against the U.S. dollar; the São Paulo stock market fell. Lula moved at once to clarify that the existing monetary stance and the law of fiscal responsibility would be maintained. He hoped, however, that Brazil would achieve a higher growth rate, which would make it easier to tackle inequality.[6]

Lula's occasionally cavalier attitude toward the PT was belied by his reliance on what he and others called the *militância*—its militant comrades—when he needed to get out the vote. Seeing him at a PT rally was to witness a sense of personal identification. But as someone who had learned to play the political game expertly, he was also aware of its democratic shortcomings. This was not only a problem with the role of money in politics, a point to which I return later in this chapter.

There was the issue of the lack of party fidelity, which caused politicians to swap labels lightly, with little consideration for their constituents or the values of different parties. On the surface, there was not much to choose among many of the parties. Indeed, it was remarkable that Antonio Carlos Magalhães, chief of the conservative PFL in Bahia, was actually a personal friend of Fidel Castro and could claim to have pioneered both education grants and food rations, which became merged in the Bolsa-Família.[7]

The Brazilian people, and therefore their political system, placed a high priority on the candidate, not the party. A lot of electors who had voted for Lula still distrusted the PT. Nonetheless, the general tendency since the 1988 Constitution had been to strengthen party loyalty. This was an effect of the verticalization rule, and could also turn out to be a result of the fusions in 2006, prompted by the expected requirement of minimum support for any party wanting recognized status in Congress. Even the unideological PMDB planned a programmatic agreement to support the reelected president. Without a lot of publicity, the Chamber of Deputies introduced a rule in 2006 under which members had to declare openly how they voted on amendments and laws.

Lula had gotten used to dealing with a multiplicity of parties; some small ones such as the PCdoB and PSB had produced valuable colleagues in his government. But by the end of his first term, possibly in reaction to exposure of greed and dishonesty among the *mensaleiro* and "bloodsucker" deputies, he was convinced of the need for political reform. Ideally he would like to achieve this by consensus, and the details would be important. The *mensalão* scandal had arisen because of the need to get a governing majority from among small parties: some had little principled interest in politics, except to see how much money they could make.

The first Lula presidency was bathed in a black shadow from the occult role of money in Brazilian politics; no one was quite sure of the extent of Lula's responsibility, except in not paying sufficient attention. His reelection took place with the faint possibility that direct connection to the president might yet result in impeachment proceedings. Yet similar issues dogged older democracies. In France, President Chirac knew that corruption proceedings relating to his time as mayor of Paris might be instituted when he left the presidency. In the United Kingdom, Tony Blair was caught up in a police investigation over the sale of honors to raise funds for his party. In the United States, Tom DeLay, the Republican majority leader in the House of Representatives, was forced to resign his leadership position in September 2005, and resigned his congressional seat in June 2006, after being indicted for wrongful campaign financing.[8]

The different scandals in Brazil were varied in causes and effects. But what worried critics were the nonchalance of their president and the fear that key players in the PT, for whom the end might justify the means, were skimming off funds from the Brazilian state in a systematic effort to hold on to power.

Lula, who had been so close to the Catholic Church in the 1970s and 1980s, was believed to have supported Dom Cláudio Hummes for the papacy after he became president.[9] But somewhere inside Lula, by 2002, an ethical dimension had gone missing. In this perhaps he was what people said was a typical Brazilian—loyal to his friends and unembarrassed when they helped themselves to money or influence. Until he started sacking the "nuts and imbeciles" who made him face a second round, he was loath to discipline those who let down the history of the PT and his own reputation.

There was a problem over party funding in Brazil, for elections had become too expensive for the income from the PT's own membership.[10] The PT itself wanted more state funding. By 2002, the Lula campaigns were certainly getting business funding, but how far he appreciated that there was nearly always a price to be paid in contracts and inflated invoices for services to state and parastatal firms is difficult to verify. He was never a man for detail. His line that nobody told him anything became a joke told at his nonappearance at the TV Globo debate on the eve of the first round in 2006: no one had told him it was taking place.

His nonchalance reached a peak in the way he dismissed the allegation that his son, Fabío Luís, the entrepreneur who had suddenly made so much money from Gamecorp, might have been exploiting his father's position. Ever keen on soccer analogies, he compared him with Ronaldinho, Brazil's star forward. In successive interviews between the two presidential rounds, he said that he could not stop his son from working and that the rules for him were the same as for 190 million other Brazilians—if he had done anything wrong, he could be sued. Every father would like his son to be a Ronaldinho, but not everyone could be a Ronaldinho. He claimed that it was more difficult for the son of a president to become a star, and that his being president had not changed his son's habits by a millimeter.

Corruption scandals were not new in Brazil, and the media and the PT had had their criticisms of the Cardoso governments. But the failure of presidential leadership, if not actual complicity, had a ripple effect on the reputation of the country as well as of Lula's own party. In the four years of his first mandate, Brazil dropped from forty-fifth to sixty-sixth place in international rankings of perceived corruption.[11] The PT, which had its own ethics committee, postponed even a generic review of the mensalão scandal until December 2006, safely after the elections.[12]

All of this mattered, because Brazilian democracy was still young and needed strengthening. This is a federal system, with a lot of state enterprises and much public procurement seen as a honey pot by lobbyists and businessmen. Although certain audit processes were strengthened under Lula, and the federal police and state prosecuting authorities gained credit for their professionalism and objectivity, some tendencies were negative.[13]

In his first three years, the government created nearly thirty-eight thousand positions, an increase of nearly 8 percent in the contingent of civil servants. There was much criticism that party favoritism was playing too large a part, particularly in senior appointments, where the PT and its allies were giving important jobs to poorly qualified people. The *mensalão* revelations highlighted the issue. The PT itself was becoming an employment machine.

Lula did have some proposals in mind. Between presidential rounds he promised to introduce a freedom of information act, to achieve greater transparency in government decision making. By the early years of the new century, more democracies were introducing such measures, although they did not always work as well as advocates hoped. In countries as different as India and the United Kingdom, bureaucracies and governments had found ways to reduce their impact, arguing that compliance was too costly and time-consuming.

In an interview with European journalists shortly after his reelection, Lula called for an "Operation Clean Hands," comparable to the effort that had cleaned up political corruption in Italy in the 1990s. He acknowledged that the involvement of PT members in corrupt practices was the hardest blow he had received, but said that from now on his government would be intransigent. "All those accused of corruption will be tried. Not one of them will have the protection of my government," he promised.

Lula also made it clear that he would like Brazil to return to the practice of a single five-year term for presidents, as laid down by the 1988 Constitution. Many agreed that with a single term there was less risk of corruption, and more politicians would pass through the presidential palace in Brasília. Lula himself had followed Cardoso's example, however, in running for a second term, and after sixteen years of the double mandate system it would require remarkable abstinence to switch back.

Winning a second term for Lula was a triumph, given the criticism his government had faced. But it could also be seen as marking the beginning of the end of the cycle of democratization that had begun with the battles against the dictatorship in the late 1970s. The *linha dura* had been at its most ruthless in São Paulo, where Lula had led the strikers and both the PT and PSDB had come into existence. Cardoso and Serra had been exiles from the military. Lula had resisted intimidation and spent a month in prison.

But the generation that had enabled Brazil to break free from a military dictatorship and start building a freer and more open society was beginning to hand over the reins to younger people. Lula himself would be over sixty-five when the presidential sash passed to his successor in 2011. It was possible that Aécio Neves, grandson of the president who epitomized the transition to civilian rule in the 1980s, would follow Lula into the Palacio Planalto.

Brazil was incomparably freer. Social inequities were being addressed. Media were diverse and, though the PT complained that journalists were often unfair to the president and his party, censorship was a thing of the past. An active and vigilant civil society kept official institutions under constant review. In significant ways, though neither the PT nor the PSDB would like the reflection, the Cardoso and Lula years should be seen as a package. Both presidents wanted to take Brazil out of the third world and put it proudly in the first.

One aspect of the postdictatorship scene irritated human rights activists. They felt that not enough had been done, either by way of trials or through truth and reconciliation commissions, to bring to justice or bring out the truth of the crimes and torture committed by the military regime. José Sarney, the first civilian president who was able to serve a full term, was conservative and wished to let bygones be bygones.

By the time Lula came to power, some military and intelligence archives were being opened, and an Amnesty Commission was set up to provide compensation for those claiming political persecution. This, combining payments and pensions, was quite generous. In four years, from 2002 on, more than fourteen thousand claimants had received or been pledged R3.25 billion; one victim received as much as R3.4 million; and twenty-seven thousand more applications still had to be processed.

Although critics complained that the applications were not checked sufficiently strictly and had not been budgeted for on such a scale, it was clear that the large number of people whose lives had been damaged by the dictatorship were now getting a remedy.[14]

The degree to which the military had been tamed was illustrated by an incident in the presidential campaign. At a certain point the Military Club (Clube Militar), to which serving officers belonged, growled that a coup against the Constitution was developing; this appeared to be aimed at the PT. A half-century earlier, the Military Club had played a key part in the Brazilian polity, its elections watched for the influence of conservative, nationalist, or leftist factions, its threats taken very seriously.

President Kubitschek in 1959, after he had broken off talks for a loan with the IMF, addressed the Club with one of his more famous speeches. "Brazil has come of age. We are no longer poor relatives obliged to stay in the kitchen and forbidden to enter the living room," he said.[15] Now, in 2006, nobody cared what the Military Club thought. It really did not matter.

There was another sense in which Brazil was moving away from the postdictatorship era. It was possible to see an end to the political dominance of São Paulo, the biggest, richest city in the country. The PSDB, even more than the PT, had been a Paulista party. It was a party of the city's middle class, whereas the PT drew its support from the industrial workers in and around the city, and from certain intellectuals. In 2006, in spite of Lula's courting of the city and state of São Paulo, he and the PT did not do well there in the presidential and governorship elections. Furthermore, although the PSDB and PFL alliance elected Serra as governor, his neighbor in Minas, Aécio Neves, did even better.

It was obvious from the start of the 2006 campaign that Lula's greatest strength was in the northeast and north, historically the most conservative, poorest, and least educated regions of the country. His social programs and the income transfer of the Bolsa-Família turned the northeast and north into regions that gave him huge majorities even on the first ballot. The PT and its allies, particularly the PSB, did well. The gerrymandering at the end of the military era, which had overrepresented the northeast in Congress, now turned out to advantage Lula. But it also made likely a shift in the balance within the PT and, allowing for parallel but opposite changes within the PSDB, potentially the whole political system.

How far was Lula, by 2006, still a man of the left? Commentators on the election results that year referred to "two Brazils." The geographical division was sharper than anything seen before, and comparable to the remarkable division in the United States in the 2000 and 2004 presidential elections. In the United States, the heart of the country had voted Republican and in broad terms the coastal, more internationally minded states had gone down to defeat with the Democrats.

In Brazil, the division was more obviously social. One Brazil, which voted for Lula, was poorer, benefiting from federal investment and income transfers. The southern Brazil, which supported Alckmin, was wealthier, with more employed by the private sector and more who had had at least a secondary education. Did this not prove that Lula, as even disillusioned supporters still hoped, was a man of the left?

Questioned about his efforts to relieve poverty during the campaign, Lula said that he would be happy for everyone to be rich. One of his achievements, acknowledged by the way the opposition guaranteed that Alckmin if elected would maintain the Bolsa-Família, was to change the terms of debate over income inequality. But Lula was not an ideological person, and he said contradictory things.

Marxists were still attacking him during his presidency for failing to give absolute priority to the working class, and for a wishy-washy attachment to plural democracy. As seen in the chapter on the elections, he was also trying to mollify middle-class voters. His thinking was largely governed by his own experience, fighting for the rights and income of industrial workers, aware of poverty in the rural northeast and in the slums around the big cities.

He had been critical of Marxists who claimed to speak for the workers, but who were not always elected by them and could not organize a mass movement. He was particularly critical of student Marxists who might come to the factories, but then returned to comfortable homes.

He was undoubtedly influenced by progressive Catholics in the 1970s and 1980s. Their theology of the liberation of the oppressed in Latin

America awarded high priority to the rights of the poor on earth before they reached heaven. But at the same time, this progressive Catholicism was opposed to the communist dictatorships of eastern Europe, which oppressed the workers. There was a period in which Lech Walesa's shipyard workers in Gdansk, struggling with Catholic backing against the Polish communist government, seemed similar to the strikers around São Paulo, up against the Brazilian dictatorship.

Previous Brazilian leaders, notably Getúlio Vargas, had shown ideological dexterity.[16] It was plain that Lula, particularly by the mid-1990s, could in no way be described as a socialist. He made significant compromises on his way to the presidency. But in the course of his presidency, he stuck to certain principles: he tried to better the life of the poor; he refused to make further privatizations, and sometimes was unenthusiastic about the public-private partnerships that Cardoso had begun to promote; he supported land reform; he backed the cause of national sovereignty and development in the international arena; he paid off the IMF; he was willing to use federal funds to promote development projects, such as the diversion of the São Francisco river in the northeast.

Given the modest growth of the Brazilian economy and the high interest rates for most of his term of office, there was plenty of ammunition for critics. He himself was arguing that the economy needed to grow by 5 percent a year. But the kind of endorsement that voters gave him in 2006 suggested that they themselves saw him as a reformist. It was the fifth poll since direct election of the president had been introduced, and voters of all types were increasingly sophisticated.

Defining what is both of the left and electable is a universal challenge in the era of globalization. Lula was lucky that he did not reach the presidency earlier, during the high tide of the so-called Washington consensus of neoliberal economics. That consensus had broken by 2002. It had caused too much poverty and chaos in the post-Soviet economies and the dependent developing world; its promised growth and the trickle down of wealth had either not happened or been too partial. Instead, policies of pro-poor development and social inclusion were fashionable at the start of the twenty-first century, coinciding with Lula's arrival in power. In Latin America there had been growing revulsion against the Washington model, shown sharply in Argentina and Venezuela, but influencing Brazil also.

Brazilian journalists wrote about *lulismo* rather as British journalists had written about "Blairism" or "Thatcherism." But Lula had no worked-out theory, and *lulismo* lacked the kind of progressive rigor that might equate on the left with Margaret Thatcher's free-market conservative capitalism on the right. Lula was steering a coalition in a country with different layers of government, and opportunist alliances could be part of the price of survival.

Whether his second term in office would be more coherent, only time would tell. Lula indicated that he would maintain his financial stance but try to stimulate more economic development with an ambitious growth package. This could pose risks for the environment, if this meant big projects dangerously exploiting the land and minerals. He was aiming for a growth rate of 5 percent a year—quite modest by Chinese and Indian standards. He promised to pursue his social programs and give more attention to education.

Issues that were not part of his own life experience were becoming more important—such as the threat of global warming, the drug-fueled lawlessness in the *favelas,* and rapid socioeconomic change that could destroy manufacturing jobs and the well-paid "monkey suits" he wanted as a young man. The astonishing growth of the charismatic evangelical churches represented a different society, and different aspirations, from the progressive Catholicism that had nurtured his career. How far could he adapt to and lead this changing Brazil?

He would still be chairing a coalition, and would maintain his alliance with small parties in Congress—including the "physiological" and conservative PTB and PP. But he would rely more on the PMDB. He would try to reach out to the opposition, especially the opposition state governors, but it was probable that the patterns of political conflict established over the previous twelve years would continue for another four. He would not let the PT dictate to him.

How had Lula performed on the international scene? He had become a star. He was determined to show that those who said that anyone who did not speak English was ineffective as a president were wrong. He might need an interpreter, but the force of his personality, his humor and directness, would always show through.

He could make strong economists cry as he recalled his family experiences. An apology for slavery could become a tear-jerking occasion. He used a mango dessert for the Japanese prime minister as a chance to persuade Japan to lift a barrier to Brazilian mango exports. He traveled more than his predecessors. He enjoyed it.

Whereas President Cardoso had established a name for himself internationally as an intellectual, Lula presented himself as an activist. In his first term he may not have succeeded in winning a UN Security Council seat or success in the WTO's Doha development round. But he had shown determination in pursuit of what were always long-term objectives.

Furthermore, he had launched important new dimensions for Brazilian foreign policy, in Africa, with the Arab world, with key developing countries in the G20, and in BRICS and IBSA. Of course, there was a PT South-South analysis lying behind much of this. But his successors would wish to build on these initiatives for reasons of national interest. The Arab world was awash with petrodollars to invest. Africa would not remain in the economic mire for ever. China and India, particularly, were motors for the twenty-first century's world economy.

It was in its detail that the foreign policy of the Lula government ran into difficulties. Lula's presence at G8 meetings was a victory for Lula and Brazil, but not necessarily seen as so brilliant for all developing countries. Rhetoric about Brazil's leadership could be counterproductive; Brazil could be seen as unilateralist and uncooperative, and other governments were unwilling to vote for Brazilians in international agencies. Significantly, following his reelection, Lula was soft-pedaling the claims to international leadership.

There were also problems with the neighbors in Latin America. There were always frictions between different countries and, as with the nationalization of oil and gas by Evo Morales in Bolivia, these could lead to confrontations with a Brazil that could be characterized as Big Brother. Lula tried to be a pragmatic good neighbor and, like his predecessors, to make Brazil a hinge for South America's development. Its geographic expanse and its economic weight provided opportunities that needed to be used with discretion.

There were several fault lines in Latin American politics. One concerned relations with the United States, where Hugo Chávez was vociferously anti, while Mexico's Vicente Fox and his successor were pro. Chile, even under a socialist president, was happy to make bilateral agreements with the United States. Although Morales was elected in Bolivia with the support of Chávez, Chávez's aggressive policy led to a reaction in Mexico and Peru, where pro-American presidents were elected in 2006. The election of Daniel Ortega, the one-time Sandinista revolutionary, as president of Nicaragua had a touch of Lula about it: the one-time revolutionary had redefined himself as a Catholic moderate, seeking foreign investment.

Lula tried to keep a foot on both sides of this divide. There was, for instance, a contested election for a Latin American rotating place on the UN Security Council in 2006. The United States backed Guatemala, and Venezuela had the support of Brazil and other Mercosul states. But it was obvious, well before more than forty ballots, that neither could get the required two-thirds majority. Brazil was always in favor of a consensus, which implied that both competitors should withdraw. When they did, Panama was elected without difficulty.

While saying after his reelection that he wanted to strengthen ties with the United States, Lula's first overseas trip was to Venezuela. He was due to open a new bridge over the Orinoco with President Chávez. But there was another reason. He wanted to confirm arrangements for the joint funding of a large new oil refinery in Pernambuco. It would take four years to build and cost $2.5 billion, to be shared equally by Petrobrás and PDVSA, the state oil company of Venezuela. It was a signal to his supporters that Lula was serious about the development of the northeast, and still friendly with Chávez. At the new bridge over the Orinoco, Lula made an outspoken speech, calling on Venezuelans to reelect Chávez in the upcoming presidential elections.

But Latin American summitry could be too much of a good thing for Lula. Immediately after his reelection at the end of October 2006, he sensibly took a four-day vacation, and was pictured on a beach in swimming trunks. Yet this coincided with an Ibero-American summit in Montevideo, which all presidents were supposed to attend. At the time, Lula was chairing Mercosul, and there was a tense row between Uruguay and Argentina over the siting of a new cellulose factory on the border. Both Uruguayan and Argentinean journalists wrote that Lula was showing disrespect to the organization.[17]

The fact was and is that Brazil is not a small developing country. Although gross domestic product per capita may only be around $2,600, it is a major factor in several world markets, some of them innovative and fast-growing. In one year, to October 2006, its exports of sugar-derived ethanol to the United States jumped 91 percent to 144 million gallons.[18]

In the middle of the presidential election, the Companhia Vale do Rio Doce, the iron and steel company founded by Vargas but privatized under Cardoso, took over Inco, a Canadian nickel and minerals firm, for $13.2 billion, to create what was said to be the second-largest minerals business in the world. Shortly after, the Companhia Siderúrgica Nacional, another Brazilian steel firm, was narrowly beaten in a takeover battle with Tata, the Indian conglomerate, for the Anglo-Dutch firm Corus. It seemed like the future of capitalism in the twenty-first century.

Globalization offers scope for the big power ambitions that Lula harbors for Brazil, as do other Brazilians who do not share the rest of his views. What does distinguish him from most of his predecessors is that he finds the contrast between great wealth and great poverty not only shocking but capable of redress. Many ordinary Brazilians ask, "If the country is so rich, why are we still so poor?" With all his failings, Lula has tried to end this poverty.

He also delves into his own life story, in a way that better-off politicians simply cannot, to make the case. Arguing for the scheme to divert the São Francisco river in northeast Brazil, he remarked, "Those who criticize the project to transfer the São Francisco never had dirty water, which I and my brothers drank when we were children in the northeast. We took the same water to cattle, and this has to stop."[19]

Lula's popularity rests on a genuine empathy with the mass of Brazilians. He frequently speaks off the cuff, not always grammatically, using northeastern idioms and sometimes swearwords. In August 2004, for instance, he made forty-seven speeches. For much of his first term he avoided general press conferences, which was why journalists tried to get him to answer questions on his overseas trips. During the *mensalão* crisis, they would annoy him by asking, "Who has betrayed you today?"

At the same time, he would make fun of the journalists. Two who traveled with him, Eduardo Scolese and Leonencio Nossa, wrote a book about their experiences.[20] They reported how on one occasion in Pretoria he called up someone to say something privately, to arouse the reporters' curiosity. When a journalist asked what this secret was, he discovered that Lula had deliberately whispered nothing in particular as a way of teasing the media.

Lula energizes himself with one-on-one meetings. From Monday to Friday, when he is at his office in Brasília, he puts aside an hour or so at around 3 P.M. to talk to people who want to see him—town councilors, former union colleagues, clergy, winners of regional beauty pageants, businessmen, and ordinary people who call because they want their photos taken with the president. It may be populism, and hark back to an older, more feudal Brazil. But it gives delight to those who get to visit him, and strengthens the president for the rest of the day.

Lula has a good sense of humor. The first time Marisa came with him to Brasília, when he was still leading the metalworkers, they were in a group of union leaders and their wives. Passing the ministry buildings and the Planalto Palace where the president has his office, Marisa asked, "And you think that the bosses of these palaces will let you and the PT come in one day?" Lula replied, "Marisa is talking like this because she is worried about who will clean all the windows."[21]

Before the 1989 campaign, Lula and his family were offered the beach house at Cabo Frio of Leonardo Boff, the liberation theologian. A large group, including campaign workers, borrowed it. Lula stuck a notice on the refrigerator of the "rights and duties of people living in this house." The rights were "to eat and drink everything to which you are entitled, and to stroll around at your pleasure." The duties were "to wash dirty dishes, to clean the house every day, and to take a shower outside the house after swimming." The notice finished, "All are equal in their rights and duties. This is the basic principle of socialism."[22]

Lula tried to keep his family out of his public life, unsuccessfully in the cases of his eldest son in 2005 and his daughter Lurian in 1989. Marisa was vehement in trying to protect the family's privacy, preventing security personnel from patrolling their private quarters in Brasília. When some in his team tried to make a point of criticizing Alckmin's daughter in the 2006 presidential campaign because of allegations against the owner of the store for which she worked in São Paulo, Lula ordered a stop to it.

While Lula seemed to be everywhere, Marisa conducted herself with discretion and decorum. She accompanied Lula on some of his overseas trips—visiting the Taj Mahal with him, for example, in January 2005, when he was a guest at India's Independence Day.[23] She made sure that attractive female security personnel were allowed nowhere near him. It was said that she discouraged him from having too much to drink. There is little doubt that Marisa's loyalty, staying power, and intelligence are a huge and undocumented part of Lula's success.

Even in the presidency, Lula had to put up with a lot of snobbery about his lack of formal education and his ungrammatical Portuguese. In other democracies, people of humble origin—Lincoln in the United States, or Ernest Bevin and Aneurin Bevan in the United Kingdom—have been celebrated for their achievements and their origins have not been held against them. It said something about the nature of Brazilian society and its sense of hierarchy that Lula could be treated in a disparaging way so long after he had become a prominent figure.

The fact that he retained a sense of earthiness was, of course, an electoral asset. When Alckmin was running against him, Alckmin looked dull competing against the very human, and not always politically correct, Lula. Lula regularly smoked ten cheroots a day—Marisa also smoked—and he would smoke on the presidential plane even though he was supposed not to. He enjoyed his glass of whisky.

But there was one aspect where Lula's lack of intellectual training may have been a handicap. This was in mastering the large quantities of paperwork that modern government throws up. This is a requirement not only in choosing big strategic priorities, but in ensuring that policies are actually being implemented and avoiding the elephant traps that can befall any administration. It has been part of the political equipment for leaders as different as Bill Clinton and Margaret Thatcher.

Here Lula's failure to get into detail and ask sharp questions hit him hard in the successive corruption scandals. Was he really reading the finance minutes of the PT, for example? The sense that he was not properly on top of administration was exacerbated by his love of travel, inside Brazil as well as out of the country. One calculation suggested that by 6 June 2006, he had been out of the Palácio Planalto, his office in Brasília, for 1,014 days out of the 1,230 in his mandate.[24] Even recognizing that some of these were day trips, and modern communications follow a president everywhere, such an epic quantity of excursion must have limited his hands-on control in Brasília.

José Serra's criticism, that he was running the government of Brazil as though it were an NGO, had an element of truth. He trusted associates he had known when he was in the union or setting up the PT—people sometimes described as his old drinking companions, who still came to share a weekend barbecue with him and Marisa. They were on a loose rein. Not all of them were capable of holding down difficult jobs in government.

It was not easy to develop coherence in a coalition government, and Lula could be seemingly frivolous or opportunist in changing ministers around. While some he kept, such as Celso Amorim in External Affairs and Gilberto Gil in Culture, he had three ministers in three years in both Education and Labor. Insiders criticized him for throwing out Olívio Dutra from the Cities portfolio to make way for a nominee of Severino Cavalcanti.

Lula relied heavily on his charm, force of character, and understanding of personalities. But there were those who saw him, even after four years as president, as naïve and an innocent abroad. "To make profound change in our country is not easy," he remarked wearily, two years into his first term.[25] A cynical Brazilian observer in the capital thought that he had simply been "oversold" in Europe, so that an overseas audience thought he was more radical, more of a miracle worker, more amazing as an individual than he really was. Domestic critics argued that the qualities needed to be a successful strike leader were not the same as those required of a head of state some twenty-five years later.

But Lula's personal qualities stood him in good stead, in that he could get on with people of the most diverse views—George W. Bush one day, Hugo Chávez the next. This conciliatory skill was part of a rich tradition in Brazil, not just in the union movement, where it is essential in negotiating agreements, but in politics and diplomacy as well. The sharp ideological quarrels of Spanish America seem alien to Brazilians.

It was typical that, after the harsh words in the 2006 election campaign, Lula reached out not only to allies among state governors and in Congress, but to opponents as well. He considered setting up an advisory group of former presidents. He was looking to build consensus for tax and political reforms, and to put more money into basic education. Although a Brazilian president is powerful, he needs support at many levels if policies are to be effective, and especially if ordinary people are to benefit.

Of all his personal qualities, stamina, determination, and ambition stand out. Without them he might have been forgotten soon after the great strikes at the end of 1970s. But he was in the thick of the effort to build a new party for workers, overcoming hostility from both the Marxist left and congressional opponents of the dictatorship. He showed amazing perseverance in doggedly running for the presidency in 1989, 1994, and 1998. Three successive defeats cannot have been pleasant, for he did not have much to fall back on. As he said periodically, "I'm only a lathe operator."

There is no doubt that Lula was personally as well as politically battered at the peak of the *mensalão* crisis, in August 2005, especially after Duda Mendonça had given some damning evidence to the parliamentary commission investigating scandals in the postal service (CPI Correios). Several ministers suggested that Lula should resign, according to a well-informed journalist in Brasília.[26]

"You are all soft. I will resist," he is quoted as saying to them. In fact, Lula knew that neither Serra nor Cardoso would be pressing for his impeachment. The PSDB was calculating that Lula and the PT would be easy to defeat the following year, and Cardoso's advice was that he should not try to run again. So although Lula shed tears at some of these crisis meetings, he was adamant that he would not throw in the towel. He also felt sorry for José Genoino, who he thought was not personally guilty, but rather was caught up in a system of corruption and was out of his depth.

Had Lula's ambition betrayed him and the hopes of his supporters? There are two main critiques, one tactical and one strategic. The tactical case is that after the 1998 defeat he made inappropriate compromises with conservative forces, with small right-wing and greedy parties, and with the demands of political advertising. People who watched the João Moreira Salles film about Lula between the two presidential rounds in 2002 thought that it was humiliating to see how dependent he was on the marketing publicist, Duda Mendonça.[27] The PP, the party of Paulo Maluf, formed part of his congressional majority. Unknown, but widely suspect, were the sources of money that had filled the illegal PT accounts from which Mendonça drew funds.

The strategic case against Lula is that he compromised too much on economic policy, so that a conservative, market-friendly approach made it hard to achieve real social reform. In earlier elections Lula had denounced Brazil's international debt; in office he paid it. Although Argentina had suffered badly at the time it was writing off its sovereign debt to private creditors, its economy had subsequently grown fast. Brazil was having to run a higher balance of payments and fiscal surplus than needed for its own economy, and domestic growth and redistribution suffered because of high interest rates.

History will judge how far these critiques are justified, and what happens in his second term will provide a better interim assessment. But one may argue that, without at least some of the tactical compromises after 1998, Lula might not have won the 2002 election. Until then he was stuck with around one-third of the electorate that would vote for him in all circumstances, and another third totally opposed. He had to win over the chunk in the middle. He became "Lula—peace and love." He justified this to himself and to his supporters as necessary if he was to gain power.

The strategic issue will be argued for a long time. The Palocci-Meirelles era was the hardest pill for PT activists to swallow. The contrast with

Argentina, which had reneged on its debt and then grown rapidly, was stark. And in 2006, both Chávez and Morales were nationalizing resource companies and utilities in ways that had gone out of fashion in the 1980s.

Lula defended the government's economic policy on several occasions, and made clear that even in a second term, focused more on development, it would be maintained. It may be that he was haunted by the hyper-inflation of the 1980s, and the PT's error in deprecating the real when Cardoso introduced it. He believed that monetary stability and lower inflation brought benefits to the working class as well as to wealthier people.

Rather like social democrats in Europe, Lula also thought that calmer, market-friendly policies made possible social investment and modest transfers of income to Brazil's large poor population. The best judgment on this came from the poor themselves. They turned out and voted for a second term for Lula. Economists will continue to argue that more can be done. But given the modest living standards of which Lula himself was well aware, small improvements can feel enormous to those who see them. Significantly, the president had also changed public debate, so that even opponents accepted the Bolsa-Família and saw that it was possible to reduce extreme poverty.

Many second terms prove disappointing. Lula had benefited from disillusionment with Cardoso in 2002, and the same could happen to him. One of the problems for Lula was that he was not only a man, but also a myth. The myth had been created originally by media coverage of his leadership in the strikes around São Paulo at the end of the 1970s. Subsequent media attacks on him had not dented the optimism of many who had joined the PT in the early years. It was almost inevitable that, once he became president, some would see him as failing to live up to their hopes for dramatic social change. The lack of preparation by the PT itself, and the diversion of time and public attention involved in the corruption scandals, ate away at Lula's own standing. Furthermore, the PT of the early years of the new century was not the idealistic force of two decades earlier.

The issues thrown up by the need to make alliances with individuals and parties that were far from radical would not go away. Lula has to go on manipulating a series of coalitions in his second term, just as in the first. Ideologically, it is not a pretty sight. But it is unavoidable in a federal system where a president is not all-powerful and has to operate a multiparty democracy. Lula has indicated that he wishes to move further in building more accountability to voters into the system, and more party fidelity. He has said he would like to make Congress more effective as a legislative body and less vulnerable to lobbyists with money.

His own work, as a builder of democracy and a more just society, is demonstrably incomplete. Four more years as a president would still be insufficient, and they could easily be sidetracked by further scandal or developments in Latin America or beyond. So far, for example, Brazil has been fortunate enough to avoid any terrorist outrage. The country is still vulnerable to a world economic downturn, and its growth has been too sluggish. Climate change remains a subtle threat, even if polluting states can be persuaded to pay to preserve Brazil's forests.

But there must have been a moment, after Lula realized that he had not won reelection in the first round of October 2006, when he wondered what he would do if he were no longer president. What would his legacy be? The questions have now been pushed back to the end of 2010. It is difficult to imagine him retiring, and he has said that Marisa would be against his ending up in a beach house in the northeast. For as long as he lives he will be an influence in Brazilian politics.

His legacy may look very different, and perhaps more positive, by 2010. Brazil may seem more important in the world, poor Brazilians better off, more parts of the country developed. Whether at the UN or in the WTO, his own and his country's diplomacy may be helping to reduce the world's injustices.

His strengths and his failings are known. The fairytale quality of his own life is as familiar to Brazilians as his missing finger. The worker president is still working.

And, by dint of his persistence, his identification with the poor, and his understanding of his fellow citizens and the political process, he had given himself another four years in which to end for others the kind of wretchedness that he knew as a child. His challenge is personal.

NOTES

1. Lula was registered by his father eight years later as having been born on 6 October. His father was absent from the birth and was illiterate, however, and Lula's mother said he had made a mistake.

2. *Lula* was a common nickname for *Luiz* in the northeast; he decided to incorporate it into his legal name—as Luiz Inácio Lula da Silva—in 1981, when he was already a national figure.

3. Party membership amounted to only three hundred by 2005, and the PT candidate for mayor (*prefeito*) came in third.

4. In this period Caetés was known as Vargem Comprida.

5. By the 1970s, *pau-de-arara* had acquired a more sinister meaning in the centers of military intelligence as a type of torture in which the victim was strung upside down.

6. Her real name was Valdomira Ferreira de Goís. She may have been as young as fourteen and was certainly no more than sixteen. Aristides was arrested twice, in Recife and Rio de Janeiro, for making off with a minor but claimed that she was his sister.

7. See Paraná, *Lula, o filho do Brasil,* especially pp. 49–52.

8. Wilcken, *Empire Adrift,* provides a readable account of this period.

9. See, among other biographies, Bourne, *Getúlio Vargas of Brazil.*

10. In fact, Petrobrás was not terribly successful in oil exploration in its initial years, although by October 2005, long after the company had lost its monopoly, Brazil became a net exporter of petroleum products. The iconic status of Petrobrás was recognized in the 1988 Constitution, which gave it special protection.

11. Paraná, *Lula*, p. 75.

12. Ibid.

13. For these and figures quoted in the following paragraph, see Corrêa de Lacerda et al., *Economia Brasileira*.

14. Lula went to one of the two big political meetings that finished the presidential campaign. On 30 September 1960 he heard the governor of São Paulo, Adhemar de Barros, speak at a concluding rally in the Praça João Mendes. De Barros, whose unofficial slogan in São Paulo was "He robs but he does," came in third in the election. Lula, wearing an Adhemarista badge after the rally, was beaten up and thrown off a tram by supporters of Quadros.

15. Ernesto Geisel, then head of the new president's military office (Casa Militar) and a president himself in the 1970s, was sent to investigate these allegations. He dismissed them. Following Brazil's move to democracy in the 1980s, however, some were proven.

16. This was the account given by Lula to Denise Paraná (*Lula*, p. 76). Paulo Markun, in *O Sapo e o Príncipe* (p. 54), blames a colleague of Lula's, probably sleepy in the early morning hours, for releasing the arm of the press while Lula was tightening a screw.

17. Information given to the author in the mid-1960s by Carlos Widmann, then correspondent in Brazil of the *Suddeutsche Zeitung*.

18. Campos, who had been a diplomat as well as an economist, was ridiculed by Brazilian opponents as "Bob Fields" for his pro-American views. The military regime was not averse to massaging economic statistics, which Campos once described as "like a bikini—more interesting for what they conceal than what they reveal."

19. In fact censorship came in at the end of Castelo Branco's term, with a law in February 1967 that instituted control of TV, music, film, theater, and books. Newspapers had been censored ever since the military took over.

20. Paraná, *Lula*, p. 154.

CHAPTER 2

1. According to Mário Morel (*Lula—o Início*, pp. 20–21), Lula was accompanied to the mortuary by a friend and fellow unionist, Nelson Campanholo, who was worried about his reaction on seeing his dead wife and baby; Campanholo went in first, and then told Lula that the corpses were not theirs.

2. See Paraná, *Lula*, p. 265. The twins had been born sick, probably suffering from a urinary condition.

3. See ibid., p. 265, for his sister Maria's opinion, and chapter 3 for the 1989 presidential campaign. Lula kept in touch with Lurian and provided money, and Maria arranged birthday presents for her.

4. Lula's own account is in ibid., pp. 95-97. His sister Maria has a more down-to earth version of his first meeting with Marisa. According to Maria, he told his assistant at the union, Luisinho, "As soon as a new widow turns up here, please tell me, as I'd like to talk to her" (ibid., p. 266).

5. Morel, *Lula—o Início*, p. 26, suggests that she was caring for a doctor's children as a *babá* (nanny) at the age of eight, and that she was working in a factory when she was thirteen.

6. At Frei Chico's suggestion, Lula took a course in public speaking at the Centro de Oratória Ruy Barbosa, linked to a university law school.

7. See Paraná, *Lula*, p. 115.

8. Codi stood for Centro de Operações de Defesa Interna. DOI stood for Departamento de Operações de Informações. The two organizations worked together to root out what they defined as internal subversion.

9. Another term used in the Geisel and Figueiredo eras was *abertura*—an opening up in politics.

10. See Baer, *A Economia Brasileira*, pp. 110, 114, and passim. In the second half of the 1970s it was estimated that the average annual growth rate was 7 percent.

11. Ernesto Geisel had been running Petrobrás, the state petroleum monopoly, from 1969 to 1973.

12. General Golbery had been one of the plotters prior to the 1964 coup. Within three months of its success he had set up the SNI, with himself at its head. He was a key behind-the-scenes figure in the military regimes and, like intelligence chiefs elsewhere, sometimes had a more realistic understanding of public opinion than ministers and other generals. See Ferreira and Delgado, *O Brasil Republicano*, p. 175.

13. The courses at the ESG were taught by qualified academics and others of similar standing, and were attended by members of the civilian elite as well as officers. An association of ESG graduates had branches throughout Brazil.

14. The Médici government set up Aerp (Assessoria Especial de Relações Públicas) as a propaganda organ that made films and ran campaigns. Among the slogans it promoted, exploiting Brazil's 1970 World Cup soccer win, were "Ninguém segura o Brasil" (no one holds back Brazil) and "Este é um páis que vai pra frente" (this is a country that is going ahead—a line borrowed from a popular song by Miguel Gustavo).

15. The military police in São Paulo were also running their own death squad.

16. There was also a significant rural guerrilla movement in Araguaia, from 1972 to 1975, supported by the Maoist Partido Comunista do Brasil, PCdoB. The PCdoB had split in 1962 from the pro-Soviet PCB, founded in 1922, because it thought Brazilian communists should pursue armed struggle in order to make a revolution.

17.   Figures from DIEESE, Departamento Intersindical de Estatística e Estudos Sócio-Econômicos, quoted in Alves, *Estado e Oposição no Brasil*, p. 185. DIEESE was a research organization for the unions.

18.   See ibid., p 181 (NB a misprint in the table).

19.   Eduardo Matarazzo Suplicy was an intellectual and a scion of the Matarazzo commercial dynasty. He was also a professor at the Fundação Getúlio Vargas and therefore must have been particularly surprised that, without explanation, the World Bank stated that the FGV inflation figures for 1973 had been mistranslated by the labor court. Later one of the founders of the PT, he was a PT senator in the early years of the twenty-first century. The original tip-off on the World Bank study had come from Paulo Francis, a Brazilian journalist in Washington. The updated loss of 34.1 percent was calculated by DIEESE (see note 17).

20.   Paulo Vidal was no longer a member of the executive; in addition to policy differences with Lula, he had had to take time out for surgery.

21.   See Paraná, *Lula*, p. 134.

22.   Controversially, Lula expelled from the union a student working at Resil who belonged to the Trotskyite Convergência Socialista.

23.   Among much media coverage were a long interview on TV Cultura, interviews in *Pasquim* and *Senhor*, and substantial reporting by Brazil's newsmagazines.

24.   The average hourly salary of autoworkers in Brazil in 1978 was 60 cents, compared with 80 cents in Colombia and South Korea, $1.50 in Peru, $1.60 in Venezuela, $2.05 in Mexico, $4.30 in Japan, and $8.65 in the United States (Alves, *Estado e Oposição no Brasil*, table on p. 299).

25.   Since the Cuban revolution in 1958, beards worn by *barbudos* had become symbols of radicalism in Latin America.

26.   Quoted by Markun, *O Sapo e o Príncipe*, p. 140.

27.   Paraná, *Lula*, p. 142.

28.   This account draws heavily on Markun, *O Sapo e o Príncipe*, pp. 135-50.

29.   Lula said he first spoke publicly of the need for a workers' party at a congress of petroleum workers on 15 July 1978 (see Paraná, *Lula*, p. 138).

30.   Dom Cláudio Hummes sheltered Nelson Campanholo, the one member of the metalworkers' executive who had escaped arrest, for a whole day in the sacristy of the mother church in São Bernardo when the police were looking for him.

31.   DOPS stood for Departamento de Ordem Política e Social.

32.   Marisa helped organize a march of the wives of unionists, spoke in public, and took part in a liturgical act for the strikers with Cardinal Evaristo Arns, but the stress made her ill. See Morel, *Lula—o Início*, p. 108.

CHAPTER 3

1. This was the year in which the PCB had been founded.

2. He spoke on 15 July 1978.

3. The two were Aurélio Pires, linked to the PCdoB, and Benedito Marcílio, linked to the largest Trotskyite group, Convergência Socialista. Others in the union delegation were Arnaldo Gonçalves of the Santos Metalworkers, Henos Amorina of the Osasco Metalworkers, Jacó Bittar of the Campinas Petrolworkers, and David de Moraes of the São Paulo Journalists. See Markun, *O Sapo e o Príncipe*, p. 173.

4. See Keck, *The Workers' Party and Democratization in Brazil*, p. 77.

5. Bittar, for example, disapproved of Lula's handling of the 1979 strike.

6. Keck, *The Workers' Party and Democratization in Brazil*, p. 93.

7. Miguel Arraes had been governor of Pernambuco prior to the military takeover and had promoted agrarian reform.

8. Frei Chico told Mário Morel that he thought in 1980–81 that there was a real danger of Lula's being murdered, and then he would be made into a martyr (Morel, *O Sapo e o Príncipe*, p. 74).

9. He was Euler Bentes Monteiro, a retired general, who attracted some ARENA dissidents to add to MDB votes. The regime, however, had fixed itself a comfortable majority in Congress in spite of opposition gains in 1978.

10. A key resource for the government was its group of unelected senators, known as "bionic."

11. *Lula* was a common nickname in the northeast for someone named Luis or Luiz; perhaps "Lu—there" translates it better than the literal translation, "squid." More recently it has become possible to run for elective office with just a nickname.

12. See Markun, *O Sapo e o Príncipe*, p. 195.

13. In fact, the *linha dura* tried to perpetrate an electoral fraud that would have prevented Brizola from winning the Rio governorship, but it was exposed.

14. One of those who set up the PT in Acre was Chico Mendes, the rubber tappers' leader (murdered in 1988), who developed the eco-friendly concept of extractive reserves. Jorge Viana of the PT was elected governor in 1998, and won again in 2002.

15. Dante de Oliveira, then thirty-two, had been a militant in the revolutionary group MR-8; his arrival in Congress illustrated the way in which, after the amnesty and the 1982 elections, former enemies of the dictatorship were entering the political system.

16. Paulo Maluf, a very right-wing figure, had been a governor of São Paulo state for the military, was later elected mayor (*prefeito*) of São Paulo city, and was arrested for corruption and imprisoned during Lula's presidency.

17. See Keck, *The Workers' Party and Democratization in Brazil*, p. 170, citing *IstoÉ*, 26 August 1981.

18. See Alves, *Estado e Oposição no Brasil*, p. 351.

19. This three-way analysis is drawn from Keck, *The Workers' Party and Democratization in Brazil*.

20. For a definitive history of the MST, see Branford and Rocha, *Cutting the Wire*.

21. A document from a preparatory meeting of the MST in 1984 stated that in the state of Paraná more than 2.5 million people left the land in the 1970s; comparable figures in other southern states were 1.5 million in Rio Grande do Sul and 600,000 in Santa Catarina.

22. In the 1970s, companies of many kinds, including Volkswagen do Brasil, took part in land speculation. In the northeastern state of Maranhão, at a time when its governor was José Sarney, firms such as the airline VARIG, the stores group Mesbla, and the supermarket chain Pão de Açucar were investing in cattle ranches and eucalyptus plantations.

23. See Branford and Rocha, *Cutting the Wire*, p. 50.

24. In Lula's first term, Brazilian interest rates were 25 percent in January 2003 when he took office, and 13.75 percent when he ran for reelection in October 2006.

25. Markun, *O Sapo e o Príncipe*, p. 215.

26. See Kotscho, *Do golpe ao Planalto*, p. 166.

27. This party was the Partido Municipalista Brasileiro. The survival of tiny parties in the Brazilian system into the twenty-first century, often built around one or two personalities and for hire, was one of its defects that the more democratic, mass-based PT sought to challenge.

28. Lula's campaign group at one point had only ten dollars to buy a meal, and wasted time discussing what they could afford (Kotscho, *Do golpe ao Planalto*, p. 162).

29. Maria Helena Amaral, a journalist, resigned from Collor's team in protest at the purchase of Miriam's claims by Leopoldo Collor for 200,000 cruzados, around $123,000 (Markun, *O Sapo e o Príncipe*, p. 233).

30. See Dimenstein and de Souza, *A História Real*, pp. 47–50.

31. This lady was widowed in 1979 when her husband was murdered, as mysteriously as Marisa's first husband.

CHAPTER 4

1. See the Web site for the Metalworkers of São Bernardo and Diadema, and, after the 1993 merger with Santo André as well, www.abcdeluta.org.br.

2. Markun, *O Sapo e o Príncipe*, p. 237.

3. Robb, *A Death in Brazil*, pp. 39–44.

4. Paragraph 4 of the resolution on "O Socialismo Petista," approved in 1990 and reaffirmed at the second PT Congress, November 1999. See the PT Web site.

5. Shortly after the formation of the PT, Lula told the journalist Mário Morel, "Sometimes I say you could call me a socialist, because at bottom we are all socialists, because we all want a more just society." But he also said he did not want the kind of socialism imposed with bayonets and torture. His dream was of a country where everyone had the same rights and did not climb over others or cause misery to their neighbors (Morel, *Lula—o Início*, pp. 166, 174–75).

6. It was not at all clear which member of the old imperial royal family would have become the Brazilian monarch if the plebiscite had supported reinstating the monarchy, but before the PT and PSDB fell out over the presidential issue it was planned that Lula would be the presidential candidate and Fernando Henrique Cardoso would be the prime minister.

7. Markun, *O Sapo e o Príncipe*, p. 249.

8. See Kotscho, *Do golpe ao Planalto*, pp. 187–90.

9. Mendonça's full name was José Eduardo Mendonça. He worked to elect Collor as governor of Alagoas in 1986.

10. See Baer, *A Economia Brasileira*, table 10.1a, p. 223.

11. Anecdote recounted in Dimenstein and de Souza, *A História Real*, p. 72.

12. Broadly speaking, the parties on the left with whom the PT found it more comfortable to ally in the 1990s and at the start of the twenty-first century were: the PDT (the party of Leonel Brizola), the PSB (the party of Miguel Arraes), the PCdoB, and the PPS (the renamed Communist Party of Brazil, PCB, for so long led by Luís Carlos Prestes), although the PPS opposed Lula in the 2006 election.

13. In just over a decade, the Brazilian economy and currency suffered from, for example, a Mexican devaluation in 1995, when more than seven billion dollars left Brazil in February and March; the "Asian flu" of southeast Asian economies in July 1997, which led to a 15 percent decline in the gross national product of Indonesia; the Argentine debt write-off in 2001–2; and the 10 percent decline in world stock markets in 2006, when U.S. and European investors took fright at inflation prospects.

14. Few sociologists were also prominent politically in the late twentieth century; another example was Ralf Dahrendorf, whose career in German politics led him to become a member of the European Commission.

15. The previous occasion was in 1961, when Juscelino Kubitschek handed the presidential sash to Jânio Quadros.

16. The real was at the time still worth one U.S. dollar; the PT deputy was Paulo Paim.

17. These figures come from Hilary Wainwright's chapter, "Porto Alegre: Public Power beyond the State," a valuable account of the participatory budget process, in Branford and Kucinski with Wainwright, *Politics Transformed*.

18. After three years exclusively in Porto Alegre, the World Social Forum took place there and in Mumbai in 2004, and was held in the city again in 2005. In 2006 it took place in Caracas, Bamako, and Karachi. In 2005, President Hugo Chávez of Venezuela was cheered by the activists, and the contrasting disillusion with Lula was widely noted.

19. For an excellent account of the movement, see Branford and Rocha, *Cutting the Wire*, especially chapter 7, pp. 129-47, which describes what became known as the massacre of Eldorado de Carajás.

20. Ibid., p. 173.

21. Ibid., p. 181.

22. See Markun, *O Sapo e o Príncipe*, p. 294. The discussion is reported to have taken place over a meal in José Dirceu's flat in Brasília.

23. Peter Mandelson, a "New Labour" guru who held various ministries in the Blair government and had a Brazilian boyfriend, was reported as saying on a visit to Brazil that Cardoso and the PSDB compared favorably to the Labour government in Britain.

24. See *EntreAtos*, a documentary film by João Moreira Salles, a well-known independent filmmaker, shot between the first and second rounds of the 2002 presidential election.

25. In 1997 in London, in an unexpected act that calmed financial markets fearful of radicalism from a Labour government, the chancellor of the exchequer, Gordon Brown, announced that the Bank of England would set interest rates without government interference.

26. Lula was also backed by Senator Benedita da Silva, no relation, who was Brazil's first black senator and an evangelical, and who had been briefly interim governor of Rio de Janeiro state in 2002. She continued to live in a *favela* or slum.

27. In the state of Maranhão, even the right-wing PFL was supporting Lula.

28. See *Veja*, 28 June 2006. The nine were the PT, PTB, the Partido Liberal of the vice president, the PSB, PDT, PPS, PCdoB, the Greens (Partido Verde), and the Partido Popular (a right-wing party).

29. See *Financial Times*, 15 October 2002.

30. Lula walked out of a lunch with Otavio Frias Filho, a proprietor of the *Folha de São Paulo*, during this campaign; the media boss had asked him insultingly whether he thought he was equipped to govern the country when he couldn't even speak English (Kotscho, *Do golpe ao Planalto*, p. 225).

CHAPTER 5

1. Interview with an education official, Brasília, 22 September 2005.

2. Palocci was a good example of party careerism as the PT became a fixed and growing part of the political scene; he was successively a town councilor,

a state deputy, a federal deputy, a mayor for two terms, and then minister of finance.

3. Criticism in January 2006 by José Serra, a defeated PSDB presidential candidate who became the mayor of São Paulo in 2004 and governor of the state two years later.

4. Prior to Lula's election as president, the PT had had only fifty-eight deputies; altogether the government majority included nine parties.

5. Many still thought that there were serious inequities in the system, with overly generous pensions for retired military officers and judges. During 2002, the state had had to allocate thirty-nine billion reais for the benefit of civil servants, while total federal spending on health was only thirty billion reais.

6. Such Labour ministers included Peter Mandelson, Stephen Byers, and Alan Milburn.

7. *Veja,* 23 February 2005.

8. In September 2004, for example, José Dirceu was chairing such commissions or "chambers" on social policy, on economic development, and on incentives for productive private investments in Brazil.

9. Such partnerships, known as PPPs, were much used in the United Kingdom as a way of creating public goods without weighing down the national balance sheet. Supporters argued that more improvements in infrastructure could be paid for if private investors joined up with public agencies; critics complained that public institutions were being saddled with long-term debt that would be hard to service.

10. Dirceu, seeing the danger that Cavalcanti might win, had actually proposed an increase in the budgets for deputies' offices from his position in the Casa Civil, but Aldo Rebelo vetoed the plan.

11. See, for example, *Folha de São Paulo,* 21 September 2005.

12. The PDT, PPS, and PV (the Greens) said they would support José Thomaz Nonô of the PFL; Fernando Gabeira, who had left the PT to join the Greens, had led the attack on Cavalcanti.

13. *Veja,* published by Editora Abril in São Paulo, prided itself on its independent investigative journalism but was not generally friendly to the Lula government. Its exposé, published 22 April 2004, that the PT had purchased PTB support for ten million reais had had nothing like the impact of its articles a year later.

14. The expressive and subtle Portuguese used in Brazil has a word for such parties—*fisiologicos*—to which the English word *physiological* cannot do justice. It connotes that such parties are part of the organism of political power in Brazil, disconnected from interest or ideology, and are part of a perpetual system of rewards and favors.

15. See *Veja,* 18 May 2005, p. 59.

16. Lula appeared to enjoy the trappings of his position—journalists dubbed a new presidential plane, bought from European Airbus rather than Brazil's Embraer, "Aerolula." The Airbus cost around $56.7 million to purchase and $2,000 an hour to fly. In a reference to the old plantations, Lula called the presidential suite at the front of the plane "the big house" and the area at the back for staff and journalists "the slave quarters." When he had to report his assets to the Electoral Commission (Tribuna Superior Eleitoral) in July 2006, they were R839,033, as compared with R422,949 in the 2002 election—an increase the PT attributed to savings from the presidential salary and good financial management (*Folha-online*, 5 July 2006).

17. For instance, in June 2005 he was saying, "We will cut into our own flesh if necessary—whoever is to blame will pay the price." But talking at a dinner in February 2006 to celebrate the twenty-sixth anniversary of the founding of the PT, he commented, "People ought not to execrate those who err. To err is human."

18. See *Brazil Network* news summary, 17 July 2006. Lula went on to say that, while Americans and Europeans had called him a leftist, in Brazil he had been called a CIA agent by the Brazilian Communist Party and "a crutch of the dictatorship" by Trotskyites. He added that these critics were now all his friends.

19. Proposal by Tony Blair, the prime minister of the United Kingdom, prior to the St. Petersburg meeting, 2006. At Gleneagles, the Scottish G8 gathering a year earlier, which focused on African poverty, the leaders of Nigeria and South Africa were also in attendance.

20. Although born in Rio de Janeiro in 1948, Vieira de Mello's connections with Brazil had become tenuous, and his family lived in Geneva, where he had spent most of his career with the UN High Commission for Refugees. He became well known when Kofi Annan gave him responsibility for guiding East Timor to independence. In 2002 he succeeded Mary Robinson as the UN high commissioner for human rights, and in May 2003 Annan transferred him for four months to head the UN office in Baghdad. The explosion there, which killed him and his staff, was a serious setback for the UN in postwar Iraq.

21. See Scolese and Nossa, *Viagens com o Presidente*.

22. See *Veja*, 9 February 2005.

23. Data released at the end of April 2006 by IBGE, the respected Brazilian statistical institute, suggested that Brazil had overtaken Mexico in 2005 to become the leading Latin American economy, and was eleventh largest in the world.

24. These World Trade Organization talks began in Doha in November 2001 and should have concluded in three years. They were described as a "development round," though many analysts questioned how far world trade liberalization would promote the growth of the poorest developing states. They broke down in July 2006.

25. *Veja*, 25 January 2006.

26. Interview, Denise Paraná, 8 September 2005. Lula's brother Frei Chico suffered a heart attack that month.

27. See *Veja*, 13 July 2005.

28. The final report of the parliamentary inquiry into the postal scandal (CPI dos Correios) withdrew a direct reference to Lulinha, though it urged the Ministério Publico to clarify the relationship between Telemar and Gamecorp (*Folha de São Paulo*, 30 March 2006).

29. The Vavá consultancy was discussed in *Veja*, 12 October 2005. An example from another country was of the legitimate role played by the brother of Gordon Brown, then the UK minister of finance, as a PR lobbyist for the nuclear industry.

30. Mercadante was one of the Catholic intellectuals who had helped found the PT. Originally a professor of economics, he had helped coordinate successive election campaigns, was Lula's vice presidential running mate in 1994, was elected São Paulo senator in 2002, was government leader in the Senate, and ran as the PT candidate for governor of the state of São Paulo in 2006.

31. See Directions for the PT Program of Government, 2006, developed at the Thirteenth Encontro Nacional in April, posted online at www.pt.org.br.

32. Speech reported in *Folha de São Paulo*, 24 July 2006.

33. Alencar had parted company with the equally tiny Partido Liberal.

34. Aécio Neves da Cunha is grandson of Tancredo Neves, who was hospitalized before he could be invested as president at the end of the military era.

35. Reported by the Spanish daily *El Pais*, 18 July 2006.

CHAPTER 6

1. "Popular restaurants" had a long history on the socialist left. In the United Kingdom during World War II, there was a chain of government-owned restaurants called "British restaurants."

2. For comments on Fome Zero, see Baer and Amann, "Economic Orthodoxy versus Social Development?" and a debate between Alfredo Saad-Filho and Sue Branford in *Red Pepper*, January 2005. The program attracted support from Brazil's glitterati: Gisele Bundchen, the model, donated a check for fifty thousand reais in 2003, which paid for thirty-five water cisterns.

3. In 1999, for example, the richest 20 percent of Brazilians had 63.8 percent of the country's income, and the richest 1 percent had 13.3 percent; the poorest 20 percent had only 2.3 percent. See Sue Branford's chapter, "The Fernando Henrique Cardoso Legacy," p. 92, in Branford and Kucinski with Wainwright, *Politics Transformed*.

4. Multinationals such as IBM, Banco Real (ABN Amro), and Dupont had taken a lead in setting employment quotas to reflect Brazil's racial diversity.

5. The study was conducted by Maurício Cortez Reis and Anna Risi Crespo for the Instituto de Pesquisa Econômica Aplicada, using national statistics. It was reported in *Folha de São Paulo,* 25 September 2005.

6. Research by Sergei Soares in 2000 and by Ricardo Henriques in 2001 had focused on educational disadvantage and unequal access. An IBGE study published in November 2006 showed that there had been a rise from 22 percent in 2001 to 30 percent in 2005 in the proportion of blacks and dark brown (*pardo*) Brazilians in higher education, and a significant increase in their numbers matriculating in secondary schools.

7. The World Bank study *Equity and Development* was released in September 2005.

8. The International Labour Organization estimates that around 25,000 people are working in slavelike conditions; from 1995 to 2006, around 18,000 farm workers have been freed as a result of the special mobile inspection unit of the Ministry of Labor (*The Sunday Times Magazine,* London, 3 September 2006). Aloizio Mercadante stated that in the first three years of the Lula government, 13,179 farm workers were rescued from servitude (*Brasil: Primeiro tempo,* p. 196).

9. In 2003 Lula created a Secretaria Especial de Políticas para as Mulheres with ministerial status, linked to the presidency.

10. The novel was first published in Brazil by Editora Schwarcz Ltda. in 1997. The feature film, directed by Fernando Meirelles and Katia Lund, was first shown in Brazil in 2002.

11. The PCC was supposedly founded in a prison in the interior of São Paulo state in 1993; Marcola won control in 2002 and took it outside of the prisons to trade drugs in the wider community.

12. Statistics on gun crime quoted here are from various sources, including Serra's article in *Folha de São Paulo* in September 2005.

13. See Scolese and Nossa, *Viagens com o Presidente,* p. 59.

14. See *Veja,* 5 October 2005, pp. 76–88.

15. This expression was widely used during the corruption crisis. Pizza parties, especially takeout, involve a sharing of food among friends. In this context it was suggested that all the politicians in Brasília were a group of friends who shared the spoils of office and were unwilling to exclude any of their own.

16. See Branford and Rocha, *Cutting the Wire,* p. 286, for a discussion of the Cardoso government's attitude to the MST; it mobilized a large force of police when the MST called a "day of action" in May 2000.

17. There is wide variation in estimates of the number of American Indians in Brazil. According to FUNAI, the responsible government agency, there are 460,000 Indians living on protected lands, with an additional 100,000–190,000

living in other forest areas, cities, and the countryside. IBGE, the national statistical institute, introduced an "indigenous" category in the census from 1991. In only a decade, the number of people describing themselves in the census as Indian rose from 294,000 to 734,000, in an estimated 225 ethnic groups (*Época*, 6 November 2006).

18. Mercadante, *Brasil: Primeiro tempo*, p. 174.

19. *Folha de São Paulo*, 8 September 2005.

20. See Mercadante, *Brasil: Primeiro tempo*, pp. 177–78.

21. Quoted in *Veja*, 1 December 2004, p. 35.

22. In the 2006 election, Blairo Maggi was easily reelected as governor in the first round, with two-thirds of the vote.

23. See *The Guardian*, 6 April 2006, quoting Greenpeace and Brazilian official figures.

24. Greenpeace tried to present him with a "golden chainsaw" at a school, but he escaped demonstrators by a back door. One of his officials, Luiz Antonio Pagot, who had left his firm to join him as the state's secretary for infrastructure, was one of those who saw environmental NGOs as part of a giant plot to hold back Brazil's development.

25. Lula flew to Mendes's funeral, even though it took place between Christmas and New Year's at the end of 1988; he had recognized the significance of Mendes well before the Brazilian press did, a factor that helped explain the PT's strength in Acre (see Kotscho, *Do golpe ao Planalto*, pp. 154–55).

26. In 2005, the Congress passed a law making it easier to sell, grow, and market genetically modified crops.

27. See *The Guardian*, 24 July 2006.

28. The claim was that 33,000 square miles of forest cover had been lost, an area larger than the state of South Carolina.

29. The dramatic impact of antilogging enforcement on towns that had prospered from the illegal trade was described in *The Guardian*, 21 November 2006; Castelo dos Sonhos in southern Pará had become a ghost town.

30. See, for example, *The Guardian*, 17 July 2006. *Veja* and the Brazilian press were carrying more reports not only about Amazonia, but also about global warming in general.

31. See Hemming, *Die If You Must*, p. 638. Hemming, who has written three magisterial volumes of history of the Indians of Brazil from the arrival of the Portuguese in 1500 to 2000, stated then that there were ten indigenous parks of more than two million hectares (approximately five million acres).

32. Report from the Instituto Socioambiental, "Povos Indígenas no Brasil, 2001/2005," quoted in *Época*, 6 November 2006.

33. The Makuxi, who also live in neighboring Guyana, are at ease with modernity. They are one of several tribes that use sophisticated lobbying

techniques to obtain their rights. Friction with FUNAI, the government's agency for Indians, is a regular feature, and two of the largest Indian coordinating bodies boycotted a May 2006 national conference of indigenous peoples set up by a national commission established by Lula. Lula also ratified certain smaller areas for indigenous inhabitants.

34.   Report from the Instituto Socioambiental, "Povos Indígenas no Brasil, 2001/2005," quoted in *Época*, 6 November 2006.

35.   This study was reported in *Veja*, 15 December 2004, pp. 120–22.

36.   Sônia Rocha, of the Instituto de Estudos de Trabalho e Sociedade, used 2004 figures to show that fewer than 4 percent of children in families receiving the Bolsa-Família were out of school up to age thirteen, but 7.1 percent of fourteen-year-olds and 12.7 percent of fifteen-year-olds did not attend. Opportunity costs for families, the attractions of the labor market for teenagers, and the fact that they were not learning much in school explained the difference. Study reported in *Folha de São Paulo*, 17 October 2006.

37.   The greater ABC district, where Lula had started his union career, got its own federal university.

38.   Earlier, Buarque had been rector of Brasília University, and was elected governor of the federal capital for the PT.

39.   Apart from a handful of private universities, such as the old Catholic universities in São Paulo and Rio de Janeiro, the fifty-five federal universities were generally seen as the best. Tuition was free, but entrance exams were hard. Parents spent heavily on private secondary schools so that their children could pass the entrance exams; the student body was overwhelmingly rich or middle-class.

40.   Mercadante, *Brasil: Primeiro tempo*, p. 145.

41.   *Veja*, 14 June 2006, pp. 138–39.

42.   Study reported in *Folha de São Paulo*, 13 December 2005.

CHAPTER 7

1.   *Turcos*, or Turks, was a common but misleading label for a group whose ancestors had come mostly from what is now Syria and Lebanon, initially in the time of the Ottoman Empire. By the end of the twentieth century, many were playing a prominent role in business and politics.

2.   When Lula only narrowly won the first round of the presidential election, Garcia offered to resign; although Garcia was put in as president of the PT after Berzoini was forced to resign over the anti-PSDB dossier, the lead in political coordination for the second round was taken by Jaques Wagner, who had served in three ministries and was the unexpected PT winner as governor in Bahia.

3. Estimates prepared by my research assistant, Carlos Feres; due to time spent on air travel, it is not possible to be absolutely precise on the periods Lula was out of Brazil. Scolese and Nossa, *Viagens com o Presidente*, p. 74, estimated that he was abroad for 159 days, or 14 percent of his first three years in office.

4. In Spanish the association is known as Mercosur; in Portuguese it is Mercosul.

5. Inaugural speech quoted and commented on by Paulo Roberto Almeida in a presentation at the Catholic University, São Paulo, 13–14 September 2006 (see www.pralmeida.org).

6. See Scolese and Nossa, *Viagens com o Presidente*, p. 270.

7. The PT had, prior to Lula's election, been pressing for the FTAA to be put to a national plebiscite, but Lula himself had already backed away from what would have become a referendum on neoliberal economics and a field day for anti-Americanism.

8. He was repeating this line when he addressed the UN General Assembly in September 2006, arguing that poverty bred violence.

9. Anoop Singh, director of the Western Hemisphere department of the IMF, press briefing at the IMF meeting in Singapore on 16 September 2006.

10. Brazil did better in recruiting Arabs than Latin Americans, as twenty-two Arab governments were represented and only twelve Latin American ones. Brazil's diplomatic history regarding Israel/Palestine had been convoluted. It was a Brazilian vote in the United Nations that achieved a majority for recognition of the state of Israel in the 1940s; by the 1970s, a military government supported the UN resolution that defined Zionism as racism.

11. Prime Minister Tony Blair speculated on this.

12. The permanent status of the United Kingdom, for example, rested on the fact that the British Empire was one of the victors, but that empire had evaporated by the 1960s.

13. Some of the embarrassments for the UN had included the massacre in Srebrenica, the genocide in Rwanda, corruption in the oil-for-food trade with Saddam Hussein's Iraq, and the UN's inability to prevent war in Iraq in 2003 or to achieve a quick cease-fire in Lebanon in 2006.

14. Information supplied by Paulo Roberto Almeida, Brasília, October 2006.

15. Neither permanent nor temporary Security Council members had impressive records in "representing" the views of their regions or associates. Some Brazilian diplomats thought that Lula would have done better to cut a deal with Argentina, under which they took turns holding a seat on the Security Council.

16. Brazil operated a much lower interest-rate regime for long-term investment in the productive sector. For instance, the government's long-term rate (Taxa de Juros de Longo Prazo) was lowered from 7.5 percent a year to 6.85 percent in September 2006, just prior to the election.

17.   *Veja* estimated that the cumulative inflation over the four years 2003–2006 would be 29.3 percent (12 July 2006, pp. 60–61).

18.   *Bovespa* is short for Bolsa de Valores de São Paulo.

19.   Aloizio Mercadante was an economist who had been professor at the Catholic University of São Paulo; active in the student movement against the dictatorship, he was one of the founders of the PT, the vice presidential running mate of Lula's in 1998, government leader in the Senate in the Lula government, and defeated PT candidate for the governorship of São Paulo in 2006. To be fair, there had been so many failures to stabilize the Brazilian currency before the real that some cynicism was justified, but the PT's opposition and Lula's misunderstanding were toxic in the 1994 election.

20.   Numbers quoted here are from a special issue of *Época*, the newsmagazine published by the Globo group, of 4 September 2006; the issue assessed the degree to which the Lula government had carried out its election promises.

21.   In 2005, according to labor ministry figures, there were 33.2 million registered jobs. The unregistered workforce is hard to estimate, but nearly 126 million adults, age eighteen and older, voted in the 2006 presidential election.

22.   *Época*, 4 September 2006.

23.   See *Veja*, 16 August 2006. The economists were: Gary Becker, Douglass North, Robert Solow, Robert Mundell, Paul Samuelson, Edward Prescott, and James Heckman.

24.   The same issue of *Veja* stated that, between 1980 and 2005, Chinese participation in world trade had grown from 3.2 percent to 13.6 percent, and India's had risen from 3.3 percent to 6 percent, but Brazil's had fallen from 3.4 percent to 2.6 percent.

25.   See Baer and Amann, "Economic Orthodoxy versus Social Development?"

26.   A study by the UN Conference on Trade and Development ranked Brazil after China, the United States, India, and Russia. It also showed that developing countries were increasingly investing abroad (reported in *Folha de São Paulo*, 6 September 2005).

27.   Study reported in *Folha de São Paulo*, 13 September 2005.

28.   A report in *Veja*, 6 September 2006, stated that productivity at Volkswagen in 2005 (thirty-three cars per worker) was less than half the productivity of the Toyota plant in Kentucky (seventy-four cars per worker).

29.   It was a tribute to the fear of China, as well as the leisurely thoroughness of Brazilian bureaucracy, that it was nearly four years after China joined the WTO before Brazil recognized the fact officially in a 329-page decree in the *Diário Oficial*.

30.   Report in *The Guardian*, 14 September 2006.

CHAPTER 8

1. See Kotscho, *Do golpe ao Planalto*, pp. 274–76.

2. In its issue of 25 May 2005, *Veja* showed that the PTB was trying to obtain R400,000 a month from the IRB, the state reinsurance corporation. The party was also raising funds from a utility firm, Eletronorte.

3. *Folha de São Paulo*, 6 June 2005.

4. See *Veja*, 29 October 2005.

5. The 10 percent could be worth R70,000, or around $35,000.

6. While only two PT parliamentarians were involved, there were 22 from the PTB, 20 from the PL, and 20 from the PP (see *Veja*, 26 July 2006).

7. By July 2006, it was alleged that Delúbio Soares, former PT treasurer, had had links with the vampire mafia.

8. Journalists in many countries, showing a certain want of imagination, have added *-gate* to words describing local political scandals since the 1970s. This tribute to the Watergate scandal was copied, for instance, in South Africa in the apartheid era in reporting of the Muldergate affair.

9. At Mercadante's meetings in the last week before the election, speakers could hope only that he would get through to a second round, but Serra had a comfortable overall majority in the first.

10. There was a strong suspicion that the release of the photos was part of a dirty-tricks operation by the PSDB, which had friends in the police; in the run-up to the selection of José Serra to run against Lula in 2002 there was a well-timed release of damaging photos of money associated with Serra's rival, Roseana Sarney, who would have been a PFL candidate for the presidency.

11. See *Veja*, 9 February 2005.

12. Reported by *Folha-online*, 22 October 2006. Many would doubt the comprehensiveness of these asset declarations to the election commission. Nonetheless, the distribution of "millionaires" among the parties was striking—PFL with 38, PMDB with 37, PSDB with 21, and PT with only 6—as it showed that PT deputies were reflecting the relative poverty of their core voters.

13. For material on the agreement between Transparency Brazil and the CGU, I am grateful to Maria Laura Canineu for research assistance.

14. Mercadante, *Brasil: Primeiro tempo*, pp. 213–14.

15. By 2006 there had been fifty-two amendments to the 1988 Constitution; each of these had had to pass both houses of Congress twice, with 60 percent voting in favor. In India, by contrast, it had taken some fifty years to reach the same number of amendments, and Australia has amended its constitution only six times in more than a century.

16. The state fund for political parties was due to distribute R118 million in 2006, according to the *Folha de São Paulo*, 3 October 2006.

17. The case was brought by the PCdoB, with the aid of seven other small parties, and the court's decision was unanimous; altogether fourteen small parties celebrated their continued privileges.

18. *Veja*, 19 July 2006.

19. Brazilian diplomat, speaking off the record, Brasília, October 2006.

20. His full name was Carlos Alberto Libânio Christo; he was a year older than Lula.

21. Interview, *Estado de São Paulo*, 24 August 2006; quoted online at www.escandalodomensalao.com.br.

22. The Ordem concluded that there was not enough evidence in 2005–6 that linked the president directly with corruption.

CHAPTER 9

1. Lula threatened to write a book about all the lies that journalists had published about him during his period in office; the author was present at this rally.

2. This was a joke that had formerly been used against the communist politburos in so-called People's Democracies.

3. Figures from the Electoral Commission reported by *Folha-online*, 7 August 2006. When the presidential election went to a second round, the costs skyrocketed, with the commission allowing Lula to spend R115 million, and Alckmin complaining when it would not let him raise his spending from R85 million to R95 million. Subsequent reports showed that, collectively, business was the largest contributor to Lula's campaign, with banks (R10.5 million), construction firms, and steel and mining companies, in that order; the pro-Lula and PT-based regional committees gave R15 million; banks gave the same amount to Alckmin as they did to Lula.

4. Research on voting patterns suggested that Lula's support base was among the poorest and the richest, but that he had lost ground in the middle class, compared with 2002. Support from the very rich suggested that they thought he had actually been good for business.

5. Half of the "thirteenth month" bonus paid to pensioners covered by the Instituto Nacional do Seguro Social was paid in September, on the eve of the election.

6. This package was a government scheme launched by means of a *medida provisoria*, the device that preempted Congress.

7. Reported by *Folha-online*, 22 September 2006.

8. See *Estado de São Paulo*, 29 September 2006; the positions of different leaders of the Conference varied.

9. The state of Acre had long been PT territory and, although preferring Alckmin as president, still elected a PT governor in the first round; in Minas Gerais, where Aécio Neves obtained 7.4 million votes as governor and two-thirds of the vote, Lula got 5.1 million votes to Alckmin's 4.1 million.

10. Tim Power, of the Oxford Centre for Brazilian Studies, demonstrated a close coincidence between the Human Development Index statistics for Brazilian states and the first-round presidential results. A calculation by *Veja* (11 October 2006) showed that the average monthly income in states that supported Alckmin was R861, compared with R570 in the states going for Lula; 27 percent of people in Alckmin's states had access to the Internet, compared to 16 percent in Lula's.

11. These estimates of progovernment and pro-opposition deputies were made by *Folha de São Paulo*, 3 October 2006; it was likely that, for "physiological" reasons, a President Alckmin could persuade some deputies to switch allegiance to a PSDB-PFL government.

12. The federal deputy results for the four big parties were the following, with previous figures in parentheses: PMDB 89 (78), PT 83 (81), PSDB 65 (59), and PFL 65 (64). Among the smaller parties were: PSB 27 (27), PDT 24 (20), PL 23 (36), PTB 22 (43), PPS 21 (15), PCdoB 13 (12), and PV or Greens 13 (7).

13. The new totals in the Senate were: PMDB 16 (19), PFL 18 (19), PSDB 15 (11), and PT 11 (14). Among the smaller parties, the best performers were the PDT 5 (5), PTB 4 (3), and PSB 3 (4).

14. The free TV program was broadcast on 21 October 2006.

15. The firm was called Vicatur, and the conspirators were alleged to have bought their dollars from it to purchase the dossier.

16. As usual, there were allegations of dirty tricks in some state elections. In Rio de Janeiro, a senatorial candidate for the right-wing PP, who looked as though he was being overtaken by a woman candidate for the PCdoB, suddenly steamed ahead after many voters received cell-phone messages that the PCdoB candidate was in favor of abortion.

17. Garotinho had had strong support from evangelicals and had been a presidential candidate for the PSB in 2002, throwing his weight behind Lula in the second round then.

18. Unemployment figures for the six metropolitan regions are collected by IBGE, the statistical institute.

19. The cost of the CVRD takeover of Inco was reported as $13.2 billion.

20. Following the second round, it appeared as if the Greens and the PDT would on the whole support the second Lula government.

21. The successful PSB candidate was Eduardo Campos.

22. *Estado de São Paulo*, 30 October 2006.

23. Some would argue that the PTB in João Goulart's day was a leftist party, but Goulart himself was a landowner, the PTB was far from democratic, and he was not elected president by universal suffrage.

CHAPTER 10

1. Ciro Gomes, who had been a successful reforming governor of Ceará and was married to a popular soap-opera star, showed that leftists too could have a relaxed attitude to party affiliation. He had earlier belonged to the PSDB and then joined the PPS (the one-time PCB), for which he was a presidential candidate in 1998 and 2002, when he threw his weight behind Lula for the second round. He switched to the PSB, and Lula made him a minister for national integration in his coalition government. While he swept back to Brasília in 2006, his brother Cid Gomes was simultaneously elected PSB governor of Ceará in the first round.

2. One of Lula's assets was the strength of his own constitution, which withstood a punishing travel schedule. He did, however, receive acupuncture from a Chinese specialist in Brasília to combat muscular pain.

3. The Bolsa-Família, linked to school attendance, was helping to reduce educational inequality. A study by Sônia Rocha, of the Instituto de Estudos de Trabalho e Sociedade showed that fewer than 4 percent of children in recipient families were out of school up to the age of thirteen, although this proportion increased sharply by the age of fifteen (*Folha de São Paulo*, 17 October 2006).

4. Kotscho, *Do golpe ao Planalto*, p. 97.

5. Positivism, a philosophy developed by the French thinker Auguste Comte (1798–1857), lies behind the motto on the Brazilian flag, "Order and Progress" (Ordem e Progresso).

6. Brazil would be aiming for a 5 percent growth rate in 2007; Lula had been stung by the opposition's criticism that the nation was falling behind other Latin American countries, let alone China and India.

7. See Gilberto Dimenstein, in *Folha de São Paulo*, 4 October 2006. Magalhães died at age seventy-nine on 20 July 2007; Jaques Wagner, the PT governor of Bahia, declared five days of mourning in the state.

8. In the 2006 midterm congressional elections in the United States, allegations of corruption reportedly affected the results in ten races for the House of Representatives.

9. Hummes, who had turned away from the theology of liberation in the 1980s, was chosen by Pope Benedict to head the Congregation of the Clergy for the Vatican two days after Lula's reelection; the national conference of Brazilian bishops announced that the pope would make a visit to São Paulo, which occurred in 2007.

10. Nearly two months after the second round in 2006, it was estimated that Lula's PT campaign still owed five to ten million reais.

11. Transparency International rankings, in which the higher a country stands the more honest it is seen to be in public affairs and business dealings (*Veja*, 1 November 2006, p. 92).

12. The thirteenth conference of the PT, in April 2006, saw a struggle to achieve any review of the scandal; the Campo Majoritario group linked to Berzoini (subsequently sacked) and Lula had tried to prevent it.

13. Lula claimed, in an interview with journalists from *La Repubblica*, *El País*, and *Le Figaro*, that the federal police had carried out three hundred anticorruption operations between 2003 and 2006, compared with forty-eight in the previous eight years under President Cardoso (reported in *Folha-online*, 4 November 2006).

14. Figures supplied by the Amnesty Commission and quoted in *Veja*, 11 October 2006, p. 74; Sergio da Silva del Nero received the large payment of R3.4 million.

15. Quoted in Bourne, *Getúlio Vargas of Brazil*, p. 202.

16. Vargas had successively led a revolution in protest that the old political system was undemocratic, then installed a fascist-style Estado Novo, then joined the Allies against the Axis in World War II, and finally reinvented himself as the "father of the poor" as founder of the PTB, the Brazilian Labor Party.

17. In fact, eight out of twenty-two leaders did not come—the lowest turnout in sixteen meetings. Hugo Chávez was one of those who did not attend, although Venezuela was now a member of Mercosul. It was said on Lula's behalf that he was resting on his doctors' orders.

18. Bloomberg report, 1 November 2006. Nevertheless, there was friction with the United States, which was protecting cereal-based biofuel against imports and subsidizing it.

19. *Veja*, 22 September 2004.

20. Scolese and Nossa, *Viagens com o Presidente*.

21. Kotscho, *Do golpe ao Planalto*, p. 152.

22. Ibid.

23. Lula could not resist a joke at the Taj Mahal. Asking the cameramen whether this was not the most beautiful thing they had ever seen, he then answered himself: the most splendid thing was himself!

24. Estimate by a blogger, Joelmir Betting.

25. *Veja*, 17 November 2004.

26. This information was published by Kennedy Alencar, an experienced correspondent of the *Folha de São Paulo* in Brasília, in *Folha-online* on 5 November 2006.

27. See the film *EntreAtos*.

SELECT BIBLIOGRAPHY

Alcoforado, Fernando. *De Collor a FHC.* São Paulo: Nobel, 1998.

de Almeida, Paulo Roberto. *Relações internacionais e política externa do Brasil,* 2nd ed. Porto Alegre: UFRGS Editora, 2004.

Alves, Brito. *A História de Lula, o Operário Presidente.* Rio de Janeiro: Espaço e Tempo, 2003.

Alves, Maria Helena Moreira. *Estado e Oposição no Brasil, 1964–1984.* Bauru, São Paulo: EDUSC, 2005.

Baer, Werner. *A Economia Brasileira,* 2nd ed. São Paulo: Nobel, 2003.

Baer, Werner, and Edmund Amann. "Economic Orthodoxy versus Social Development? The Dilemmas Facing Brazil's Labor Government." Paper, University of Manchester and University of Illinois at Urbana-Champaign, 2005. Posted online at www.business.uiuc.edu/Working_Papers/papers/05–0108.pdf.

Bourne, Richard. *Getúlio Vargas of Brazil, 1883–1954: Sphinx of the Pampas.* London: Charles Knight, 1974.

———. *Political Leaders of Latin America: Che Guevara, Alfredo Stroessner, Eduardo Frei Montalva, Juscelino Kubitschek, Carlos Lacerda, Eva Peron.* London: Pelican, 1969.

Branford, Sue, and Bernardo Kucinski, with Hilary Wainwright. *Politics Transformed: Lula and the Workers' Party in Brazil.* London: Latin America Bureau, 2003.

Branford, Sue, and Jan Rocha. *Cutting the Wire: The Story of the Landless Movement in Brazil.* London: Latin America Bureau, 2002.

Bruce, Iain. *The Porto Alegre Alternative: Direct Democracy in Action.* London: Pluto Press, 2004.

Cavalcanti, Luiz Otávio. *O que é o Governo Lula*. São Paulo: Landy Editora, 2003.

Conti, Mario Sergio. *Notícias do Planalto: A imprensa e Fernando Collor*. São Paulo: Companhia das Letras, 1999.

Corrêa de Lacerda, Antônio, João Ildebrando Bocchi, José Márcio Rego, Maria Angélica Borges, and Rosa Maria Marques. *Economia Brasileira*. São Paulo: Editora Saraiva, 2005.

Dimenstein, Gilberto, and Josias de Souza. *A História Real*. São Paulo: Editora Ática, 1994.

Fausto Neto, Antonio, Eliseo Verón, and Antonio Albino Rubim. *Lula Presidente: Televisão e política na campanha eleitoral*. São Paulo: Hacker Editores, 2003.

Ferreira, Jorge, and Lucilia de Almeida Neves Delgado, eds. *O Brasil Republicano: O tempo da ditadura—regime militar e movimentos sociais em fins do sécolo XX*. Rio de Janeiro: Civilização Brasileira, 2003.

Hemming, John. *Die If You Must: Brazilian Indians in the Twentieth Century*. London: Pan Books, 2004.

Isidoro, Ursulino Dos Santos. *O Lula da TV, o Lula real e a morte do capitalismo selvagem*. São Paulo: Ícone Editora, 2004.

Keck, Margaret E. *The Workers' Party and Democratization in Brazil*. New Haven, CT: Yale University Press, 1992.

Kotscho, Ricardo. *Do golpe ao Planalto*. São Paulo: Companhia das Letras, 2006.

Kucinski, Bernardo. *As Cartas Ácidas da Campanha de Lula de 1998*. São Paulo: Ateliê Editorial, 2000.

Markun, Paulo. *O Sapo e o Príncipe*. Rio de Janeiro: Objetiva, 2004.

Mendes, Candido. *Lula: A opcão mais que o voto*. Rio de Janeiro: Garamond, 2003.

———. *Lula entre a impaciência e a esperança*. Rio de Janeiro: Garamond, 2005.

Mercadante, Aloizio. *Brasil: Primeiro tempo*. São Paulo: Editora Planeta, 2006.

Morel, Mário. *Lula—o Início*, 3rd ed. Rio de Janeiro: Nova Fronteira, 2006.

Paraná, Denise. *Lula, o filho do Brasil*. São Paulo: Editora Fundação Perseu Abramo, 2002.

Robb, Peter. *A Death in Brazil*. London: Bloomsbury, 2004.

Scolese, Eduardo, and Leonencio Nossa. *Viagens com o Presidente*. Rio de Janeiro: Editora Record, 2006.

Velloso, João Paulo Dos Reis. *Novas prioridades e desenvolvimento sustentado*. Rio de Janeiro: José Olympio Editora, 2003.

Wilcken, Patrick. *Empire Adrift: The Portuguese Court in Rio de Janeiro, 1808–1821*. London: Bloomsbury, 2004.

USEFUL WEB SITES

The Brazilian presidency: www.presidencia.gov.br
Época: www.epoca.com.br
State of São Paulo: www.estadao.com.br
Folha de São Paulo: www.folhaonline.com.br
IstoÉ: www.terra.com.br/istoe
Partido dos Trabalhadores: www.pt.org.br
Veja: http://vejaonline.abril.com.br

INDEX

Text: 10/14 Palatino and Bauer Bodoni
Display: Akzidenz Grotesk and Sackers Gothic
Compositor: International Typesetting & Composition
Indexer: Sharon Sweeney